W9-APV-667

KYLENE BEERS & ROBERT E. PROBST

Notice & Note

STRATEGIES *for* CLOSE READING

HEINEMANN
PORTSMOUTH, NH

Heinemann
361 Hanover Street
Portsmouth, NH 03801-3912
www.heinemann.com

Offices and agents throughout the world

© 2013 Kylene Beers and Robert E. Probst

"Dedicated to Teachers" is a trademark of Greenwood Publishing Group, Inc.

The authors and publisher wish to thank those who have generously given permission to reprint borrowed material in this book:

"Thank You, Ma'm" from *Short Stories* by Langston Hughes. Copyright © 1996 by Ramona Bass and Arnold Rampersad. Reprinted by permission of Hill and Wang, a division of Farrar, Straus and Giroux, LLC, and Harold Ober Associates Incorporated.

Excerpts from *Crash* by Jerry Spinelli. Copyright © 1996 by Jerry Spinelli. Used by permission of Alfred A. Knopf, an imprint of Random House Children's Books, a division of Random House, Inc.

Excerpts from *A Long Walk to Water* by Linda Sue Park. Copyright © 2010 by Linda Sue Park. Reprinted by permission of Clarion Books, an imprint of Houghton Mifflin Harcourt Publishing Company. All rights reserved.

Excerpts from *Hatchet* by Gary Paulsen. Copyright © 1987 by Gary Paulsen. Reprinted with the permission of Atheneum Books for Young Readers, an imprint of Simon & Schuster Children's Publishing Division, and Flannery Literary Agency.

Excerpts from *Hope Was Here* by Joan Bauer. Copyright © 2000 by Joan Bauer. Used by permission of G.P. Putnam's Sons, a division of Penguin Group (USA) Inc., and SLL/Sterling Lord Literistic, Inc.

Cataloging-in-Publishing Data for this book is available from the Library of Congress

ISBN 10: 0-325-04693-X
ISBN 13: 978-0-325-04693-8

Editor: Debra Doorack
Production: Stephanie J. Levy
Cover and interior designs: Lisa Fowler
Typesetter: Eclipse Publishing Services
Manufacturing: Steve Bernier

Printed in the United States of America on acid-free paper

16 15 14 13   ML   4 5

Dedication

For Louise Rosenblatt

Dedicated to the lifelong work and ongoing inspiration
of friend and mentor

1904–2005

Contents

I'm not under the illusion that the schools alone can change society. However, I can reaffirm the belief uttered so many years ago: We teachers of language and literature have a crucial role to play as educators and citizens. We phrase our goals as fostering the growth of the capacity for personally meaningful, self-critical literary experience. The educational process that achieves this aim most effectively will serve a broader purpose, the nurturing of men and women capable of building a fully democratic society.

from "Retrospect" by Louise Rosenblatt, found in
Transactions with Literature: A Fifty-Year Perspective,
edited by Edmund J. Farrell and James R. Squire (NCTE, 1990)

Introduction

We Begin

Notice and Note presents a suite of new lessons for helping students read literary texts with deeper understanding. We've been working on these lessons since 2008. With a publication date of fall 2012, you could possibly think we're slow. We prefer to think we're thorough. (Our editor might side with you.) Actually, some of the thinking for the ideas presented in this book probably was planted long before 2008, perhaps when we both—separately—met Louise Rosenblatt in person and through her seminal texts: *Literature as Exploration* and *The Reader, the Text, the Poem*.

These books, and Louise herself, shaped our thinking about reading and about the role of literacy in creating a democracy. Meaning can't reside in the "ink spots on paper," she said. Meaning emerges as readers, with all their own thoughts and experiences and predispositions, interact or—to use Rosenblatt's word—transact with those squiggles. The text awakens associations in the reader's mind, and out of the mix, meaning is created. It resides neither in the text nor in the reader's mind, but in the meeting of the two.

How might we affect those moments in which reader and text come together so as to improve the reading experience and deepen a student's understanding of the text? That question has guided much if not all our professional work and certainly has

> **The text awakens associations in the reader's mind, and out of the mix, meaning is created. It resides neither in the text nor in the reader's mind, but in the meeting of the two.**

shaped this material you now have in your hands. As we wrote, we constantly had students and teachers in our minds. We know that as you read this, our words are those ink spots on a page, and your prior experiences will shape the transactional moments you will share with us through these words. And when you share ideas with your students, you will help them read at a deeper level; you will help them learn how to notice and note.

What We First Noticed

In early 2008, we started reflecting on reading instruction in our country. We've both been public school teachers and university teacher-educators. Additionally, for decades, either separately or together, we have walked into schools, sat in classrooms, occasionally taught in those classrooms, and worked with teachers and administrators from across this nation. We've watched the change from mostly whole-class instruction to instructional practices that include large-group minilessons, small-group guided-reading instruction, literature circles, and readers' workshops. We've watched the evolution of materials in the classroom: one basal reader for all, trade books, big books, small books, and leveled texts. We've seen the format of these materials change: hardback, paperback, e-book.

And we've seen an explosion of professional texts that support teachers who are trying to improve the literacy skills of students. We're hard-pressed to walk into a principal's office or a teacher's classroom and not see at least an entire shelf of professional texts (sometimes even our own). And these books have been *read*. Sticky notes are on the pages, passages are underlined, coffee stains are on the covers. These texts have contributed a great deal to what teachers do in their classrooms, shaping the lessons that are taught and moving kids toward a literate life. Yet there we were, in 2008, thinking it's just not enough.

We want them inside the text, noticing everything, questioning everything, weighing everything they are reading against their lives, the lives of others, and the world around them.

Our concern was that we still saw too many readers who plow through a book giving it little thought; too many readers who finish the page or the chapter and then, rather than express a thought, ask a question, or leap into conversation, look up at the teacher and wait. They seem not to have noticed anything, responded to anything, been touched or troubled or amused by anything. Some wait patiently—or passively—for the teacher to tell them what to do next and then do that, just that, and nothing more. Others, those who have substituted the word *finishing* for the word *reading*, perhaps simply shrug and ignore whatever the teacher has said to do next. If we're lucky, we get kids standing at our desk saying, "I don't get it," for then we see students who at least recognize that there is something they didn't get, that there is something else they might have done with the book besides stare mindlessly at it.

What we want are kids who are curious, who dive into a text and can't begin to think of coming up for air until they know what happens to Brian and his hatchet or Kenny and the people who thought bombing a church filled with little girls would be a good idea; until they figure out what's happened to Sal's mom; until they understand why it is both the best and worst of times; until they feel as Anne felt hidden in an attic or get angry like Atticus or know regret and redemption like a boy who grew up among kite runners. We want them inside the text, noticing everything, questioning everything, weighing everything they are reading against their lives, the lives of others, and the world around them.

What We Did Next

And so we began asking each other questions—questions about the shape and nature of reading today, about what it means to be literate in the twenty-first century, about the new emphasis on text-dependent questions and rigor and text complexity. We asked what it was we might do that we had not yet done to help students notice something about the text that would lead them deeper into it and, simultaneously, deeper into themselves. We believe it is the interaction, the transaction, between the reader and the text that not only creates meaning but creates the reason to read. Eventually, all our questioning and thinking led us to wondering if we could identify something in the text that we could teach students to notice so that their responses might become more nuanced and more reasoned.

> We believe it is the interaction, the *transaction*, between the reader and the text that not only creates meaning but creates the reason to read.

THE TWENTY-FIVE MOST COMMONLY TAUGHT NOVELS, GRADES 4–8

- *Among the Hidden*
- *Because of Winn Dixie*
- *Bridge to Terabithia*
- *Bud, Not Buddy*
- *The Cay*
- *A Christmas Carol*
- *The Diary of Anne Frank*
- *Esperanza Rising*
- *Freak, the Mighty*
- *The Giver*
- *Hatchet*
- *Holes*
- *Maniac Magee*

- *Night*
- *Number the Stars*
- *The Outsiders*
- *Riding Freedom*
- *Roll of Thunder, Hear My Cry*
- *Stargirl*
- *Tears of a Tiger*
- *To Kill a Mockingbird*
- *Touching Spirit Bear*
- *Tuck Everlasting*
- *Walk Two Moons*
- *The Watsons Go to Birmingham— 1963*

As you look at this list, some of you will think, yes, we read that book in seventh grade, while others will consider the same book and say that book is read in eighth grade or sixth or fifth or fourth. In other words, while many respondents to our study mentioned *Esperanza Rising*, it was just as likely to be mentioned at fifth grade as it was at seventh. You can read more about this survey below.

Figure 1: The Twenty-Five Most Commonly Taught Novels, Grades 4–8

We owe much to teachers who helped us, and we offer words of thanks in the Acknowledgments, which begin on page 263.

We began by surveying about a total of 2,300 teachers in two separate surveys, one in 2008 and the second in 2010, to find out what books are most commonly taught in grades 4–10 (those are listed in Figures 1 and 2). We then read these books repeatedly, and in those re-readings we began to notice some elements—which we eventually called *signposts*—that occurred in all the books across genres. For each signpost, we crafted a series of questions (brilliant questions, we thought) that students could ask themselves once they spotted a signpost. Next, we developed lessons for teaching the signposts and answering their questions and started sharing them with particular groups of teachers for feedback as they used them with their students. At the same time, we took these lessons into classrooms and taught them ourselves. We listened when teachers said there were too many signposts, and we culled the list, reducing it from twelve to a critical six. We responded when Jennifer Ochoa took us out in the hall of her New York City middle school and said, "Give them only

THE TWENTY-FIVE MOST COMMONLY TAUGHT NOVELS, GRADES 9–10

- *1984*
- *The Adventures of Huckleberry Finn*
- *Animal Farm*
- *Brave New World*
- *The Crucible*
- *Fahrenheit 451*
- *Frankenstein*
- *Great Expectations*
- *The Great Gatsby*
- *Heart of Darkness*
- *Jane Eyre*
- *The Kite Runner*
- *Lord of the Flies*
- *Monster*
- *Night*
- *Of Mice and Men*
- *Othello*
- *Pride and Prejudice*
- *Romeo and Juliet*
- *The Scarlett Letter*
- *A Separate Peace*
- *Their Eyes Were Watching God*
- *Things Fall Apart*
- *The Things They Carried*
- *To Kill a Mockingbird*

We weren't too surprised at this top twenty-five. It should be noted, though, that many teachers mentioned *Tears of a Tiger, Hunger Games, The House on Mango Street, The Book Thief, Al Capone Does My Shirts, Miracle's Boys, The Absolutely True Diary of a Part-Time Indian*, and Bluford series books. Teachers noted that these books were read in "regular" or "non-academic" or "non-pre-AP" classes or were for "struggling readers." We say more about this survey on page 48.

Figure 2: The Twenty-Five Most Commonly Taught Novels, Grades 9–10

one question for each signpost," and cut the list of accompanying questions for each signpost from ten to one.

When we shifted to one anchor question for each signpost, we saw two things happen. First, students began using these questions more quickly on their own without our prompting. Second, students began generating more of their own questions. That, of course, was our goal. Indeed, our ultimate objective is to have students asking their own questions. We'd like to see them independently, confidently, and competently noticing those points in the story that they think might yield the most insight into the text, the author's intentions, and the character's motives; we want them to notice those moments that trigger their own memories and thoughts about their own lives, about other texts they have encountered, and about events in the world. And we hope to see them pausing there to reflect, to articulate the questions that arise, and to speculate about possible answers and explanations.

In other words, we hope that they will be alert, observant, responsive, responsible, self-reliant readers, respecting their own perspectives and values but also willing to change their minds when evidence and reason demand. These signposts and their accompanying anchor questions are nothing but a scaffold to move them toward that ultimate goal. And on the road toward that destination, as their responses and questions emerge, we must honor them and address them. Do not assume that our questions should replace questions students ask. That is not our intent or purpose. But for students who have learned to sit passively and wait for teachers to ask the questions, the anchor questions can become the first questions they own, a first step toward finding their own questions and thus toward becoming active and independent readers.

Independent reading is not merely the ability to decode a text with minimal errors. Nor is it simply the ability to answer correctly the teacher's questions. Independent reading is the ability to read a text on one's own with deep engagement, with attention to what might sway the reader's judgment or acceptance one way or the other. Independent readers are not only able to read without depending on the teacher to help them make sense of the text, but also are able to stand independent of the text itself, choosing on their own, with evidence from the text to justify the decision, to agree or disagree, to accept the author's vision and thinking or reject it. We hope the signposts and their anchor questions will empower readers to struggle successfully and productively with texts on their own, without relying upon the teacher—and, ultimately, without needing or relying upon these six signposts and questions.

They will need you to put the right books in their hands, books in which they can lose themselves and books in which they can find themselves.

The Work That Resulted

All that reading and work with teachers and their students eventually led to this book you now hold. We've divided it into three parts:

- Part I, *The Questions We Pondered*, shares our thinking about some critical issues in literacy today.

- Part II, *The Signposts We Found*, explains the Notice and Note Signposts and the anchor question that accompanies each signpost.

- Part III, *The Lessons We Teach,* provides model lessons for teaching the signposts.

We hope that *Notice and Note: Strategies for Close Reading* will help students come to enjoy the pleasures of reading attentively and responsively. They will need you to put the right books in their hands, books in which they can lose themselves and books in which they can find themselves. And they'll need you, and other teachers like you, to invite them into the conversations that will transform them into close and thoughtful readers whose entire lives will be enriched by books.

The questions which one asks oneself begin, at least, to illuminate the world, and become one's key to the experience of others.

James Baldwin, American Essayist,
Playwright, and Novelist, 1924–1987

The Questions We Pondered

Anything new is likely to begin with questions about the old. We look at what is and begin to wonder about the possibilities for what might be. Questioning, wondering, and then exploring may lead us to new understandings, new ways of doing things. And so, tentativeness about where we are and what we're doing now—even if it seems to be, so far as we can tell, "best practice"—is a desirable quality, leaving us open to new possibilities, receptive to ideas, willing to change. Our own tentativeness about our teaching, our uncertainties about our theories and practices, led us into the ideas that we'll explore in this book. So we invite you to be uncertain with us, think about some of the questions that started us along this path (and other questions that will occur to you), and consider some possibilities that arose.

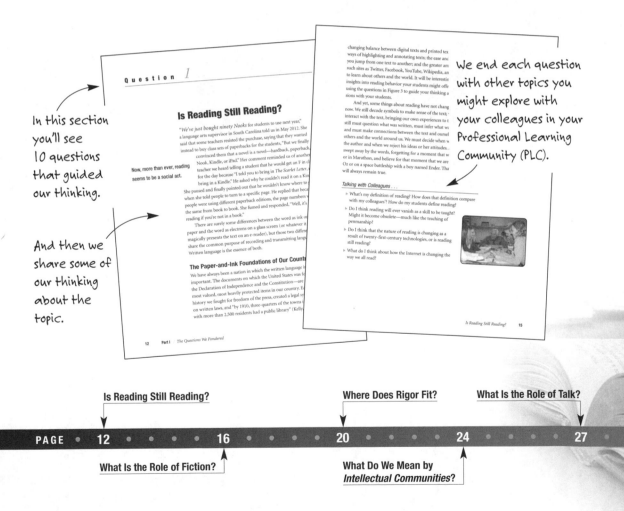

In this section you'll see 10 questions that guided our thinking.

And then we share some of our thinking about the topic.

We end each question with other topics you might explore with your colleagues in your Professional Learning Community (PLC).

Is Reading Still Reading?

"We've just bought ninety Nooks for students to use next year," a language arts supervisor in South Carolina told us in May 2012. She said that some teachers resisted the purchase, saying that they wanted instead to buy class sets of paperbacks for the students, "But we finally convinced them that a novel is a novel—hardback, paperback, Nook, Kindle, or iPad." Her comment reminded us of another teacher we heard telling a student that he would get an F in class for the day because "I told you to bring in *The Scarlet Letter*, not to bring in a Kindle." He asked why he couldn't read it on a Kindle. She paused and finally pointed out that he wouldn't know where to go when she told people to turn to a specific page. He replied that because people were using different paperback editions, the page numbers weren't the same from book to book. She fumed and responded, "Well, it's just not reading if you're not in a book."

Now, more than ever, reading seems to be a social act.

There are surely some differences between the word as ink on paper and the word as electrons on a glass screen (or whatever it is that magically presents the text on an e-reader), but those two different media share the common purpose of recording and transmitting language. Written language is the essence of both.

The Paper-and-Ink Foundations of Our Country

We have always been a nation in which the written language is vitally important. The documents on which the United States was founded— the Declaration of Independence and the Constitution—are arguably the most valued, most heavily protected items in our country. Early in our history we fought for freedom of the press, created a legal system based on written laws, and "by 1910, three-quarters of the towns in America with more than 2,500 residents had a public library" (Kelly, 2010).

We still have public libraries, but now they are filled not only with books and periodicals but with e-readers. By 2011 "nearly two-thirds of public libraries offer[ed] e-books" and libraries now spend their time dealing with the issues around circulation of those e-books, issues such as the publishers' restrictions on the number of times the digital version of a book can be circulated via an e-reader (*American Library Association*, 2012). And of course, more often than they borrow e-books from a library, people are buying their own. On February 27, 2012, *Publishers Weekly* reported that "while adult hardcover and trade paperback sales in 2011 were off 17.5% and 15.6%, respectively, [and] the YA/hardcover segment sales fell 4.7% and paperback sales fell 12.7% . . . e-book sales rose 117% for the year, generating revenue of $969.9 million."

There are surely some differences between the word as ink on paper and the word as electrons on a glass screen (or whatever it is that magically presents the text on an e-reader), but those two different media share the common purpose of recording and transmitting language.

All those dollars would suggest that someone is reading a lot; but the 2007 National Endowment of the Arts report *To Read or Not to Read* confirmed what many teachers in many classrooms have known—that there is a decline in time spent reading, especially pleasure reading, among teenagers and adults in America. At the same time, those who are reading, and specifically those who are reading digital texts, seem to be reading differently.

Reading Today

It's probably worth our time to consider how the practices and the demands of reading have changed. It seems to us that digital texts certainly have changed our practices. We find that digital reading allows us to more easily make reader-to-reader and text-to-other-reader connections. Digitally delivered texts allow us to quickly highlight, extract, annotate, and then share our thoughts about what we're reading with others through social networking sites. With digital texts we can see highlighted passages from other readers, and if they've made their notes public, see those as well. And with social networking sites, we can share what we have read, are reading, want to read, and think others ought read. For example, in February 2012, Otis Chandler, the CEO of the online site Goodreads, stated in his presentation at the Tools of Change Conference that seven million people use Goodreads, launched in 2006, to share their reading habits and thoughts with others. Now, more than ever, reading seems to be a social act.

And it's not just Goodreads that folks are using. Here's a short list of social networks created to help book lovers connect to books and to one another:

- Shelfari
- LibraryThing
- BookCrossing
- Reader2
- Booktribes
- Revish
- ConnectViaBooks

READING HABITS SURVEY

- How often do you read each day?
- Do you usually read printed texts or digital texts? If digital texts, do you use an e-reader?
- How is reading with an e-reader different from reading printed books?
- What sort of material do you read online or on an e-reader or mobile device? Is this different from what you choose to read in print?
- Do you read any blogs or Websites on a regular basis? If your answer is yes, how large a part of your reading life are they?
- Do you use any social bookmarking sites to communicate with others about what you are reading? How have these sites changed how you think about what you are reading?
- Have you read anything that includes other types of media (video) as a part of the story?
- Do you listen to audio books? Do you consider this reading?
- What do you think are the major challenges of online reading?
- What are you curious about when it comes to reading today?
- Have you talked about these same issues with your students? If not, when will you start? Because they are, in some way, reading online. We promise.

Figure 3: Thanks to our friend and colleague Franki Sibberson for suggesting some of these questions. Follow Franki on Twitter at @frankisibberson. This survey, slightly modified for students, appears in the Appendix.

And it seems to us that as we move more and more to digital texts we must recognize some new demands of reading. Screen reading, unlike book reading, may include video and sound; on the monitor images float past us, words move around, videos pop up, and music joins in; we scan and jump and scroll. Screen reading is likely to be faster and less contemplative than book reading. And reading on an Internet-connected device gives us immediate, almost instantaneous access to information, other perspectives, and fact-checking sources that aren't as readily available when we're in a paper-and-ink book. Of course, that same questioning and verifying sometimes leads us away from the primary text we should be contemplating. . . .

In fact, some would say that as a result of all the online reading we now do, our reading is becoming more and more shallow (Carr 2010). At the same time, others would say that because of our reading on the Web, we are getting smarter (Cascio 2009). As you consider those conflicting views, you might ask yourself and your students, "What has changed, and what remains the same as before, when it comes to how we read?" You're likely to find that you and your class talk about such matters as the changing balance between digital texts and printed texts; the changing ways of highlighting and annotating texts; the ease and speed with which you jump from one text to another; and the greater amount of reading on such sites as Twitter, Facebook, YouTube, Wikipedia, and Wonderopolis to learn about others and the world. It will be interesting to see what insights into reading behavior your students might offer you. Consider using the questions in Figure 3 to guide your thinking and your discussions with your students.

And yet, some things about reading have not changed, at least for now. We still decode symbols to make sense of the text; we still must interact with the text, bringing our own experiences to the words; we still must question what was written, must infer what wasn't written, and must make connections between the text and ourselves and others and the world around us. We must decide when we agree with the author and when we reject his ideas or her attitudes. And we still get swept away by the words, forgetting for a moment that we are in Houston or in Marathon, and believe for that moment that we are in Narnia or Oz or on a space battleship with a boy named Ender. That, we hope, will always remain true.

Talking with Colleagues . . .

▶ What's my definition of reading? How does that definition compare with my colleagues'? How do my students define reading?

▶ Do I think reading will ever vanish as a skill to be taught? Might it become obsolete—much like the teaching of penmanship?

▶ Do I think that the nature of reading is changing as a result of twenty-first-century technologies, or is reading still reading?

▶ What do I think about how the Internet is changing the way we all read?

What Is the Role of Fiction?

There is obviously a push, coming from the new Common Core State Standards and elsewhere, for teaching more expository and less narrative material in the schools. Nonetheless, there are still important reasons for teaching this genre. Children come first to reading through poetry, picture books, and stories. Narrative is their first way of making sense of the world. They tell you who did what to whom long before they explain the reasons for that behavior. Listening to and telling stories is their way of making sense of the world. In fact, it is probably the way all of us—young children and adults—make sense of the world. We think that logical, scientific thinking is valuable but that we come to know much of this information—perhaps all information—through our narrative thinking. And much—not all, but much—of the narrative we encounter is fiction. Fairy tales at first; children's books later; classics eventually. These works of fiction, the products of imagination, carry for us truths that throughout our lives not only entertain us but sustain us.

Visiting the school library—something we see far more in elementary schools than middle and high schools—gives kids a chance to roam among the stacks, to fall in love with the feel of a book, to rush in wondering if that wanted book is available, or simply to make a choice.

Indeed, it is imaginative literature that offers readers a chance to think about the human issues that concern us all: love, hate, hope, fear, and all the other emotions, problems, situations, and experiences of living. Granted, we need to be able to read the repair manuals, and we certainly need to be able to think critically and analytically about what our politicians offer us as evidence and reason. Both of us regularly reach for nonfiction. One of us likes to read nutrition books, while the other prefers books about diesel engines, and both of us devour books about education and how the Web is changing the world; but more often, we turn to fiction. We have to, and want to, because with fiction we continue to think about what it is to be human. As Kylene has written, "Nonfiction lets us *learn* more; fiction lets us *be* more."

Furthermore, because the issues in imaginative literature are so fundamental and universal, we have a much better chance of finding texts with broad appeal. The young student who dreams of being a surgeon may not care about the inner workings of the automobile engine, the aspiring architect may not be interested in the book about military history, and the budding computer programmer may not care about either. But all three of them will care about fear, loneliness, friendship, and the other themes to be confronted in novels, plays, and poems. So we're more likely to be able to keep our entire class of seventh graders engaged with *Among the Hidden* rather than with the text on hot rods or astronomy.

> "Nonfiction lets us *learn* more; fiction lets us *be* more."

When we want to know about great fiction and connecting kids to this fiction, we turn to *The Book Whisperer*, by Donalyn Miller, and *Reading Ladders*, by Teri Lesesne; we read the nerdybookclub blog (http://nerdybookclub .wordpress.com); and we follow @donalynbooks, @professornana, and @PaulWHankins on Twitter.

The *Power* of Fiction

There's another reason for continuing to share fiction in our classrooms. It seems that not only is it a genre with broad appeal, but current research shows that it also affects the way we interact with one another. And so, science now aids the humanist in defending the power of fiction. The argument for reading fiction isn't simply the effort of one who loves literature, believes that it's a force for good in the lives of our students, and is desperate to defend it in an era that seems to be growing increasingly hostile to the genre. It's also the conclusion of many who are studying the psychological consequences of reading. Contemporary research in psychology and brain functioning confirms the value of fiction in our intellectual and emotional lives, telling us that the effects of reading fiction are far more significant than the mere pleasure of vicarious experience and the temporary and insignificant release of momentary escape from the present. A good book does more than entertain and pass the lazy hours on a beach or the boring hours on a long plane ride; it can change us.

Keith Oatley's extensive studies of the effects of reading fiction, reported in a 2011 issue of *Scientific American*, suggest several measurable outcomes beyond sharpened understanding of literary elements. He reports "Recent research shows . . . that reading stories can actually improve your social skills by helping you better understand other human beings. The process of entering imagined worlds of fiction builds empathy and improves your ability to take another person's point of view. It can even change your personality" (Oatley, K. 2011). Oatley builds on the work of Jerome Bruner, who has long argued that understanding—and creating—narrative requires a particular way of thinking.

Medical technology now lets us understand how our brains process what we're reading, and it seems that as we read fiction, we not only learn about the characters but also learn more about ourselves, others, and how we might relate to one another. Living for a time in the book's imaginary world may make us better able to live in our real world. Research on the functioning of the brain confirms the findings of psychologists such as Oatley. Annie Murphy Paul (2012) summarizes that research by observing, "Reading great literature, it has long been averred, enlarges and improves us as human beings. Brain science shows this claim is truer than we imagined." Reading great literature, Paul asserts, makes us better people.

The humanities, it turns out, do tend to humanize.

> **The humanities, it turns out, do tend to humanize.**

Talking with Colleagues . . .

▷ What's the role of fiction in my life? What about nonfiction? When do I turn to one or the other? How do I help my students think about the role of both genres in their own lives?

▷ How well do I strike some sort of balance with fiction and nonfiction in my classes?

▷ What type and what amount of reading do students do in my classroom? In their content area classes?

▷ How do I help students consider or document their changing interests in genre?

▶ Do I use nonfiction to extend students' thinking about ideas developed in novels?

▶ Do my students read *literary* nonfiction—the human interest essay, biography, autobiography, journalism, historical and scientific documents that are written for a broad range of audiences and often with a narrative structure (i.e., think *The Great Fire* for upper elementary or *Black Potatoes* for middle school/high school or *The Winter of Our Disconnect* for yourself)?

▶ Do my students read *informational* nonfiction texts that follow an expository structure rather than narrative? Why do they read informational texts? To learn about something that interests them? For assignments?

We're finding it harder and harder to find any text that is only expository or only narrative (save our income tax booklet or a novel). Here's a tip of the hat to Tom Romano for his smart book *Blending Genre, Altering Style: Writing Multigenre Papers* (2000) that forecasted this several years ago.

Where Does Rigor Fit?

FROM KYLENE: *Rigor* is, without doubt, the buzzword these days, though Bob first emphasized the importance of rigor in *Response and Analysis* in 1984, offering what I would say is a much more nuanced understanding of what all this word implies. Today, it's a term bandied about so often that some wickedly smart folks created a funny video about it. Go to YouTube and search for "Rigor in the Classroom by Xtranormal" for a wonderful moment of levity on an otherwise heavy topic.

Rigor in the classroom—or rather lack of it: That's the problem, we're now told. When the Common Core State Standards were originally envisioned by the National Governors Association and the Council of Chief State School Officers, those new standards were to be (1) research- and evidence-based, (2) aligned with college and work expectations, (3) rigorous, and (4) internationally benchmarked. But once written, the single issue that has drawn the most—and most contentious—attention from the policy makers and the press has been the issue of rigor. Those who attribute the downfall of Western civilization in the United States (and perhaps the shrinking of the polar ice caps) to lack of rigor in the classroom have seized the opportunity to renew their condemnation of education's past failure and express their dwindling hopes for the future. Other issues, other criteria, seem almost to have been dismissed or forgotten.

Where Rigor Resides

More rigor is probably a good idea. There is surely a lot of wasted time in the school day—too many minutes spent on drills and pointless work-sheets; too much time spent making sure students are prepared to pass high-stakes tests; countless days wasted on Accelerated Reader quizzes. The problem is that *rigor* is a term too easily misinterpreted by critics who have little direct contact with schools. A careless and ill-conceived effort to increase rigor in the classroom is likely to have exactly the opposite effect. If we infer, from the Common Core Standards' call for the teaching of more complex texts at all grades, that we simply need to teach harder books, we will make a serious mistake.

Rigor is not an attribute of a text but rather a characteristic of our behavior with that text. Put another way, rigor resides in the energy and attention given to the text, not in the text itself. We can breeze through

War and Peace hastily and thoughtlessly, or we can labor through it, finishing with nothing more than the most basic understanding pulled from the pages. Either way, that challenging text will not have been read rigorously.

On the other hand, we can read, as an adult, Mem Fox's *Wilfred Gordon Macdonald Partridge*, a child's picture book, exploring deeply and thoughtfully its subtleties and implications, and that simple straightforward book, accessible to a first or second grader, will have provided us the opportunity for a rigorous reading. A professional football player lifting a 100-pound weight ten times would not be justified in calling that a rigorous workout; an eighth grader trying to get into shape for the football team probably would. And the fourth grader, who could not lift the weight at all, would, like the professional football player, be hard-pressed (pun intended) to have said his workout was rigorous. The quality, *rigor*, does not reside in the barbell but in the interaction with it.

> **Rigor is not an attribute of a text, but rather a characteristic of our behavior with that text. Put another way, rigor resides in the energy and attention given to the text, not in the text itself.**

It's Rigor, Not Rigor Mortis

In one high school with which we are familiar, the English teacher intentionally chose the least accessible and most difficult translation of *Beowulf* for her students to read. There was another version of the story, much more readable, much more enjoyable, much more likely to interest readers and invite them into a conversation about the tale, but she ignored that one. Her reason for rejecting it was that it was too readable, too enjoyable, too likely to be interesting. She selected the other one, she explained, because it was inaccessible and difficult.

When the text is *too* tough, then the task is simply hard, not rigorous.

Presumably, she had reasoned that the more difficult and painful the work was, the better it would be for her students. We doubt that she was motivated by malevolence and a simple, sadistic desire to inflict pain. Rather, she wanted her students to be better prepared, to be intellectually tougher, and to be capable of dealing with all the Old English the world might later throw at them. The pain and suffering would be good for them, make them better people, and build her reputation as a hard, tough, demanding teacher. Rigorous. She probably would have been satisfied that she was honoring the Common Core State Standards call for more complex texts and more rigor in the classroom.

But the result was *diminished* rigor. Some of the students labored through the text, doing what they could with it. Some students read one of the guides designed to make reading the actual text unnecessary by summarizing and explaining it. Some just accepted the bad grade that resulted from ignoring the text completely and hoping that anything they learned by listening in on class discussion would at least keep them afloat with a C or a D. The text was harder; the work less rigorous.

Those students who did struggle with the assignment, trying their best, were not doing rigorous intellectual work, rigorous reading. They were asking questions like *What does this word mean?* and *How do you say this word?* Or they were trying to figure out simply, *What's happening? Who is doing what to whom?* They weren't wrestling with the theme, with the picture of a time presented by the story, with the issues of danger and the courage it demands, or with any other ideas that might have been awakened by the text. Doing so would have been rigorous reading— expressing responses, asking questions, speculating about implications, discussing values and choices, considering similarities and differences between ancient times and our own, debating different interpretations of passages, and so on. Instead, they were working hard at an intellectually low level. The text was hard, the work was painful, and those who attempted it struggled mightily. But the struggle wasn't productive, and therefore the reading wasn't rigorous, at least not in the way that we would hope it might be.

The Essence of Rigor

The essential element in rigor is engagement. The rigor has to be achieved by engaging the readers in a process that is sufficiently interesting or rewarding that they'll invest energy in the work. If they are to read rigorously, students must be committed to understanding some intriguing character, to solving some problem, to figuring out what a writer believes or values and how those thoughts compare with their own, or to understanding how other readers have made sense of a text. Granted, students should learn over time to cope with more and more difficult texts. We know of no teachers who do not want students to be able to read more and more complex texts as the year progresses. But students are more likely to do that if they are invited to read texts with which

The essence of rigor is engagement and commitment.

they can become engaged and are lured into the sort of thinking that might be both challenging and enjoyable.

Rigor, in other words, lies in the transaction between the reader and the text and then among readers. The essence of rigor is engagement and commitment. A classroom that respects what the students bring to it, what they are capable of and interested in, and that welcomes them into an active intellectual community is more likely to achieve that rigor.

Talking with Colleagues . . .

- ▶ What is my own definition of rigor?

- ▶ How do my colleagues define rigor?

- ▶ What do I think—can a student be encouraged to think rigorously about a text that is at his or her independent reading level?

- ▶ If I needed to make a checklist of practices that new teachers could use to help them decide if their classrooms would be called rigorous, what would I include?

We, too, made a checklist—one we've titled Rigor and Talk. You can see it on page 33— after you've made your own!

What Do We Mean by *Intellectual Communities*?

Whether sitting outside on a college campus or inside your own school, intellectual communities are rooted in talk.

We suggest that for rigorous work to occur, we need to see our classrooms in a new light. We want to see them as intellectual communities. That's the intent, we're sure, when policy tells us not to leave any child behind or to race to the top. That's the intent, we hope, when federal dollars are offered if districts promise to tie teacher salaries to student achievement. But we fear that the notion of the classroom as an intellectual community gets lost when conference rooms by the principal's office are turned into data rooms—rooms in which walls, floor to ceiling, are covered with test scores of every child in the school—and "Days Until the TEST" banners greet students and parents as they enter the school. That, at the very least, suggests the school (or at least the principal) is more interested in making sure students pass a test than in creating an intellectual community.

The Glitch in Becoming an Intellectual Community

In many ways, keeping the focus on our real purposes of education, rather than on the test scores, is the struggle. Daniel Pink, author of the bestselling book *Drive*, explains that "when the profit motive becomes unmoored from the purpose motive, bad things happen" (Pink, 2010). We think that line might offer an explanation for at least some of the student apathy (and teacher frustration) we see in schools today.
The purpose of schools ought to be to create intellectual communities where students are encouraged to be risk takers, to be curious, to be willing to try and fail, and to be more interested in asking questions than providing answers. The profit for *that* purpose—that goal—ought to be satisfaction in creating places where we all want to work and students want to attend; places where engagement is high and rigor results from

students wanting to know more; where work is challenging because the attempt—the challenge—won't penalize you with a low test score; where work is relevant and so attendance goes up, discipline problems decline, and as a result of all that, test scores climb.

We fear, though, that profit—a word most often associated with dollars, which are countable and measurable—now, in far too many places, is about scores, another thing that can be counted and measured. Many schools—probably not yours, but many—measure success, *profit*, by how many students have passed that test so that the school can get a good grade and now, so that teachers can keep their jobs. No one mentions, though, that even with that success, too many kids are bored in school, too many others still drop out of school, and too many good teachers keep leaving the profession. No one mentions that too many schools look like test-prep places and certainly not intellectual communities. The test was passed; the grade was met; and thus the profit was achieved.

We doubt, no matter how great any standard—common or other-wise—is deemed to be, that any student will arrive in the classroom aching to use detail to support her opinion or rushing to compare and contrast two stories. We don't think new standards will fix this. New standards, without addressing old problems, won't change anything. What might make a difference is to stop teaching students simply to pass a test, something every teacher, administrator, parent, and most certainly student in this country would applaud. What might make a difference would be schools becoming the intellectual communi-ties that they ought to be but can't be when the penalty for not teaching to the test is so high.

We can't address, in this book, all the policy issues that must be discussed for that to happen. But we can offer some ideas for creating an intellectual community so that students learn more and as a result pass the damned test. And we know that intellectual or otherwise, a community is formed with discourse. Take away communication, and all you have are thirty people sitting in the same classroom or same bus or same stadium. Add talk, though, and you have a chance of creating a community. And if the people understand how to conduct themselves in an exchange of ideas, if they know how to listen appreciatively, how to frame their own thoughts with evidence and examples, how to extend

> What happens in your school after the state test is given? Is it harder to motivate students to work? Do you see an attitude that says, "This doesn't count because the test is over?" Those are signs that students have decided that the point of school is only to take one test.

New standards, without addressing old problems, won't change anything.

their own thinking and that of others, how to weigh ideas and reach conclusions, how to speculate and hypothesize, how to evaluate and analyze, and how to think independently while working collaboratively, then the community might become an intellectual one. But not without the talk.

Talking with Colleagues…

▶ Do you think of your *school* as an intellectual community?

▶ Do you think of your *classroom* that way?

▶ Do your students see their classrooms as intellectual communities?

▶ What happens if the answers to these questions are *yes*? More important, what happens when our answers are *no*? Most important, what happens when students fail to see their classrooms this way?

▶ What could you and your colleagues do to help parents, students, and any visitor to your school realize—almost upon entering the front doors but certainly when walking into classrooms—that this place is different, that it is a community where people come together to think, explore, question, try, and create?

Question *5*

What Is the Role of Talk?

We want kids to leave school ready to do whatever it is they want
to do next—whether that be college or career—but we also want more.
We want them to be ready to participate *fully* in a democratic society.
A democracy is not about blindly following but about questioning,
pushing, exploring, and ultimately knowing for ourselves what we believe
is good and right and just. In fact, John Dewey said that the "vital habits"
of democracy include "the ability to follow an argument, grasp the
point of view of another, expand the boundaries of understanding, [and]
debate the alternative purposes that might be pursued" (Moyers 1992).
These vital habits are best developed through discourse with one another.
In other words, through talk.

Listening when students turn
and talk with one another
gives you the opportunity
to check for understanding.

For that reason, we built this project on the importance of talk
because we think it's easier (not easy, just easier) to inspire and to feel
inspired when there is conversation, not lecture; when there is dialogue,
not monologue. We think that when kids are engaged, when they are
active co-constructors of their knowledge, then they are more likely to
take ownership, to discover relevance, and to ask why and why not; they
are more likely to feel inspired when they realize their voice matters and
their questions count more than their answers. But it's not *any* talk that
does the trick. The funny quips designed to take the class off track or the
quick agreements with someone else's comments or the digressions that
lose their way to an important point will most certainly (and we would
even say hopefully) occur from time to time, but this isn't the classroom
talk that helps us change as thinkers, that helps us create intellectual
communities.

The talk we are striving for must be engaging. We think that's critical
because students must be interested and committed if they are to grow
intellectually. And if interested, they are more likely to think about their
perspectives and their arguments, and we may be better able to help

If you've not read *Talk About
Understanding*, by Ellin Keene,
we certainly recommend it.

them learn to cite evidence from the text and their own experience, to reason cogently and persuasively, and to listen respectfully and thoughtfully to the ideas of others. If they are engaged, we may be able to gradually lead them to deal rigorously with more and more challenging texts.

Monologic and Dialogic Talk

The critical phrase in the preceding sentence is "if they are engaged." Not all classroom talk leads to deep engagement or to rigor. Talk is a valuable tool for improving understanding, and yet, too many times, classroom talk about a text can best be described as monologic rather than dialogic.

Monologic talk is authoritative and presumes that the goal of the listener is to agree with or learn from the speaker. Monologic talk doesn't open the door for "Well, that's interesting, but I thought the text was saying. . . ." It is the talk that happens in school all too often when a teacher lectures, explains, and imparts (even if through carefully guided questions) as students listen, nod, and are expected to accept. We delude ourselves that such talk is a conversation—and there might even be some give-and-take with students—but there is a right answer (the one in the book), and the goal is simply to transfer this knowledge to students. These teacher-centered classrooms see the student as the passive recipient of knowledge and not as a co-constructor of meaning.

On the other end of the discussion continuum is the dialogic conversation. These conversations expect that speaker becomes listener and listener becomes speaker, that through give-and-take new ideas might emerge, one might change one's mind when the other is convincing, and the other might reshape an opinion when the first is persuasive. Neither is privileged and both are responsible for bringing clarification to the table. The teacher is no more responsible for initiating and sustaining questions about a text than the students. In fact, one easy way to tell if classroom talk is monologic or dialogic is to see who asks questions (teacher versus students).

We know we're using educational jargon here, but that's purposeful. We could have said *lecture* or even *teacher-centered talk* for *monologic*. But that's not quite it. *Monologic* really does imply that something is being transmitted and the listeners are not supposed to question the

If you're a parent, you know that many conversations with your children are monologic. You are transmitting information to them. "Eat your meat so your body will grow strong." In this monologic moment, we want our child to accept the information we offer and comply with our instructions. At some point our talk about the same issue may become more dialogic. When your 14-year-old child asks if you have heard of the inhumane treatment of cattle or the dangers of eating meat from genetically modified animals, you may be entering into a dialogic conversation that has no predetermined conclusion.

authority of the statements, though they may question for clarification. We also use the jargon because we like the authority in these terms. When your principal walks through one day and all the kids are in small groups engaged in lively conversations and he wants to know why your room is so noisy, explain to him that dialogic conversation increases engagement and improves achievement more than monologic talk. He'll nod and leave quickly.

Interestingly, when teachers ask questions about a text, almost all already know the answer; by contrast, when students ask questions, they almost never already know the answer. Asking questions for which you already know the answer is inauthentic, yet that's the type of questioning that goes on in most classrooms. We would suggest that this inauthentic type of conversation—monologic in its function (to get the right answer out for all to hear)—explains why so many students fail to be engaged. Authentic questions, by contrast, are questions for which you really don't know the answer. The responder understands that her contribution truly helps shape your understanding and is much more willing to become engaged in that dialogue. Sadly, most research confirms that classroom conversations are overwhelmingly monologic, with the teacher putting students through paces of scripted questions that are, all students realize, inauthentic. Research also reveals that in dialogic classrooms, students do more of the questioning, and as a result, achievement increases (VanDeWeghe 2003).

Asking questions for which you already know the answer is inauthentic, yet that's the type of questioning that goes on in most classrooms.

Tips for Improving Student-to-Student Discourse

We expect that you already have things you do well that improve student-to-student discourse in the classroom. Here are some things we do that, if not on your list, you might try.

1. *Listen to the conversations in your classroom, asking yourself if there is evidence of rigorous thinking.* Take a look at Figure 4 (p. 33), a checklist we've titled Rigor and Talk. Rigor can't, of course, be reduced to a checklist. But as you are encouraging more dialogic talk, it's important to make sure it is rigorous talk—accountable talk—and this type of checklist could help you determine how talk in your classroom might need to change.

2. *Step back and let students pose questions.* The easy way to teach is to ask a lot of questions that we hope guide students to understanding, but that would guide them to *our* understanding, *our* knowledge. That's a transmission model of education, and we're more comfortable with a transactional model. That's not to say that we accept all student responses without question. We value them, but that's not the same as validating them. We push students to the text all the time to support their thinking. We correct when they misread. We ask for students' thoughts because we want them thinking, not repeating, not parroting, not hunting and giving what they believe we want. We want them analyzing, synthesizing, evaluating, applying, speculating, inferring, and confirming. When students have misread or have interpreted with no justification, you don't have to accept. Help them reread and rethink. And do that through talk.

3. *Give various students prompts that can keep the conversation going.* As long as we are the ones asking the questions, no matter how many students do jump in to respond, we're still in control. To give yourself more opportunity to watch and listen, put conversation prompts or questions on note cards and distribute them to a few students. Tell the students to ask the questions when there is a lull in the conversation. This directs answers to them, and if you give the questions to your more reluctant students, you give them a way to enter the conversation without the fear that what they say might be wrong.

4. *Record small-group conversations, using either an audio recorder or a video camera.* We like putting a small video camera with each group and letting them record their own conversations. You'll be surprised how this alone encourages staying focused. Once they've finished their conversations, small groups can plug their cameras into a computer, watch their own clips, and choose the three or four minutes that best illustrate something—how they solved a difficult moment, how they came to a new understanding, how they used the text to clarify something, how they took turns, how they made connections between parts of the text.

5. *Give students specific feedback about their comments as a natural part of the conversation:* "I liked the way you connected your comment about Jonas with what Andy just told us" or "You not only told us what you visualized at this point, but you pointed out that it was the author's use of details that helped you see the action." Specific feedback (not merely "good point") is what helps others. And let

this feedback further the conversation. The tendency is simply to affirm or improve an answer and then move on. Even doing something as simple as using students' names or referring to previously made comments encourages students to stay engaged. Teachers working to do this might say something like, "That reminds me of what Sha'Mia said earlier about Jonas and Gabriel both having pale eyes."

6. ***Encourage students to elaborate.*** Their first comments—like first drafts in writing—usually need revision. When the student says, "I thought the Giver should have gone with Jonas" and then stops, don't rush in. Give him some space. If he doesn't naturally add more and no one else asks for more, then you probe. For some students that means simply saying, "Tell me more" or "Add an example." For other students you'll need to model the elaboration you are seeking: "I see what Jim's suggesting here, and when I look back at this part of the chapter, I can see another example that would support what he's said."

7. ***Ask high-level questions of all students.*** Sadly, too often we turn to the lowest-level questions for our underachieving students. The research supports, though, that higher-level questioning encourages deeper engagement and aids in our understanding of even lower-level facts (Cotton 1998).

8. ***Encourage students to use the vocabulary of the discipline.*** Listen to kids in band and they talk about *sections* and *squads* and *the drill*. Stand beside kids who skateboard and you'll hear them talk about *ollies* and *kick-flips*. Read a text message and see 404 (*I haven't a clue*) or ABT2 (*about to*) or CIL (*check in later*). They know how to use the vocabulary of the discipline! But too often when it comes to talking about books, we let them slide. If they say "The book was dumb," don't argue that it was good, but do push them to more precise language. Was the plot too predictable? Were the characters static? Was the theme didactic? Yes, they will have to learn these words, but they had to learn *ollie* and *squad* and *ABT2*. Help them out by making sure you model the language you want them to use.

9. ***Arrange desks so that students see one another's faces instead of backs of heads.*** That might be as simple a move as asking students who sit in the first several rows (if desks are in traditional rows that all face front of room) to turn their desks around so that they now face those sitting in remaining rows.

> ▶ What was the last great discussion I participated in? What made it a good discussion?

> ▶ Why do I hold class discussions? To check for understanding? Check completion of reading? Allow students to raise questions? Encourage them to learn from one another? Encourage students to explore their own thoughts?

We think it's important to hear what students have to say about classroom discussions. In the Appendix, we've provided a survey for students you might want to use.

> ▶ Who sets the topic for discussions—me, the students, or an outside source such as a textbook?

> ▶ Do I think my students approach classroom conversation with a predisposition to learn from it, or do they think it's a way to show what they have already learned?

> ▶ What's my plan for improving discussions in my classroom?

Students and Dispositions

☐ Students are curious, as shown by comments such as "Tell me more . . ." and "Show me how . . ." and "What if we did this . . . ?"

☐ Students are reflective, as shown by comments such as "To me, this means . . ." and "As I understand what you're saying, . . ." and "After thinking about this some more, . . ." and "When I reconsider . . ."

☐ Students tolerate ambiguity, letting multiple ideas or positions exist side by side while evidence is being presented or sorted.

☐ Students are patient, giving ideas and others a chance to grow.

☐ Students are tentative, meaning they *offer* rather than *assert*, are open-minded rather than narrow-minded, are more interested in questions that are to be explored rather than questions that are to be answered.

Students and Texts

☐ Students use texts to expand, deepen, challenge, and clarify their own knowledge.

☐ Students use evidence from one or more texts to back up claims.

☐ Students make connections within a text.

☐ Students make connections across texts.

☐ Students refer to what was learned in previously read texts.

Students and Ideas

☐ Students change their minds about ideas from time to time.

☐ Students hypothesize.

☐ Students are able to consider alternative positions and are willing to ask "What if?"

☐ Students identify topics that they need to know more about before reaching conclusions.

Students and Reasoning and Evidence

☐ Students provide evidence for their statements and opinions.

☐ Students present information in some sort of logical order—cause and effect, sequential, lists of reasons or examples.

☐ Students avoid "just because" statements.

☐ Students recognize faulty assumptions and helpfully encourage each other to examine those assumptions.

☐ Students recognize persuasive techniques.

☐ Students question the author's motives when appropriate to do so.

Students and Vocabulary

☐ Students use language that reflects their understanding of the vocabulary specific to the topic under discussion.

☐ Students ask for clarification of words they see and hear but do not understand.

Figure 4: Rigor and Talk Checklist

What Is Close Reading?

Questions about rigor lead naturally to another focus of the Common Core State Standards: close reading. Sometimes rigor and close reading are equated, on the assumption that a rigorous reading means a close reading. Occasionally, close reading is understood to mean a narrow focus on the text to the exclusion of all other factors. When it is interpreted that way, the reader is asked to focus on and think about only the text—the words on the page, the understandings that can be derived from analysis of the relationships and patterns found, as some have described it, within the four corners of the page.

The intent in adhering to such a conception of close reading is noble. Advocates of this notion of close reading want us to:

- Observe carefully what the author has presented to us.

- Avoid imputing to the author any visions, arguments, or ideas that aren't evident in the text.

- Avoid wandering from the experience in the text to think only about experiences of our own, substituting our ideas or story for the author's.

- Avoid parroting the judgments and interpretations of others for our own assessment of the text.

These are respectable goals. We do not want to make the mistake of claiming that the writer asserts something that she has not, in fact, asserted. We do want to attend carefully to what she has given us, exploring her vision, her ideas, her logic, her story. In essence, we want to respect the text.

The danger in this narrow vision of close reading is that it may ignore what Rosenblatt and others have shown us about the nature of all reading. Meaning is created not purely and simply from the words on the page, but from the transaction with those words that takes place in the reader's mind. The advocate of close reading may legitimately complain that the student who, while reading *Anne Frank*, is asked "How would you feel if you had to hide in a closet with little food for a long time?" can answer that question without reading the diary at all. He might suggest that to achieve a close reading the question should be "How does Anne feel about hiding in the attic, and where are the passages that provide the evidence?" That question, he may argue, will force the child back to the text, requiring the reader to find the answer "within the four corners of the page." That, he may say, is close reading, denying the lazy student the opportunity to avoid the text, tell us about his own feelings, and pretend that he has read when in fact all he has done is remember.

Meaning is created not purely and simply from the words on the page, but from the transaction with those words that takes place in the reader's mind.

The problem in *this* conception of close reading is that it denies the reader the chance to use the very resources he or she needs to do the reading and forbids the processes that might make sense of the text. Readers of Anne's diary can only begin to grasp the experience the text offers if they can imagine such confinement. They cannot look up *confinement* in the dictionary, learn that it means to be "restricted to tight quarters," and apply that to the diary. The resource readers need is a *sense* of confinement, a knowledge of the feeling one has when locked in a closet or restricted to a small room for a long time. Similarly, they need to know that *hungry* means "feeling the need for food," but they also need to recall the pain and discomfort of being hungry themselves if they are to understand what Anne endured.

They will not understand the diary if all they can do is report, "When Anne was confined to the attic she felt . . . as she says in these lines . . . on pages. . . ." They may be able to search the text and find the pages that show that she was hungry at this point, find later pages showing that she was hungrier still, and find even later pages demonstrating that she is near starvation now. That, close reading as it might be, does not reveal much understanding of the text.

To understand Anne's experience, readers need to attend to both their own experience and hers as it is presented in the text. They need to conjure up, from their own memory, a time when they were hungry (or separated from others or afraid, or . . .). They have to remember what it felt like, what physical and emotional effect it had on them, how it affected their thinking, If they are able to call up that experience—while attending closely to Anne's words—they may be able to begin to feel and understand what she went through. *Only* begin, we hope.

So one of the resources readers need in order to understand the diary is their own experience and memory. And the process they must be invited to engage in is the bringing together, closely, of that experience and the words on the page. Readers can better struggle with what Anne faced if they can remember hunger. To substitute the story of the time a reader missed lunch for the story of Anne's experience in the attic would be, of course, ludicrous, farcical, and embarrassing. And to substitute quoting from this page or that one for the richer process of reading, as Rosenblatt has explained reading, is equally ludicrous.

Characteristics of Close Reading

Close reading, then, should not imply that we ignore the reader's experience and attend closely to the text and nothing else. It should imply that we bring the text and the reader *close* together. To ignore either element in the transaction, to deny the presence of the reader or neglect the contribution of the text, is to make reading impossible. If we understand close reading this way, when the reader is brought into the text we have the opportunity for relevance, engagement, and rigor.

Close reading should suggest close attention to the text; close attention to the relevant experience, thought, and memory of the reader; close attention to the responses and interpretations of other readers;

Close reading occurs when the reader is deeply engaged with the text.

and close attention to the interactions among those elements. To focus exclusively on any one of them to the neglect of the others is simply foolish. Likewise, to suggest this is how we read every passage of every text is unreasonable. What we want is to *notice* those elements of the text that are, for example, surprising or confusing or contradictory, so that then we pause and take *note*, think carefully, reread, analyze— read closely.

> Close reading should suggest close attention to the text; close attention to the relevant experience, thought, and memory of the reader; close attention to the responses and interpretations of other readers; and close attention to the interactions among those elements.

The practice of close reading has the following characteristics:

It works with a short passage. We might do a close reading of a short poem but probably not of *The Odyssey*; of a paragraph or page from *War and Peace* but not the entire novel. Ideally, this passage is identified by the students themselves (the purpose of the signpost lessons we present in Part II is to teach them some of the characteristics of passages worth reading closely), but at times the teacher will want to call attention to passages the class may have missed or read too casually.

The focus is intense. It may begin with responses, including feelings, memories, and thoughts evoked by the passage, but it will return to the passage itself, exploring the significance of individual important words, the sequence of events or ideas, the connections among elements inside the passage (perhaps the relationship between two characters, for example).

It will extend from the passage itself to other parts of the text. This may allow students to make connections across passages and then to draw inferences from those connections. For example, a closely read climax in the story may lead readers to look back at passages that foreshadowed that scene.

It should involve a great deal of exploratory discussion. Much of that talk will be among students, but the teacher will lead the class at times through some analysis. It should not, however, become a question-and-answer session in which the teacher drags the class through *her* interpretative steps only, preventing them from seeing the text in any way other than the way in which she has construed it.

It involves rereading. Less skilled readers rarely see the value in reread-ing, and when they do reread, they do so indiscriminately. That rarely proves effective, so they give up on it as a part of close reading or as a fix-up strategy. When you are confused by something you've read, you reread, but you reread with purpose, with questions in mind, with a hypothesis about the meaning that you were trying to confirm. By contrast, less skilled readers *might* reread the same paragraphs, but they reread with no questions in mind, no particular points of concern, eyes just moving over the same words again. Eventually, as that proves to be ineffective, they give up on what is a critical reading strategy and a necessary part of close reading.

The signpost lessons we present in this book are designed to encourage close reading. They attempt to teach students to be alert for the features in the text that identify passages that merit close, intense, thoughtful analysis. They each provide a question that should initiate that close attention and elicit tentative answers and further questions that will enable the teacher to help students through the text.

Talking with Colleagues . . .

- ▶ What is my own definition of close reading? How does this compare with what my colleagues say? With what is presented here in this text?
- ▶ What do I do when I closely read a text I've selected myself?
- ▶ Does a text have to be "complex" for one to read closely?
- ▶ What habits and dispositions do I need to instill in students when they are reading multimedia texts so that they read those closely? Are they different habits and dispositions from those used when reading a print text?
- ▶ In your own reading, what motivates you to pay particularly close attention to a portion of a text? What do you do during that close reading? Take notes? Underline? Look back at other parts?
- ▶ Is close reading different for fiction and nonfiction?

Do Text-dependent Questions Foster Engagement?

If you're in a state that has adopted the Common Core State
Standards, you know that the standards "virtually eliminate text-to-self
connections" (Gewertz 2012), so the questions you are now to ask about
a text are what one architect of the CCSS (and recently named College
Board president) David Coleman has dubbed "text-dependent questions."
These are questions the answers to which may be found in the text or
deduced from evidence in the text. So, to return to our example of
The Diary of Anne Frank, Coleman might tell us, "Don't ask students
how they might feel if they had to hide for a long period of time in an
attic with little food and constant fear of being found; instead, ask how
Anne felt having to do just that." Now students must depend on the text
to answer that question, setting aside their own thoughts about this situation. One of our concerns about the push to use mostly text-dependent
questions is that there is a likelihood that students will see these questions
as inauthentic. Since the teacher will already know the answer, the talk
will become monologic—the teacher doing all the asking and students
merely hunting through texts to find answers.

We Probably Need Some History Here

This approach to the teaching of reading in which one discounts the
personal responses of the reader to instead focus only on the information
provided in the text isn't a new idea. In the early 1900s through about
the mid-1970s, it was the prevalent methodology in English/language
arts classrooms and was supported by a group of academics called the
New Critics. They were "new" because prior to their emergence, literary
critics focused on the biography of the author or the history of the time
to figure out what a text meant. So, to understand a poem titled "Forgive

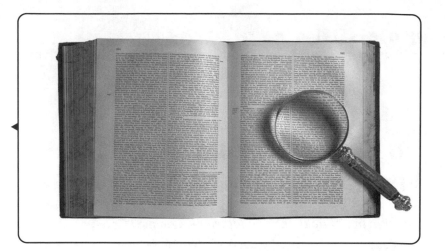

New critics maintained that meaning resided in the text, not in the interaction with the text.

My Guilt," by Robert Tristram Coffin, you needed to know that he was a lieutenant in the artillery in World War I. Without knowing that, your understanding of the poem was shallow because you would think it was a poem about a boy who shot a bird and then later regretted it. Knowing that Coffin was in battle enabled you to understand it as a poem about a young soldier who had killed other young soldiers, or so would say biographical critics.

The New Critics argued that biographical and historical criticism wasn't that important, that readers should learn to deal directly and only with the words on the page. Is there evidence on the page to suggest that this is a poem about a soldier? If not, then it's back to being a poem about a boy who shot a bird.

That created several generations of students who went to school knowing they were to hunt for the meaning. We saw the development of CliffsNotes because students—particularly college students—realized that it was easier and more efficient to read the analysis of the text than to read the actual text. Reading literature became a hunt for meaning, and meaning was hidden there, somewhere on the page. Teachers became skilled at guiding students through a series of questions that would eventually let them see the meaning—which the teacher understood because she had the teacher's guide that gave her the answers.

Though written in 1938, it wasn't until the early 1980s that *Literature as Exploration*, by Louise Rosenblatt, began to strongly influence how we thought about the teaching of literature. Rosenblatt maintained that what the text said was important—it provided the words on the page after all—but that the reader was also critical in creating meaning. It was the transaction—the interaction—between the reader and the text that created the meaning. So if the reader came from an alcoholic, abusive family, then Theodore Roethke's poem "My Papa's Waltz" might evoke images of pain and feelings of fear. If, on the other hand, the reader had a loving family with a dad who loved to let his children dance with him, standing on his shoes as he romped with them through the kitchen, then the poem more likely encouraged fond memories and smiles. The words give us some information—there's a dad, hands dirty, dancing in the kitchen with a child while mom looks on with a frown—but the *meaning* doesn't emerge until each reader brings his thinking to bear upon it. Until then, the words are, as Rosenblatt (1938/1995) would say, "merely ink spots on paper."

If our goal in reading, she explained, is to simply carry away information—as one might read the instructions on a fire extinguisher when needing to put out a kitchen fire—then we should read with an efferent stance. But if our goal is to enter deeply into the text, to see ourselves and decide if we agree or disagree with the text, to find out more about ourselves and others and the world around us, then we need a more aesthetic stance. This stance seems to encourage us to enter into a dialogue with the text. "Really?" we might ask. "I disagree," we might jot in the margin. "I remember when something similar to this happened to me," we might think. "This word suggests fear," we might note. The reader's response to the text is important in shaping the reader's understanding of the text.

It wasn't only critics such as Rosenblatt (1938/1995), Iser (1978), Bleich (1975), and Holland (1968) who thought the readers' views in creating the meaning of the text were important. Look at what T. S. Eliot, poet, playwright, literary critic, and winner of the Nobel Prize in Literature, had to say to a critic who thought the director of one of his plays had misinterpreted Eliot's meaning.

> INTERVIEWER: I had no idea the play meant what [the producer] made of it. . . . I was astonished.
>
> MR. ELIOT: So was I.
>
> INTERVIEWER: Then you had meant something very different when you wrote it?
>
> MR. ELIOT: Very different indeed.
>
> INTERVIEWER: Yet you accept Mr. Doone's production.
>
> MR. ELIOT: Certainly.

FROM BOB: One Christmas eve, when my now grown sons were youngsters, I found myself sitting on the floor of the garage at about 2:00 a.m., with the parts of an unassembled bicycle strewn around me. The instructions, considerately translated into English for me, began, "Assembly of Japanese bicycle require great peace of mind." It continued in that vein, and I found myself reading happily, enjoying the Zen meditation into which I had been invited. After a while I went in from the garage to share the charming instructions with my wife. She listened patiently for a moment, looked at the unassembled parts, looked at the clock that was fast approaching the time our young boys would be up, and suggested, *nearly* nicely, that I adopt a less aesthetic, more efferent stance and get the bikes assembled. In other words, the text might encourage a stance, but the reader—or in this case the reader's wife—will set the purpose, which trumps all.

INTERVIEWER: But . . . but . . . can the play mean something you
didn't intend it to mean, you didn't know it meant?

MR. ELIOT: Obviously it does.

INTERVIEWER: But can it then also mean what you did intend?

MR. ELIOT: I hope so . . . yes, I think so.

INTERVIEWER: But if the two meanings are contradictory, is not
one right and the other wrong? Must not the author be right?

MR. ELIOT: Not necessarily, do you think? Why is either wrong?

—(Rowntree 1977, p. 86)

Writers have always understood that although they put the words
on the page, those words carry different meanings for different readers.

The most rigorous reading the student can do involves more
than simply drawing upon the basic definition of words; it
involves exploring the understandings of those words that
the student brings to the text and weighing them against the
apparent understandings of the author. It is this testing of
our own conceptions against what we can see or deduce
of the writer's conceptions that enables us to refine and sharpen our
thinking. The most rigorous reading is to find what those words on
that page mean in our own lives.

> **The most rigorous reading is to find what those words on that page mean in our own lives.**

And so in the last part of the twentieth century and first part of
the twenty-first century, a new focus in teaching literature, often called
reader response, emerged. And, because we often leap before we look,
some embraced this without truly understanding it. Some teachers
thought we should only ask students, "Did you like it?" "What did it
remind you of?" "Have you ever felt this way?" Students could answer
these questions without reading the text at all. That's not what Rosenblatt
was encouraging, and to think that's true is to ignore much of what she
wrote. She valued both the reader and the text.

In her final publication, *Making Meaning with Texts* (2005), she
wrote, "Meaning—whether scientific or aesthetic, whether a poem or a
scientific report—happens during the interplay between particular signs
and a particular reader at a particular time and place" (p. x). It seems
to us that Rosenblatt was calling for readers to take note of the text, to
notice particular moments, and to consider them against the backdrop
of their lives to reach a full and meaningful understanding. As Ed Farrell
(2005) explains: "In *The Reader, The Text, the Poem*, [Rosenblatt] posited

two criteria for validity of interpretation: that no interpretation can be valid (1) if it has no verbal basis in the text or (2) if it can clearly be refuted by the text" (p. 68). Rosenblatt would never encourage teaching that ignores the text itself.

But we're not a nation of moderation. Not in our politics and it seems now not in our classrooms. Instead of recognizing the background of the reader in the construction of meaning, we're now told to set that aside, return to the New Critics (perhaps now Old New Critics), and only use questions that can be answered from within the "four corners" of the page (Coleman and Pimentel, 2012, p. 4).

> **We worry that a focus on text-dependent questions may create a nation of teacher-dependent kids.**

We disagree. More important, we worry that a focus on text-dependent questions may create a nation of teacher-dependent kids. Text-dependent questions usually suggest that a teacher has crafted the questions and the order of them to lead students to a predetermined meaning of a particular passage. With *this* understanding of text-dependent questions, students come to rely on the teacher to ask the questions.

Letting Students Create Text-Dependent Questions

Here's another way to consider text-dependent questions, one in which students are in charge of creating the questions.

1. *Find a short text that you think might be challenging for your class.* A poem will work or a short story (one or two pages) or a passage from a book they are reading or might later read. This is where you can push students to read more complex texts than they would read independently.

2. *Read the selection aloud to students as they follow along or, if appropriate, tell the students to read it on their own.* Forewarn them that they might find it tough so that they aren't distressed when they see the passage.

3. *Tell them that as they read they should simply mark those spots where they feel confused, have a question, or wonder about something.* Just mark it. Don't do anything more.

4. *Ask them then to reread the selection.* This time they should pause at each mark they've made to write a question about the text or a comment about the confusion they felt at that point.

> You might tell students you want them to mark three (or any number of) places. Giving some boundaries always helps, and keeps some students from marking everything and others from marking nothing. You know who those students are. . . !

This vision of text-dependent questions contrasts with how architects of the CCSS have defined this term. For them, text-dependent questions are a series of questions the teacher has crafted to lead students to a particular "aha." We support the idea of pushing kids into a text for evidence, but believe students need to, as often as possible, craft their own questions. This protocol allows that to happen.

5. *Pull the whole class back together and collect, on the board or flip-charts, the questions that have been generated.* You will probably see that almost every question springs from a reader's response to something in the text, sending the student back into the text to find evidence to formulate and support his or her answer.

6. *Next, in pairs or trios, ask them to look at the questions they think most interesting or important, discuss them, and make notes about their thoughts.* This step pushes them back into the text, encouraging yet more rereading of passages.

7. *Pull the class back together and work through some of the most interesting questions, asking for the ideas produced by the pairs/trios, and expanding or refining them with contributions from others.* At this point, you have a chance to see how well they are able to bring their own experiences and the words on the page together and to help them grow more skillful and rigorous in their analysis.

8. *Decide what follow-up is needed.* You might have students continue to answer questions they generated. You might have them choose the most interesting question and explore the answer in an essay. You might pull together a small group that seems to be struggling to consider particular passages within the text. You might have students simply jot some thinking in their response journals and then turn to another text. You choose what needs to happen next.

This structure has students reread the piece three to five times (depending on how often you return to it in the full-class discussion late in the lesson), has them generate their own questions (which are very likely to be text-based), asks them to collaborate in speculating about possible answers, gives you an opportunity to insinuate your own questions into the conversation, allows you to lead at times without taking responsibility entirely out of the hands of the students, and invites students to do a personal and private summing up of the passage and their discussion of it in the writing at the end of the class. All that it lacks is the opportunity for the student to identify the passage upon which to focus, and that opportunity will come often enough after they learn the signposts.

▶ What do I think about the role of the reader in constructing meaning?

▶ Do I think that texts carry a single meaning? Should I focus my instruction on helping students figure out the author's intent in the text, or should the focus be on helping students decide what the text means in their lives? Is it really possible to know the author's intent without asking the author? Perhaps revisit the T. S. Eliot interview on pages 41 and 42 as you discuss this question.

▶ What happens to engagement if I set aside text-to-self and text-to-world questions to focus on text-dependent questions?

▶ Can we be an intellectual community if the students depend on me to ask the questions?

Jim Burke also explores ways of helping students write questions that are grounded in the text in *What's the Big Idea?* (2010).

CLASSROOM CLOSE-UP

Putting It All Together: Rigor, Close Reading, Dialogic Talk, and Text-Dependent Questions

In a high school Advanced Placement English class, students were about to read Edward Taylor's "Huswifery," a poem that challenged all of the students. (We've included this poem in the Appendix on page 203.) The teacher had taught this poem for several years to many AP classes and reported that she followed the same basic structure each year in each class: She would read the poem aloud to students, students would then read it on their own, and then they would answer a series of text-dependent questions she had prepared (or, as she admitted, that the textbook she was using had prepared). Occasionally students answered the questions in groups, other times on their own, and sometimes in a discussion she ran that was "really just me asking the questions and students answering." When students didn't respond as she expected (i.e., as the teacher's edition suggested), she said she would respond, "Not quite. Who else will try?" or "That's interesting, but let's see who can improve that." She said that she realized this meant that students knew she wasn't asking a question she really didn't know the answer to (a key sign of monologic talk), and she intuited that this meant many were willing to let others keep "hunting around for the right answer" while they waited.

We asked her, in this one class for this one time, to share the poem using the steps explained on pages 43–44. She did. At the end of the class, she reported that "these students had the best discussion of this poem she had ever heard" and "their analysis was amazing and more students than ever participated." One student, she shared, even asked, "Can we always read this way?"

Here's a list of some of the questions that students generated:

- What's huswifery?
- What's a distaff?
- Is he talking about a real spinning wheel?
- Swift Flyers? Shoes?
- Reel? Fishing pole or something with spinning wheel?
- Wind quills? Quills like pen and quill? Is it *wind* like breeze or *wind* something up? If breeze, does it mean HS [Holy Spirit] would pierce you, like a quill? That would put the Holy Spirit inside you.
- Is this a prayer?
- Is he super religious?
- Is the narrator really just saying to God to turn me into what you want? Like giving up free will?
- So would this narrator believe in free will?
- Is he blaming God for everything that happens—not my fault because I'm just the spinning wheel?

These questions—text-dependent questions—were generated by the students and therefore were authentic, meaning the ones doing the asking didn't already know the answers. While some were knowledge-level questions ("What's a distaff?"), many others moved to inference and evaluation ("So would this narrator believe in free will?"). The conversation was dialogic, and students were highly engaged. At the end of the class, students wanted to "do this again."

So the teacher then decided to share the same poem with her "regular" class, which she described as filled with "good" kids but not "very motivated," and "most don't do much in class." This time she distributed three markers of different colors to each student. She told students the poem would be challenging, read it aloud to them, and then had them use the three colors to mark passages that were too easy, too hard, and just right as she read it to them a second time. Then she had them read it on their own a third time and write questions in the margin. Here are some of their questions:

- What's huswifery?
- What's a distaff?
- Why's distaff capitalized?
- What are affections? Like love?
- What are Swift Flyers? Like a wagon?
- What does this poem mean?
- What does "and reel the yarn thereon spun of thy Wheel" mean?
- What are Ordinances?
- What are Fulling Mills?

This text was so complex for these students that the reading wasn't rigorous. It made a comparison with parts of a spinning wheel—something that students had never seen—and students became frustrated with decoding and vocabulary challenges. The teacher then put up on the whiteboard an illustration of a spinning wheel with all the parts labeled. She didn't read it to them or bring one in or have them draw one or give them a worksheet to complete by labeling the parts. She just put it there. After students studied it for a while, she had them read the poem again (and they did!). This time you could see students pausing, pointing at words, looking up at the illustration, marking through questions, writing new ones, drawing arrows on their papers—in short, you could see evidence of rigorous reading. Then she told them to write any other questions they had. Look at the new questions.

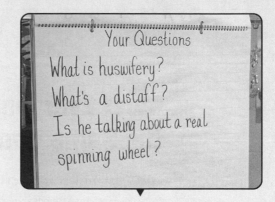

The teacher captured students' questions on chart paper.

- Is this religious? About becoming religious?
- So is becoming religious like becoming a spinning wheel?
- Is this saying that if you do everything God wants then you are "clothed in Holy robes for glory?"
- Do you have to become super religious to be complete?
- What if you say to God to do all this stuff to you but then nothing changes, like no holy robes, does that mean God failed?
- So, God is doing the spinning? Then does that mean that you have no decisions to make, no free will?

These students then all began talking, continually going back to the text or the illustration on the whiteboard. When some would wander in their comments too far from the text ("I had an aunt and she was like crazy religious and like praying all the time"), the teacher simply redirected them: "Is there evidence that this narrator is crazy?" Their questions and conversation—after building some background knowledge—indicated a rigorous, close analysis. They were having (to use our jargon) a dialogic discussion, and all were engaged; the text was complex, the questions were text-dependent, and the teacher was, for the most part, silent. And stunned.

Must Everyone Read the Same Book?

Our short answer is yes, at least from time to time.

The national surveys we conducted in 2008 and 2010 suggest that most teachers agree with us and do, at some point, teach one book to the entire class. In these surveys, we found:

You saw the titles the respondents of those surveys told us they most frequently taught on pages 4 and 5.

- Approximately 70% of the respondents teach a novel to the whole class with everyone moving through the novel at roughly the same pace. This occurs at least once per year and often up to six times per year, with the most common number of novels taught to the entire class being two.

- About 20% use a readers' workshop approach where all students are always reading self-selected novels.

- About 10% said they share novels with students by teaching four to six novels at a single time as small groups each read a different book. They reported doing this two or three times a year.

We hope that throughout a school year, your students will have some opportunity to read self-selected novels. We hope that occasionally you'll bring four or five books into your class and let students choose from that group, read the book, and then discuss it with others who have read the same one, sometimes in a small-group, guided-reading situation where you scaffold comprehension and other times in a literature circle where students are in charge of the conversation. And we see value in everyone reading the same book at the same time several times during the school year.

We should say more about that because some of you (though our surveys would tell us this isn't the majority of teachers) will disagree with that statement. You may say that students should only read books at their independent or instructional level and that those should be books they have chosen to read. You might argue that when the entire class must read the same book, then the book will be too hard for some, too easy for others, and uninteresting for many.

We agree—to a degree. We think that there are many benefits when we all share a common reading experience; the first one is simply *that*—we shared the same experience. It's hard to be a community without such moments. We also know that the most challenging books we read require conversation, guidance, and interaction with others. Reading on our own is for, well, reading on our own. When we want students to read more challenging texts, they will not be on the students' independent reading levels, so we'll be needed to provide support.

Furthermore, we know that as adults, we get together in book clubs or just sit with friends at a coffee shop to discuss *the same book*. Oprah Winfrey encouraged tens of thousands to read the same book when she began her wildly popular book clubs (an idea espoused as early as 1914 by Percival Chubb, a high school English teacher in Brooklyn). Thousands and thousands of people all read the same book, sat in small groups to discuss it, and tuned in to Oprah's show when that book was featured. Some people liked the book; some didn't. Some found a particular book hard; others didn't. But people wanted to be a part of the community of readers, and so they read the book.

What we learned from Percival and Oprah was . . . choose wisely. So, think about your students. Mostly boys? Probably choosing a romance isn't your best bet for quickly capturing those students. Mostly struggling readers? Probably choosing a book with difficult vocabulary and complex syntax, multiple shifts in point of view, lots of flashbacks, hundreds and hundreds of pages, or a setting from the early twentieth century (or earlier) means their struggle might not be productive, their reading anything but rigorous.

Whichever book you ultimately choose to share with a group, be prepared to help students through it in multiple ways. Some of your students will simply need to know that they should show up a week from Thursday with the book read and they are off! Others will need time in class each day for you to let them read silently. In other words, they can read it on their own, but they won't. And some will need for you to support their reading: you'll read aloud some of it to them; they might listen to some of it on tape; they might

When you've chosen the right book, or students themselves have made the selection, then it's hard to get them to stop reading.

We also know that the most challenging books we read require conversation, guidance, and interaction with others.

The best way to know if a book is at a student's frustrational, instructional, or independent level is to do a miscue analysis. We like the book *Miscue Analysis Made Easy*, by Sandra Wilde (2000). It was probably the "Made Easy" part of the title that first attracted us to the text.

buddy-read; if there is a movie of the book, it might help them to see a bit of the movie first so that they get some help in visualizing characters and setting. The problem isn't that we ask all students to read the same book. It's that we expect them to read it in the same way.

Also, know that when you have some students reading a book that is not at their instructional or independent reading level (meaning it's causing them some frustration), then you are not improving their reading *fluency*. Fluency improves when students read at their independent level. When you choose to have students read a book that you know will be a tough challenge for some, be prepared to support their reading.

Parents do this all the time as they read to their young children. Consider the parent who reads *Charlotte's Web* to her seven-year-old. In all likelihood, that seven-year-old would not be able to read the book on her own, but as the parent reads it to her, together they laugh at Templeton, are amazed at Charlotte, and come to love Wilbur. Together they cry when Charlotte dies, and together they learn something about the value of friendship, the pain of loss, and the knowledge that each of us, in one way or another, goes on. Sure, that child's decoding fluency didn't improve, but her vocabulary did, and we'd argue that she learned a lot about the way stories work, about the good guys and the bad guys, about friendship and love, about life and death, and perhaps even about herself.

The problem isn't that we ask all students to read the same book. It's that we expect them to read it in the same way.

The reality is, though, we don't know how you might choose to share any particular novel. Some of you use literature circles in which different groups of students all read the same book; some of you prefer a readers' workshop in which all students read their own novels; and some of you use small-group guided reading that also means different groups reading different books, or if reading the same book, they proceed through it at various rates. So, when you get to Part III, you'll see comments on how to help all students use the signposts this book introduces, regardless of your instructional practice.

Becoming a Community of Readers

We know that some argue strongly, even vociferously, for independent reading of self-selected books, for absolute and total freedom of choice by the individual student. We know how important choice is. We know that when we ask a group of students—small group or large—to read the same novel there will be challenges. And yet we still say it is important to do. We think it's because there's a need for community, for learning to listen to someone else's opinion, for learning to disagree respectfully, for discovering how to support ideas with reason, for discovering that when you talk with another about a book, you learn more than when you think it through alone. You learn more about the book, more about your neighbor, and perhaps even more about yourself.

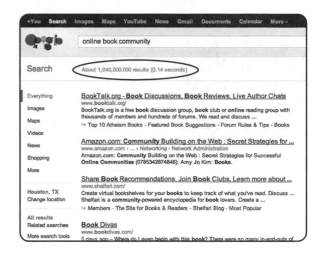

We think this world is hungry for community. In March of 2012 we googled the phrase "online book communities." In less than a quarter of a second, we had a list of 1,040,000,000 sites. Over a billion sites. We didn't review them all. In fact, we gave up after the first twenty, so we aren't sure how many of these sites truly are about participating in an online book club. Let's say it's only 50%, which brings it down to 520,000,000. People are searching for others with whom to share thoughts about books. And perhaps people are simply searching for others. For instance, as of May 2012, Facebook (which was launched in 2004) reported having over 900 million active users (Sherman, 2012). If you want to put that into perspective, Europe, with Russia included, has a population of 727 million. Everyday, people reach out to connect. They "like" and "friend" and "follow" and "tag" and "comment" and "Digg" and "share"—all of that to connect.

We are both a part of online communities, and we find them valuable for connecting us with people across the globe. We want your students to Skype with kids in Africa, to participate in global projects such as the Flat Classroom Project (http://www.flatclassroomproject.org); we want students, these digital natives, to become digital sophisticates. But we think some of what makes one an ethical member of the global online community begins in a smaller community. In the home. And in our classrooms. In groups discussing Scout or Charlotte or Lenny.

You can follow us on Twitter: @KyleneBeers and @BobProbst.

▶ Why do I teach novels the way I do? Am I mimicking the way I was taught? Am I following a practice I agree with? Don't agree with?

▶ Do I always use the same instructional design (small-group guided-reading, literature circles, large groups, readers' workshop)? What advantage for my students might there be to doing something else occasionally?

▶ How often do I ask students for input on how they would like to read a novel?

▶ How could I team-teach a novel with a colleague?

▶ What instructional setting (large group, small group, individual) works best for my students?

▶ Have I started using online book communities in my classroom?

How Do I Judge the Complexity of a Text?

We know that some of you are in districts that level books in one way or another. Some of those leveling systems are based only on numerical analysis of the text. Those formulas do indeed tell you something about vocabulary and syntax, but they tell you nothing about content. We prefer systems that take into account many factors, factors similar to those in the Common Core State Standards' discussion of text complexity. The Common Core Standards recognize that there are elements beyond the measurable aspects of texts that need to be considered in judging the suitability of a text for a grade level or for a particular child. Their vision broadens the thinking about reading levels well beyond formulaic analysis of text features. As the Standards present the issue, there are three aspects of text complexity: quantitative measures, qualitative measures, and reader-task considerations. Because we think that the connection between the reader and the text is most significant, we'll deal very briefly with the other two and turn most of our attention to "reader-task considerations."

A great text that provides a historical perspective on quantitative measures as well as information on the other dimensions is *Text Complexity: Raising Rigor in Reading,* by Nancy Frey, Diane Lapp, and Doug Fisher (2012).

Quantitative Measures

The first aspect, quantitative measures, includes, as you would expect, concrete countable and measurable elements, some of which we are familiar with from the older formulae. There are the factors we remember from the Fry and other readability rating systems: numbers of syllables per word, numbers of words per sentence, and numbers of sentences per paragraph are the obvious ones. Today, quantitative measures of complexity take into account many more features— frequency of colons and semicolons, use of dashes and italics, number of dependent clauses, for example—and the calculations are sophisticated enough to require computer analysis. We teachers are unlikely to attempt to do this sort of analysis of texts on our own but will rely (often skeptically) on the analyses presented to us.

Qualitative Dimensions

The qualitative dimensions broaden the considerations beyond the measurable. These are aspects of a text that computers are unlikely to be able to assess. In the Standards documents, this dimension consists of four aspects: levels of meaning; structure; language conventionality and clarity; and knowledge demands. Those are elusive terms, but they are discussed at some length in the Frey, Lapp, and Fisher book, so we'll do little more here than define and quickly characterize them.

Features of Qualitative Dimensions

"Levels of meaning" refers to the complexity of ideas in a text. In a text of lower complexity relative to this aspect, the ideas would be simple, concrete, few in number, and explicitly presented, requiring little complicated explanation or argument. Little or nothing would be hidden from the reader or left to the reader's inference. In a text at the high end of the spectrum, the ideas are complicated, abstract, subtle, perhaps raising questions about personal beliefs and attitudes with which readers will have to wrestle. At a still higher level of meaning would be a text designed not simply to inform but to persuade or move the reader. At the highest level would be the text that hides its motive— perhaps to sell or to delude—hoping to work its effects with the readers scarcely aware that they are being led.

"Structure" refers to the design of the narrative or exposition. At the low end of the spectrum on this dimension a text provides a great deal of structural support. A narrative might consist of short chapters, each possibly with titles, and an expository text, at the low end, will provide many subheads, perhaps define vocabulary at point of use, and offer many illustrations and diagrams that support or extend meaning. There is probably only one point of view, either third person or that of a reliable narrator, and any changes in point of view are clearly indicated. The story is presented chronologically (or in exposition with one clearly explained organizational pattern, meaning the author might say "There are three reasons why . . ."), in a straightforward, clear manner. Little inferential reasoning is demanded of the reader. At the higher end, texts may have several subplots—interwoven stories—that the reader must connect. (In the expository text, there may be a blending of organizational structures.) Characters might interrupt the flow of the narrative with memories or flashbacks, or the story might otherwise vary from chronological or other more regular patterns of organization. There may be two or more points of view presented, perhaps even multiple narrative voices.

"Language conventionality and clarity" refers to vocabulary, sentence patterns, style, and register. In texts at the easier end of the spectrum on this aspect, vocabulary is simple (tier 1 words); the sentences are mostly short, declarative sentences; and the voice and register are contemporary and colloquial, perhaps conversational. In the more demanding texts, there will be more academic vocabulary (tier 2 words) and content-specialized vocabulary (tier 3 words) and longer and more varied sentence structures. The language may be more formal and less colloquial, there may be more dialectical variation, and there may be more figurative language.

"Knowledge demands" refers to the experience and knowledge necessary to deal with the text. In the easier texts, the subject matter of the story will require no special information or experience beyond that which might be assumed for most readers. It is vitally important to become aware of cultural differences or personal histories that might call some of those assumptions into question. The characters will be in many ways recognizable to readers, and their unique features or important differences from the norm will be clearly presented. The setting will be familiar or easily imagined, and changes during the story will be marked. More challenging texts may expect readers to have particular knowledge, perhaps acquaintance with certain historical events or figures, social forces, or religious beliefs. They may require understanding of certain natural phenomena or scientific findings, disputes, or inquiries. When high-demand texts don't assume such knowledge or experience, they may present it in the context of the story, requiring readers to absorb information even as they follow the narrative, sometimes even going outside the book itself to acquire what they need to know.

The background knowledge that each reader brings to the text shapes his interaction with it.

Reader and Task Considerations

This is the crucial issue. A text is just ink on paper until a reader comes along, picks it up, and reads it. A quantitative measure of a text generates a number, but that number may indicate that the prose is boringly simple for one person and hopelessly inaccessible for another. Who picks the text up matters. A qualitative assessment may indicate that a text has multiple levels of meaning, many complications in structure, and unconventional language, and may demand some arcane knowledge. One reader may find that those features have made the text impenetrable, while another may find that they make it a joy to explore. Indeed, who reads the text matters.

One reader may find that those features have made the text impenetrable, while another may find that they make it a joy to explore. *Who* reads the text matters.

When we move from quantitative to qualitative, the reader knocks at the door, and no matter how much we want to focus on features of the text, we have to hear the knock and sense the reader's impatience to be recognized and admitted.

When we turn to the third dimension, reader and task considerations, we know that the reader has beaten down the door and is now hovering over our shoulder, reaching for the book. At this point, we finally have to face the fact that the most complex factor in text complexity is the transaction between the reader and the text. And in this dimension teachers are on their own, with only their students to help them make decisions. At this point, a great many immeasurables and intangibles come into play. The number of syllables per word, we could count and average. With work and a tolerance for ambiguity and imprecision, some consensus on structural complexity and the other aspects of the qualitative dimension might be reached. With those two issues addressed and enough experience with adolescents behind us to have shaped a general impression of students' capacities

We finally have to face the fact that the most complex factor in text complexity is the transaction between the reader and the text.

at different ages and ability levels, we might be able to offer some tentative recommendations about where a book might fit in the classroom. But when thirty or forty students beat down the door, all bets are off. Or at least hedged, as much as possible.

Issues to Consider

Interest is critical. If the reader isn't interested in the text and can't be enticed to take an interest in it or at least give it a try, then the two other factors hardly matter. It's at this point that the individual teacher needs to know something about the individual student. If he likes adventure stories, tells you about the action movies he goes to, or simply appears to think of himself as one who would be out exploring the woods if school didn't interfere, then you might direct him to *Hatchet*. If she is a contemplative young student who thinks a great deal about social and emotional issues, then perhaps you send her to *Walk Two Moons*.

The student's background and ability are, of course, also of great importance. Our increasingly diverse population complicates this issue for us and at the same time enriches our classrooms. We can't assume that all students come from the same type of home with two parents in a traditional marriage, 2.7 children in the household, one dog, two cats, and three goldfish as pets. Single parents, same-sex parents, grandparents, foster parents, teens-as-parents: our students come from all types of homes. Additionally, some of our students may have immigrated within the last year or two, from Cambodia or Haiti, and may be struggling not only with the English language but also with a Western culture alien to their own experience, urban surroundings vastly different from their places of origin, and people whose attitudes, values, customs, and manners are vastly different from their own. Some may not have even set foot in a school until the day they arrived in your classroom. Others may have come to class on that first day directly from the plane, arriving home after their third summer in Europe, still speaking French and carrying their tattered copy of Flaubert's *Complete Works*.

As you think of the reading you'll ask your students to undertake, whether independently, in small groups, or as a whole class, you may want to consider several issues:

- How will the experiential background of these students guide the selection of texts and shape their responses to them? Will their background enable them to understand the book?

- Do they possess the knowledge necessary to comprehend the situation or the events presented? If not, can it be easily shared with them, or is it too complex or mature for them to deal with at their level of maturity?

It isn't just interest in the text, but interest in the task that is important. In 2011, Linda Rief's eighth-grade students in Oyster River Middle School in Durham, NH, worked on a project that had them building model submersibles. The hands-on, highly engaging, problem-solving work these students did meant they were reading highly complex expository texts with great determination and engagement. They were willing to read these how-to texts because they were using the texts to put the words into action. What we ask students to do can be so motivating that they are willing to struggle through the text, because the struggle results in a product that is meaningful to the student.

- Do they have the vocabulary and the linguistic sophistication to handle the prose? It may be challenging to find works for those students who are older and more sophisticated and experienced in many ways but whose language skills have lagged. They may not be able to read independently more complex books that present characters and issues in which they might otherwise take an interest, and they may be too mature for the content of those books written at their independent reading level.

In addition to ability and background, you will want to consider the attitudes and maturity of the students.

- Are they intellectually and emotionally mature enough to address the issues in the text successfully? Or does their greater maturity enable them to read a simpler text, one whose quantitative measures indicate that it is below their level, but deal with it in a satisfying way because they are able to ask interesting questions and engage in rewarding conversations about the issues?

- Does the book confront the students with issues that might unnecessarily embarrass or disturb them?

Text Complexity

This vision of text complexity may suggest that there is much to consider beyond the more obvious indicators of difficulty in a text. Glancing at a text and noting that the words are multisyllabic, the sentences complex, and the paragraphs long will tell us something but not enough. And the importance we have placed on the reader-text considerations in judging text complexity should suggest that the unique and personal elements the individual readers bring to the text are just as important, perhaps even more important, in assessing the suitability of a book for a student.

This concept of text complexity, moving as it does beyond the measurable elements to include attention to qualitative issues and to the connection between reader and task, transfers a great deal of responsibility to the teacher and the media specialist and implies great respect for their judgment. The quantitative measures we'll be happy to leave to computers in some distant city, but the other two dimensions are obviously beyond the capability of a machine. Judgments such as these have to be entrusted to a person. The respect this shows for your

Riding Freedom (Muñoz 2007), for instance, has a Lexile level of 720L. MetaMetrics now says this means this book is in the grade two to three band. The language isn't complex and challenging, the chapters are short, the story is narrated chronologically and directly. But the issue—gender expectations that force a young woman to live her entire life disguised as a man—actually makes this book appropriate for older readers.

professional judgment has been missing in much public discussion of education for too long, and it seems to us to be one of the few strong points of the Common Core Standards.

Figure 5 (shown on pages 60–61) is a worksheet we've created to help you think through these three components of text complexity. This figure is also reproduced at full size in the Appendix. If you want to try using this worksheet to assess some of the books you're considering teaching, we strongly urge you to try it with a few colleagues. Alone, it's a daunting task. But if you can gather a small group of teachers together around a few good books and work your way methodically through the four aspects of the *qualitative dimension* and then discuss the issues in *reader-task considerations*, you might find yourself enjoying the work. You will be, after all, talking about books and students, probably two of your favorite topics of conversation.

This concept of text complexity, moving as it does beyond the measurable elements to include attention to qualitative issues and to the connection between reader and text, transfers a great deal of responsibility to the teacher and the media specialist and implies great respect for their judgment.

Talking with Colleagues . . .

▶ If we use a leveling system for books in my school, do I understand how it was chosen?

▶ What's the research that supports the system we use? Was the research on the leveling system done by a group that isn't financially connected to the system? If not, have I been sufficiently skeptical of the findings?

▶ Am I reading enough children's literature, young adult books, and adult books that young adults will like that I'll know what books I might want to recommend to any particular student?

▶ Do my colleagues and I get together on a regular basis to talk about books and matching kids to books?

▶ What do my colleagues and I have to say about the new Lexile band recommendations for the following texts: *Monster*, 670L; *Speak*, 690L; *Hunger Games*, 810L? What do we think about *The Grapes of Wrath* having a Lexile score of 680L while *Understanding the Grapes of Wrath* has a level of 1270L?

Grade Band	Current Lexile Band	"Stretch" Lexile Band
K–1	N/A	N/A
2–3	450L–725L	420L–820L
4–5	645L–845L	740L–1010L
6–8	860L–1010L	925L–1185L
9–10	960L–1115L	1050L–1335L
11–CCR	1070L–1220L	1185L–1385L

New Lexile levels as of August 15, 2012.

Worksheet for Analysis of Text Complexity of a Literary Text

Title of the Text: _____

Quantitative Measures: Lexile (Other) Score _____ Grade level suggested by quantitative measures: _____

Qualitative Dimensions:

Complexity of Levels of Meaning

EASIER				DEMANDING
Simple, single meaning. Literal, explicit, and direct. Purpose or stance clear.	Much is explicit but moves to some implied meaning. Requires some inferential reasoning.	Multiple levels, use of symbolism, irony, satire. Some ambiguity. Greater demand for inference.	Multiple levels, subtle, implied meanings and purpose. Abstract, difficult ideas. Use of symbolism, irony, satire.	

EVIDENCE:

Complexity of Structure

EASIER				DEMANDING
Clear, chronological, conventional. May support through subheads, definitions, glossary.	Primarily explicit. Perhaps several points of view. May vary from simple chronological order. Largely conventional.	More complex. Narrow or perhaps multiple perspectives. More deviation from chronological or sequential order.	Complex, perhaps parallel, plot lines. Deviates from chronological or sequential. Narrator may be unreliable.	

EVIDENCE:

Complexity of Language Conventionality and Clarity

EASIER				DEMANDING
Explicit, literal, contemporary, familiar language. Vocabulary simple. Mostly Tier One words.	Mostly explicit, some figurative or allusive languge. Perhaps some dialect or other unconventional language.	Meanings are implied but support is offered. More figurative or ironic language. More inference is demanded.	Implied meanings. Allusive, figurative, or ironic language, perhaps archaic or formal. Complex sentence structures.	

EVIDENCE:

Complexity of Knowledge on Demands

EASIER				DEMANDING
Requires no special knowledge. Situations and subjects familiar or easily envisioned.	Some references to events or other texts. Begins to rely more on outside knowledge.	More complexity in theme. Experiences may be less familiar to many. Cultural or historical references may make heavier demands.	Explores complex ideas. Refers to texts or ideas that may be beyond students' experiences. May require specialized knowledge.	

EVIDENCE:

Qualitative dimensions indicate text makes demands that are: Mostly easier _____ Mostly more demanding _____

Grade level suggested by qualitative assessment _____

Figure 5: As you and your colleagues consider qualitative demands and reader-and-task considerations, this worksheet might be helpful.

Reader-Task Considerations

This is perhaps the most important element in judging the complexity of the text, and the most subtle. At issue is the suitability of a particular text for a particular reader. What follows are some questions to consider in making such a judgment. As you think about these questions with students in mind, make comments in the space provided.

Interest
- Is the student/class likely to be interested in the character, theme, topic, issue, subject matter, or genre?

Background and Ability
- Does the student/class have background knowledge or experience necessary to deal with the text and the task?

- Is the student/class intellectually capable of dealing with the issues presented in the text and the task?

- Does the student/class have vocabulary and inferential skills necessary for this text and the task?

Attitudes and Maturity
- Is the student/class sufficiently mature and sophisticated to deal with the subject matter?

- Does the book raise issues that might embarrass readers or be in some other way problematic?

Potential for Stimulating Thought, Discussion, and Further Reading
- Is there potential in the reading of this text for good conversation among readers?

- Does this text raise issues or questions likely to inspire the student/class to further reading, research, and writing?

Comments Summarizing the Assessments on the Three Dimensions

- How much support will be needed with this text at grade _____?

- Final recommendation for use and placement of text: _____
  Grade level? Early or late in the year? For independent reading, guided group instruction, full class?

Are We Creating Lifelong Learners?

This first part of Notice and Note *has been about* some of the questions we have asked one another in the past several years. We've not shared here our questions about how the Internet has changed the way we work, made the world smaller, and made collaboration critical. We didn't list our frustrations about cutting fine arts from the school day. We didn't share our deep concern about bullying and the failure by some students to make ethically responsible decisions. We didn't offer our questions about the writing students do (or don't do) or the technology skills they are (or are not) developing, about the new assessments teachers and students are facing, about budget cutbacks, about tying teacher evaluations to assessment scores, or—well, there are always questions.

But the questions we've discussed in this section were the ones that guided our thinking about the biggest question of all: Are we creating lifelong learners?

Helping students be ready for college or for a career is certainly an important mission for schools. We think, though, that there's another mission, perhaps one that, if accomplished, makes the world a better place by making each of us a better person. School ought to be a place where you go to develop a passion for learning—for a lifetime of learning. You ought to leave at the end of twelve years with a profound sadness that a time in your life when your primary obligation was to learn, to discover, to wonder, to try, to fail—and then to try again—has ended. School should never be called "jail" or "dumb" or "boring." There should never be "burn parties," those events where kids gather at the end of the year to burn their schoolwork in celebration of the year's end. Those first graders who can't wait to

> School ought to be a place where you go to develop a passion for learning— for a lifetime of learning.

begin this grand adventure called school should become twelfth graders who don't want it to end.

As a nation—perhaps not in your individual school or your own classroom—we have a long way to go in reaching that goal. We think a part of reaching it is helping students become independent, engaged readers—readers who will, for a lifetime, want to turn to books to learn more about themselves, others, and the world around them. Readers who always *notice and note*.

Talking with Colleagues . . .

▷ How often do I say something to students about becoming lifelong learners?

▷ Do I describe myself to students as a lifelong learner?

▷ How would students describe school? A place to hang out with friends? A place to learn more? A place to stretch and grow? Jail? Boring? A place they make you go?

▷ In this country, public education is a right given to all school-age children. What are we doing in our school to help students value this right and see it also as a privilege? If they fail to see it this way, why? What could we do in our school, what could I do in my classroom, to change any negative attitudes toward school?

Students from the lowest quartile of family income are seven times more likely to drop out than students from the highest quartile (U.S. Department of Education, 2010).

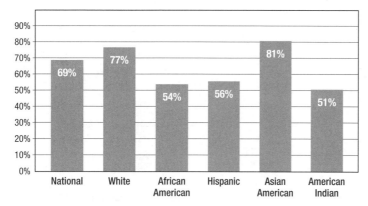

National Graduation Rate for Class of 2007

National: 69%
White: 77%
African American: 54%
Hispanic: 56%
Asian American: 81%
American Indian: 51%

This chart shows graduation rates by ethnicity. To turn that into numbers, about 1.3 million students do not graduate each year.
Source: Editorial Projects in Education, 2010.

The Signposts We Found

While thinking about the questions covered in Part I, we began reading the books listed on pages 4 and 5. We were looking for text features—beyond those we all already teach, such as the importance of titles, characters' names, setting, and the opening lines—that would help students read passages closely so they might better understand the text. We did indeed find features worth teaching, features we now call the Notice and Note Signposts. We then wrote a single question for each signpost that students should ask themselves once they notice it.

Part II shares those signposts, the anchor questions, comments about teaching the signposts, issues regarding assessment, and questions you might have.

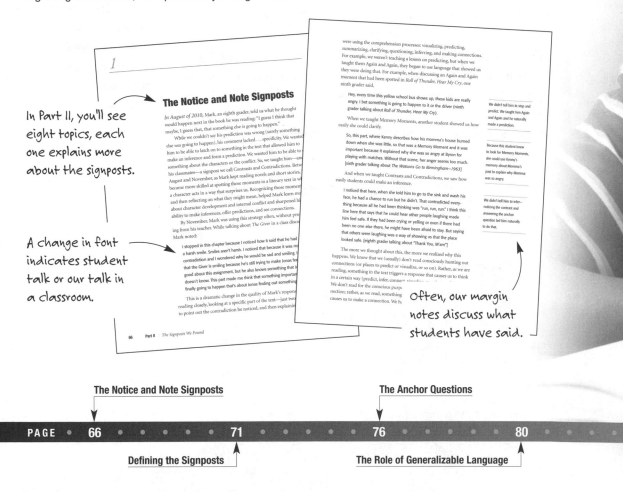

The Notice and Note Signposts

The Anchor Questions

PAGE • **66** • • • • • • • **71** • • • • • • • **76** • • • • • • • **80** • • • • •			

Defining the Signposts

The Role of Generalizable Language

1

The Notice and Note Signposts

In August of 2010, Mark, an eighth grader, told us what he thought would happen next in the book he was reading: "I guess I think that maybe, I guess that, that something else is going to happen."

While we couldn't say his prediction was wrong (surely something else *was* going to happen), his comment lacked . . . specificity. We wanted him to be able to latch on to something in the text that allowed him to make an inference and form a prediction. We wanted him to be able to say something about the characters or the conflict. So, we taught him—and his classmates—a signpost we call Contrasts and Contradictions. Between August and November, as Mark kept reading novels and short stories, he became more skilled at spotting those moments in a literary text in which a character acts in a way that surprises us. Recognizing those moments, and then reflecting on what they might mean, helped Mark learn more about character development and internal conflict and sharpened his ability to make inferences, offer predictions, and see connections.

By November, Mark was using this strategy often, without prompting from his teacher. While talking about *The Giver* in a class discussion Mark noted:

> I stopped in this chapter because I noticed how it said that he had a harsh smile. Smiles aren't harsh. I noticed that because it was really a contradiction and I wondered why he would be sad and smiling. I think that the Giver is smiling because he's still trying to make Jonas feel good about this assignment, but he also knows something that Jonas doesn't know. This part made me think that something important is finally going to happen that's about Jonas finding out something.

This is a dramatic change in the quality of Mark's response. He's reading closely, looking at a specific part of the text—just two words— to point out the contradiction he noticed, and then explaining why he thinks the character (in this case, the Giver) smiled harshly. Comparing his November comments with his August statement, we see that he's reading more thoughtfully, using both what his experience has taught him and what's in the text to form a prediction, make an inference, and analyze a character. Without doubt, Mark can still tighten his language, but when we compare this analysis offered in November to his earlier comment, "I guess that, that something else is going to happen," we are pleased. So, what is this signpost Contrasts and Contradictions, and how did we come to start teaching it—and the other signposts—to students? Let's begin with how we identified them.

Establishing the Criteria

As we were reading the novels that teachers told us they commonly taught (see pages 4 and 5), we began to identify particular features, features that helped us understand character development, internal conflict, and even theme. We kept comparing notes on what we were finding until one day, when talking about *Among the Hidden*, we both mentioned that we had noticed that the author had revealed Luke's internal conflict by having the character ask himself some tough questions: Is it really a life if you're hidden? Why do I have to hide? What will I do when Mother and Father die? We started rereading to see if this feature—the central character asking himself tough questions—occurred in other books. In each book we reviewed, we found scenes where the main character asked himself, or someone else, questions that revealed his innermost struggle.

Once we taught students the Contrasts and Contradictions lesson, they had a lot to say about the text they were reading.

Another time, while discussing *Tuck Everlasting*, we noticed the scene in which Tuck, the father, takes Winnie out into a boat and discusses the cycle of life with her. This scene, in which he shared wise words, revealed the author's theme, or at least one of them. Were there similar moments in other books in which a wise character shared a life lesson? Again, we reread and again we began to find such scenes.

As we looked for those features, we established three criteria that had to be met for us to conclude that the feature was worth teaching.

1. ***The feature had to have some characteristic that made it noticeable, that caused it to stand out from the surrounding text.*** We were looking, after all, for something in the text that even our less skillful and less enthusiastic readers could learn to spot, not for those clues that were subtle and easy to miss.

2. ***The feature had to show up across the majority of books.*** We realized that any particular author might in any particular book use a device unique to his or her idiosyncratic writing style. We want students to notice that, of course, but we were looking for text clues that consistently appeared across most books. It is this consistency across texts that makes the text feature important to learn and that gives us what we came to call *generalizable language*. This language provides students a principle they can apply across texts.

3. ***It had to offer something to readers who noticed and then reflected on it that helped them better understand their own responses, their own reading experience, and their own interpretation of the text.*** The textual element had to provide some insight into or raise some question about a literary element (character, setting, conflict, or theme), or it had to help readers predict, visualize, make connections, or draw an inference—any one of the comprehension processes.

Eventually we found features that met *all* three criteria. Most surprising, we found that not only did these features appear in *most* young adult books—they appeared in *every* young adult novel we read. Then we began to cull the list down to a critical six. Because these six features seemed to be particularly noticeable points in a text, passages that almost demanded that the reader pause and reflect, notice them and make note of them, we called them, as a group, the Notice and Note Signposts, and we named the signposts individually:

- Contrasts and Contradictions
- Aha Moment
- Tough Questions
- Words of the Wiser
- Again and Again
- Memory Moment

The Relationship Between Signposts and the Comprehension Processes

Before we define each of these (although we suspect that you can deduce what each means just from its name), we want to share something that happened as we taught students to notice them, something we never expected. The more students noticed these signposts, the more they were using the comprehension processes: visualizing, predicting, summarizing, clarifying, questioning, inferring, and making connections. For example, we weren't teaching a lesson on predicting, but when we taught them Again and Again, they began to use language that showed us they were doing that. For example, when discussing an Again and Again moment that had been spotted in *Roll of Thunder, Hear My Cry*, one ninth grader said,

> Hey, every time this yellow school bus shows up, these kids are really angry. I bet something is going to happen to it or the driver (ninth grader talking about *Roll of Thunder, Hear My Cry*).

We didn't tell him to stop and predict. We taught him Again and Again, and he naturally made a prediction.

When we taught Memory Moment, another student showed us how easily she could clarify.

> So, this part, where Kenny describes how his momma's house burned down when she was little, so that was a Memory Moment and it was important because it explained why she was so angry at Byron for playing with matches. Without that scene, her anger seems too much. [sixth grader talking about *The Watsons Go to Birmingham—1963*]

Because this student knew to look for the Memory Moment, she could use Kenny's memory about Momma's past to explain why Momma was so angry.

And when we taught Contrasts and Contradictions, we saw how easily students could make an inference.

> I noticed that here, when she told him to go to the sink and wash his face, he had a chance to run but he didn't. That contradicted everything because all he had been thinking was "run, run, run." I think this line here that says that he could hear other people laughing made him feel safe. If they had been crying or yelling or even if there had been no one else there, he might have been afraid to stay. But saying that others were laughing was a way of showing us that the place looked safe. [eighth grader talking about "Thank You, Ma'm"]

We didn't tell him to infer— noticing the contrast and answering the anchor question led him naturally to do that.

The more we thought about this, the more we realized why this happens. We know that we (usually) don't read consciously hunting out connections (or places to predict or visualize, or so on). Rather, *as* we are reading, something in the text triggers a response that causes us to think in a certain way (predict, infer, connect, visualize, question, and so on). We don't read for the conscious purpose of finding and labeling a connection; rather, as we read, something in the text triggers a memory or causes us to make a connection. We have to be alert for those noticeable moments in the text that trigger the connection, and then we explore the significance of that interaction.

Now, think back to Mark's comments about the Giver's harsh smile. Mark said, "I stopped here because I noticed how it said that he had a harsh smile. Smiles aren't harsh." Mark didn't stop and say, "I'm going to make a connection. My connection is that I don't think smiles are harsh." That's not natural language, and it's not natural thought. What's natural is to talk about the trigger and our reaction to it. Mark didn't set out to read the book with a plan to "make connections"; instead, he set out, alert and responsive, looking for moments that surprised and interested him, and in particular for the moment we've called Contrasts and Contradictions. He found one—"harsh smile"—and then he talked about that. If you'll look carefully at what he said, you'll see that he's made a connection and he's drawing some inferences.

If you need Mark to think metacognitively about the thinking he is doing while he reads, then you could respond to him with, "When you talk about what you think of harsh smiles, you show me that you are making an inference and making a connection. Perhaps you are even visualizing as you think about what smiles do and don't look like." Eventually, you could ask Mark—after he's made his comments about the text— to tell you what type of thinking his comments reveal he is doing.

2

Defining the Signposts

The lessons for teaching the six signposts we've identified appear in Part III. Here, though, is a brief explanation of each one. A chart of these appears on page 75, in Figure 6.

Contrasts and Contradictions: This is a point in the novel at which a character's actions or thoughts clearly contradict previous patterns or contrast with patterns the reader would normally expect, suggesting a change or offering new insight into the character. We see an example in *The Watsons Go to Birmingham—1963* when Byron, the near juvenile delinquent, kills a bird. When he thinks he is alone, he cries. This tender behavior contradicts the tough-guy exterior we've seen through the early pages of the book, suggesting that he may be more than simply a bully. Other contrasts and contradictions might offer insight into internal conflict, theme, or relationship of the setting to the plot.

Aha Moments: These are moments when a character's sudden insight or understanding helps us understand the plot's movement, the development of the character, or the internal conflict he faces. An Aha Moment is almost always revealed with very direct language students can be taught to watch for. Characters say, "I realized . . ." or "I suddenly understood . . ." or "It came to me that . . ." or "Now I knew. . . ." Luke, in *Among the Hidden*, is very direct with his aha: "The answer was there instantly, as if he'd known it all along and his brain was just waiting for him to come looking" (pp. 145–146). When students notice these Aha Moments, they see the character figure out something that almost always changes the character and therefore the plot.

Tough Questions: This is one lesson we haven't seen as often in adult literature but see consistently in children's and young adult literature. It is the point when the main character—a child or teen—pauses to

We present the definitions of the signposts in this order because this is the order in which we teach them to students. We've chosen this order because we find that every book has multiple instances of Contrasts and Contradictions and Aha Moments but perhaps only one or two Memory Moments. So, we want to introduce students to the signposts they'll see most often before those they'll see less often.

ask, of himself or a trusted other, tough questions. Sometimes, these questions appear not as questions but as statements, often with the word *wonder*: "I wonder what I should do about. . . ." These moments of uncertainty give readers insight into the character's development, his internal conflicts, and perhaps theme. The lesson of Tough Questions is easy to teach because you simply encourage students to be on the lookout for the big questions a character asks, all of which will be obvious. For instance, Esperanza, in *Esperanza Rising*, asks of herself, "Why did Papa have to die? Why did he leave me and Mama?" (p. 38).

Elementary school teachers tell us that their students understand this signpost quickly when they call it "The Heart Lesson." Use the language that works for your students. There is nothing magical about the names we've chosen.

Words of the Wiser: This is the scene in which a wiser and often older character offers a life lesson of some sort to the protagonist. This lesson often emerges as a theme of the novel. Sometimes the Words of the Wiser consist of only one line: Vern telling Charlotte in *Riding Freedom* that "You gotta do what your heart tells you" (p. 38). Other times the lesson emerges in a longer scene as in *Tuck Everlasting* when Tuck takes Winnie out on a pond in a rowboat and tells her that:

> It's a wheel, Winnie. Everything's a wheel, turning and turning, never stopping. The frog is part of it, and the bugs, and the fish, and the wood thrush, too. And people. But never the same ones. Always coming in new places, always growing and changing, and always moving on. That's the way it's supposed to be. That's the way it is. (p. 62).

The Words of the Wiser moment in a novel is often announced by placing the younger main character off alone with the older, wiser character in a quiet, meditative, often solemn moment. It's usually obvious from the setting that a serious conversation is about to ensue, and that conversation is usually the Words of the Wiser. When students notice these scenes, these moments when the wiser character imparts his or her wisdom, they see a guiding lesson that transcends the conflict in the novel; they gain insight into a theme.

Again and Again: This is an image, word, or situation that is repeated, leading the reader to wonder about its significance. Repetition might provide information about a character, about the conflict, about the setting, or about the theme. The object or phrase or event that is repeated might serve as some sort of symbol. In *The Giver*, readers see the word *release* repeatedly. In *Bud, Not Buddy*, the main character—Bud—repeatedly examines the small bag of rocks with strange numbers on them that his mother had collected. In *Hatchet*, Brian keeps calling to mind something he calls "the Secret."

Memory Moment: A Memory Moment is a scene that interrupts the flow of the story and reveals something important about a character, plot, or theme. It is the intrusion of the remembered event into what's happening in the present that marks this moment for the reader (and it is because the memory seems to interrupt the ongoing narrative that readers often skip it, eager to get on with the tale). In *The Outsiders*, early in the book Ponyboy remembers when his friend Johnny was badly beaten. This memory gives readers important background about Johnny's fears, the situation in Ponyboy's community, and the relationship between two rival gangs.

Other Signposts in Texts

We know that these are not the only moments in a text to pay attention to and wouldn't encourage students to sleep through the passages in between. Rather, we see these as the features most easily spotted and most likely to reward reflection. If students begin to notice these, question them, and note what they learn, they are likely to become observant and thoughtful at other points in the book as well.

Over the several years we've worked on this project, the number of these signposts has varied, once rising as high as twelve or thirteen. For instance, for a long time we had a *Last Lines* signpost. We asked students to be alert for a last line of a chapter or section that seemed to be unique. It might be extraordinarily short—perhaps even just one word—or it might begin with a conjunction (*and* or *but*). Such a last line often pointed to something important, perhaps indicating an imminent change. But too often it was simply a hook to compel the reader to move on to the next chapter, so even though that text feature appeared frequently, it didn't seem to be as helpful as others. For a while we worked with *Mind the Gap*, that point in the story at which the author makes obvious the character's ignorance of some crucial information (and probably the reader's ignorance, too). Later we decided that in many cases the gap in understanding was made evident through one of the other signposts. We finally settled on the six described above as the ones that best met the criteria.

If you see other signposts that you want to add to the list, do so (taking care not to make the list unmanageably large for your students). See this list of six as a starting place. As we begin to work on signposts in expository texts, we are very likely to add several that aren't in this collection.

As you think about each of these signposts, you'll see that they appear not only in texts but also in our lives. When your significant other mentions *again and again* that the garbage needs to go out, there's a subtext to that message—and it has to do with rising anger! When the friend who always checks on you suddenly begins to ignore you, then the *contrast* with what you expect, the *contradiction* of an established pattern, makes you wonder what is wrong. If you're now a parent, you can look back on those long talks with your own parents not as "another boring lecture" but as your parent's attempt to spare you some pain, to impart the *words of someone wiser*. When a friend asks you what your teen thought of the party that weekend, you suddenly realize—*aha*—that your teen's sad face over that weekend tells you she hadn't been invited.

> We think that these signposts show up in novels because they show up in the world.

We think that these signposts show up in novels because they show up in the world. Fiction does imitate life, and as a result we shouldn't be surprised to find that the patterns that help us understand the world around us also help us understand the world of the book in front of us.

The Notice and Note Signposts and Definitions	The Clues to the Signpost	What Literary Element it Helps Readers Understand
Contrasts and Contradictions A sharp contrast between what we would expect and what we observe the character doing; behavior that contradicts previous behavior or well-established patterns	A character behaves or thinks in a way we don't expect, or an element of a setting is something we would not expect.	Character development Internal conflict Theme Relationship between setting and plot
Aha Moment A character's realization of something that shifts his actions or understanding of himself, others, or the world around him	Phrases, usually expressing suddenness, like: "Suddenly I understood. . . ." "It came to me in a flash that. . . ." "The realization hit me like a lightning bolt. . . ." "In an instant I knew. . . ."	Character development Internal conflict Plot
Tough Questions Questions a character raises that reveal his or her inner struggles	Phrases expressing serious doubt or confusion: "What could I possibly do to . . . ?" "I couldn't imagine how I could cope with. . . ." "How could I ever understand why she . . . ?" "Never had I been so confused about. . . ."	Internal conflict Theme Character development
Words of the Wiser The advice or insight a wiser character, who is usually older, offers about life to the main character	The main character and another are usually off by themselves, in a quiet, serious moment, and the wiser figure shares his wisdom or advice in an effort to help the main character with a problem or a decision.	Theme Internal conflict Relationship between character and plot
Again and Again Events, images, or particular words that recur over a portion of the novel	A word is repeated, sometimes used in an odd way, over and over in the story. An image reappears several times during the course of the book.	Plot Setting Symbolism Theme Character development Conflict
Memory Moment A recollection by a character that interrupts the forward progress of the story	The ongoing flow of the narrative is interrupted by a memory that comes to the character, often taking several paragraphs to recount before we are returned to events of the present moment.	Character development Plot Theme Relationship between character and plot

Figure 6: The Notice and Note Signposts

3

The Anchor Questions

We began sharing these signposts with teachers—especially a great group of about 250 South Carolina teachers who came from across that state four times to meet with us in Columbia. We taught them the lessons and they returned to their schools and shared them with their students. Later, they would return to Columbia with comments. Almost immediately it was apparent that students—elementary, middle school, and high school students—did begin noticing the signposts. What we also discovered was that when students identified a signpost, teachers did what we all know how to do: they began asking students all sorts of questions. *Why do you think Byron was crying? How do you think this made Kenny feel? Would Byron have continued crying if he knew Kenny was watching him?* Suddenly something that was supposed to make students independent of the teacher was making them dependent.

The Power of One

We didn't want to lose the power of asking questions, because questions have almost always been a teacher's primary way of helping students analyze a text. In the past, we had often spent long hours devising a series of questions that would lead students, inductively, we hoped, through the analysis of a text they had read. Those questions could be powerful and revealing, but they never became the *students'* questions. There was no way that could have happened. There were too many questions, we'd worked hard to arrange them, and we didn't ever try to teach them to the students. We used them for the text of the day and then devised another series for tomorrow's lesson. *We* owned the questions, and they were not helping our struggling readers become independent readers. After all, we had convinced them that it was the answers, not the questions, that were most important. Somehow we had to reverse that.

Students need to assume ownership of the question. For them to become independent readers, they need to have the question in *their* repertoire, they need to be able to apply it appropriately, and they need to let it lead them to other questions. In short, they need fewer questions, not more. They aren't going to assimilate long strings of questions. They could, however, learn and remember fewer questions, questions useful with any text. If those questions are more powerful, they will serve well. We decided to try to develop one question for each of the signposts. If students could depend on that question, if they came to realize that it led to insight, and if they learned that out of that question many other questions might naturally emerge, then they'd have a useful tool to bring to other texts.

As we went into classes, we began experimenting with questions and eventually decided upon those in Figure 7 (page 79) as our anchor questions.

The Signposts *and* the Anchor Questions

The Notice and Note Signposts represent what we want students to do as they read. They notice something in the text and then stop to note what it might mean. Thinking about what the signpost might mean requires that students ask themselves the anchor question, so don't just teach students the signposts; also teach them the anchor question that goes with each. Thanks (again) to Jen, who shared with us the bookmark she now gives her students as they read so they can keep both the signposts and the anchor questions in mind.

When you talk with students about any of the signposts, you'll hear them pointing out contradictions or tough questions and thinking they've done enough. For example, one student, while reading *Bridge to Terabithia*, pointed out, "Now that I'm looking for things that happen again and again, it seems that Jess keeps having bad dreams that are in some way about water." The teacher was so impressed with his comment (and so were we) that she forgot to follow up by

Notice and Note Signposts Bookmark Front and Back
A template is found on pages 206–207 in the Appendix.

asking, "Why do you think this keeps happening again and again?" When we prompted her to ask that question, her student responded, "Well, you get the idea that something bad is going to happen because his dreams are all bad and it's going to be something with water. Maybe there's going to be a flood." When prompted to consider the anchor question, the student began making inferences, making connections, and offering a prediction. It's the question that moves students into deeper thinking. Noticing the signpost is necessary but insufficient; the readers also have to question it and make note of what they learn from it.

Noticing the signpost is necessary but insufficient; the readers also have to question it and make note of what they learn from it.

The Notice and Note Signposts	The Question That Follows	Why We Ask This Question
Contrasts and Contradictions	Why would the character act (feel) this way?	Contrasts and Contradictions show us other aspects of a character or a setting. This question encourages conversation about character, motivation, or the situation he is in.
Aha Moment	How might this change things?	An Aha Moment reveals change. This question focuses on that change—for the character or the setting.
Tough Questions	What does this question make me wonder about?	Tough Questions almost always reveal internal conflict and understanding that conflict generally offers insight into the theme. We want readers thinking about these big issues—the ones that shape the tough questions. By asking themselves this anchor question, readers are making a connection between the author's thinking and their own thoughts.
Words of the Wiser	What's the life lesson and how might it affect the character?	Words of the Wiser suggests the theme. We use this question to help the reader think about this theme in the context of the character's life. We hope that students might then think of it in terms of their own life, but didn't want to start with that question as that might be too probing for some students.
Again and Again	Why might the author bring this up again and again?	Recurring images, events, or words offer insight into character motivation or theme; this question encourages readers to speculate on that insight.
Memory Moment	Why might this memory be important?	Memories generally explain character motivation. They might explain why a character acts a certain way, or they might serve as guidance for a situation that a character eventually finds herself in. If they offer insight into the theme, they often become Again and Again moments. This question asks students to consider the relationship between the memory and the character or plot.

Figure 7: Notice and Note Signpost Anchor Questions

4

The Role of Generalizable Language

When we began teaching the signposts, we also saw how important it was to teach them with what we call *generalizable language.*

You know the saying about the choice between giving a man a fish and teaching him how to fish. We think some teachers do only give students a fish. In other words, they tell students an answer, or explain whatever it is the students don't understand, rather than teach them how to figure it out themselves. We think that *more* teachers, though, are trying to teach their students *how* to fish. For example, we see teachers tell students about the importance of predicting or visualizing (or any of the other comprehension processes) as they discuss a text. For instance, we heard a teacher stop and think aloud about a scene from *Among the Hidden*, saying something like:

> I'll stop here because I can imagine how hard it is for Luke to decide if he wants to risk going over to the other house. He knows he might get himself and his family in a lot of trouble if he does this, yet he has realized that he can't stay in his house forever. I can almost feel his nervousness. When we can make connections like this, we better understand the characters.

This teacher was trying to show her students how to better understand the story, *how* to fish. She was emphasizing the process of making a connection ("When we make connections like this, we better understand . . ."). The problem was, she only really taught them how to understand this specific text, how to fish for this one fish. That's because she failed to show them something in this text (about this fish) that could be applied to any other text (any other fish).

When she told them "When we can make connections like this," some of her students were left to wonder, "Like what? Connections to nervous characters?" What her students needed, even more than an understanding of Luke and his fears, was the understanding of a guiding principle that would help them understand what in a text—any text—might trigger their connection to the scene and their envisioning of the scene. A student who learned *that* overarching rule might then be able to confront the next text—one that doesn't have a nervous Luke—and better understand what's happening in it. What the student had to learn was not to spot Luke's nervousness—that's too specific and unlikely ever to appear again in another text—but rather to spot a *kind* of moment, an event with certain characteristics.

In this case, what the student needed to learn was that when a character does something that contradicts what he has been doing, that's likely to reveal something about the character and his situation. So, in this example, we wish the teacher had said something like this:

> I'll stop here because I've noticed an important contradiction. *When authors show us a character acting in a way that contrasts with or contradicts what he has been doing, I know I need to pause and ask myself, "Why is the character acting this way?"* Luke has been too afraid to leave his house and now he's contemplating breaking all the rules and going to another house. In this scene, Luke knows he might get himself and his family in a lot of trouble if he does this, yet he has realized that he can't stay in his house forever. I think he's acting this way because. . . ."

The italicized words are the generalizable language, the language that students can keep in their heads as they read any text. Then you move to text-specific language, language that shows how this plays out in this one text.

Creating a Habit of Mind

What we are trying to teach our students at this point is, from one perspective, very simple. All our students know what a contrast is, for example, or what an "aha" is. The notion of the tough question is not that elusive. All of them—even those who struggle almost hopelessly with texts—know the concept of repetition, of something happening again and again. Those are not difficult ideas.

Nor are these six text signposts hard to grasp when pointed out in a story. When we help a class notice the repetition of the word *release* in the first pages of *The Giver*, not a single child asks us what we mean by "again and again." They see the word on this page, the next, and the one after that, and say, essentially, "Yes, she's using the word *release* again and again." Most are distinctly unimpressed by that observation.

Nor do they find the anchor questions impossible to deal with, although many are slow at first to speculate, infer, or even guess. Perhaps they are too accustomed to questions that require them simply to extract from the text, whole and intact, a word or phrase or fact, or to questions that demand only a yes or no answer. Whatever the reason, many are slow, reluctant, or timid when asked a question that begins "What might . . ." or "Why would. . . ." That may take some prompting and patience.

The problem is that we aren't simply teaching the six text signposts. Nor are we fishing for good answers to the anchor questions when we ask them. Instead, we are trying to instill some reading habits and shape a pattern of reading behavior in our students. We want to teach our students to be alert for certain features as they read, to take responsibility themselves for pausing and reflecting when they spot them, to own and ask a few potentially powerful questions at those moments, and to be willing to share and revise their thoughts in responsible conversation with others.

> We want to teach our students to be alert for certain features as they read, to take responsibility themselves for pausing and reflecting when they spot them, to own and ask a few potentially powerful questions at those moments, and to be willing to share and revise their thoughts in responsible conversation with others.

Thus the importance of generalizable language in our lessons. We need to keep emphasizing the text feature that reveals the signpost and the question students should consider. We need to keep reminding the students, explicitly, what we are asking them to do—notice, pause, reflect. And we need to make sure that the language we use doesn't just help them learn more about any one particular text but is generalizable to other texts.

Our Generalizable Language

Let's look at the role of generalizable language in the teaching of the Notice and Note Signposts, using Contrasts and Contradictions. We'll begin by looking, first, at comments a teacher made in a think-aloud of the first paragraph of *Among the Hidden*, found in the Appendix on page 208. This think-aloud lacks generalizable language.

> I'll stop here because I want to think about how Luke must feel, never being able to go outside again. I had to stay indoors once, for several weeks, after some surgery, and that was difficult. But I can't imagine never going out again. That's just odd. I don't know why he's going to have to stay indoors, so let's keep reading.

Now look at what happens when we make the signpost lesson explicit by adding the generalizable language:

> I'll stop here because *I know that when authors show me a character acting in a way that contrasts with how I would expect someone to act, the author is showing me something important about that character.* Here, Luke says he will never be allowed outside again. I can't imagine why he would say that; it certainly contrasts with the life I've lived. *When authors show us such a contrast or contradiction, then I want to pause and ask myself, "Why would the character act this way?" As I think about this question, I wonder if it might be . . . .*

Notice that this think-aloud not only talks about what is in the text, but it gives students the lesson—the generalizable language—they can carry with them to the next book they read. You can see the generalizable language we use for all the Notice and Note lessons in Figure 8. Also notice that in our think-aloud we don't spend time stating the name of the signpost. We don't think that the names are critical. What's important is that the reader notice something and then stop to consider what it

The teacher has told her students she wants to think about Luke, but why? Why stop here? Her comment doesn't help the struggling readers, who need help transferring what is said about one text to another.

Italicized words are the generalizable language. Now students have a rule— if you will—to keep in mind as they read.

And this is the anchor question.

means. We're hearing students call Contrasts and Contradictions "C & C," and one teacher told us that she's changed the name "Contrasts and Contradictions" to "Lessons of the Unexpected" and that her students call "Words of the Wiser" "Life Lessons." That's fine. The label is just a way to identify the signpost. Noticing the signpost and then considering the anchor question is what counts.

The Signpost	Our Generalizable Language
To help students think about **Contrasts and Contradictions . . .**	When authors show you a character acting in a way that contrasts with how you would expect someone to act or that contradicts how that character has been acting, you know the author is showing you something important about that character. You'll want to pause and ask yourself, "Why would the character act this way?" As I think about this question, I wonder if it might be. . . .
To help students think about **Aha Moment . . .**	When a character realizes or finally understands something, then you want to pause because you know this realization means something. It might be showing you something about character development or a new direction of the plot. You want to ask yourself, "How might this change things?" Now that this character realizes this, I think that. . . .
To help students think about **Tough Questions . . .**	You know that when a character pauses to ask himself or a friend some really tough questions, then you are getting a glimpse of what's bothering him the most, and those questions often show you what the character will struggle with throughout the story. When you see these tough questions, stop and ask yourself, "What does this question make me wonder about?" These questions she was asking herself make me think that. . . .
To help students think about **Words of the Wiser . . .**	When a wise character—who is often older than the main character—shares his or her understanding, insight, or advice on an issue or topic, stop and think about that. These insights or this advice usually reveals something important about the theme. Ask yourself, "What's the life lesson, and how might it affect the character?" The important lesson offered here is that. . . .
To help students think about **Again and Again . . .**	When you see repetition in a novel, you can bet that it's important, but you might not know, right away, what it means. Repetition might give insight into the setting or a character or perhaps a symbol of some sort. You have to ask yourself, "Why does this keep happening again and again?" Here, I see. . . .
To help students think about **Memory Moment . . .**	When we share a memory with someone, it's usually because that memory has something to do with what's happening at that moment; the memory of the past helps explain the present moment. So, when an author has a character pause to think about a memory or share a memory with someone, I know that the memory can tell me something about what's happening right now. That memory might give me insight into what bothers or motivates a character; or it might help me understand something happening in the plot; it might even give me information about the theme. When you notice a Memory Moment, stop and ask yourself, "Why might this memory be important?" This memory seems important because. . . .

Figure 8: Generalizable Language for Each Notice and Note Signpost

This is our generalizable language for the Notice and Note Signposts. Do we repeat all this language all the time? No, but this is the essence, and we keep trying to capture this when we model with students.

6

Explaining the Signposts

Before you begin explaining the signposts to students, you need to think through a few things. Considering these issues now will save you time later on.

Decide Upon an Order for Teaching the Notice and Note Signposts

Consider starting with Contrasts and Contradictions, Aha Moments, and Tough Questions. They appear reliably and frequently, struggling readers can learn to identify them fairly easily, and the anchor question for each almost always provides significant information or insight or awakens curiosity about an unanswered question that readers can hold on to as they read.

Then move on to Words of the Wiser because it offers a critical lesson about theme. Although most novels have only one Words of the Wiser scene, that one scene is always vitally important, and it often continues to show up as an Again and Again moment as the character keeps calling to mind the lesson she or he has learned. Finally, we move to Again and Again and Memory Moments.

That said, if the novel you are about to teach has many Memory Moments, then start there, or start with Contrasts and Contradictions (because it will have those, too) and then jump to Memory Moments. In other words, think about the order we've suggested, but don't use that order if it doesn't make sense with what you're teaching.

Set Aside Time to Teach Each Signpost Lesson

Notice that we've never referred to the signpost lessons as minilessons. They aren't. In fact, we think that this is one of the most overused terms in education. Not everything should be taught in seven to twelve minutes. Reviews should be minilessons. Introducing new concepts, well, that requires time. You'll need about thirty to forty minutes for the model lessons we've provided.

Model lessons are found in Part III.

Teach Each Signpost Lesson with a Text That Illustrates the Targeted Signpost

In the model lessons that follow in Part III—one lesson for each of the Notice and Note Signposts—we've provided the text we use when teaching the lessons, but you should of course choose others if you think they'll work better for your students. Because you'll be reading these short selections aloud, you don't have to find texts at your students' independent reading levels, but students do have to be able to deal with the content. Choose something that you can read aloud in ten to fifteen minutes so that the lesson won't take more than about forty minutes in all.

If you choose your own texts, look for a selection that illustrates the signpost several times (see "Thank You, Ma'm" in the lesson on Contrasts and Contradictions for an example of one signpost appearing repeatedly). You may have to pull scenes from several places in a single book, as we did in the Tough Questions lessons. For Words of the Wiser, which usually occurs only once in a book, you will probably have to choose scenes from *several* books.

A Long Walk to Water, the book we use to teach Tough Questions, is filled with moments where the main character asks himself tough questions. To teach this signpost, we pulled passages from pages 9, 58, 59, and 72.

Some of you enjoy teaching with picture storybooks, and these short texts often provide examples of some of the lessons. For example:

- *Alexander and the Terrible Horrible No Good Very Bad Day* is a great example of Again and Again and Words of the Wiser.

- *I Want My Hat Back* offers an example of an Aha Moment.

- *Chrysanthemum* offers examples of Contrasts and Contradictions, Again and Again, and Words of the Wiser.

- *Ira Sleeps Over* includes Tough Questions, Again and Again, and Words of the Wiser.

- *The Three Questions* illustrates Tough Questions and Words of the Wiser.

When we teach signposts, we teach one at a time, and we use a text that will easily highlight that signpost. Here, we're teaching Contrasts and Contradictions with an article from *Time for Kids*. We were happy to see it worked well.

Recognize That the Model Text You Choose Might Be One That Is Not at a Student's Independent Reading Level

In Part III and the Appendix, we provide the text we use when teaching each signpost lesson, but you should of course choose others if you think they'll work better for your students. Just remember that you don't have to find texts at your students' independent reading levels—as long as you think they can deal with the content. Again, choose something that you can read aloud in ten to fifteen minutes so that the lesson won't take more than about forty minutes.

Use a Gradual Release Model

A gradual release model seems to work well. Demonstrate; then turn over part of the task to the class; then have them do it on their own.

Roughly, here are the steps in the lesson.

Most Support From You	**1 Explain the signpost and the anchor question.** As you do so, make a poster with the name of the signpost, the text features that identify it, and the anchor question.
▼	**2 Tell students you'll show them how the signpost you are teaching works by sharing a short text.** Make sure they have a copy of what you'll be reading.
▼	**3 Read aloud to the first occurrence of the signpost you are teaching.** Point out that what you saw in the text that caused you to pause is the signpost you're teaching, and remind students that authors use this signpost to give readers information. Then ask yourself the anchor question and share your thoughts about possible answers.
▼	**4 Read the second section, stopping at the next instance of the signpost.** Point it out to students, and ask them to turn and talk in pairs about the anchor question (two to three minutes). Share some responses in the full group. This time, you've pointed out the signpost but turned over talking about the anchor question to them.
▼	**5 Read the third section, and perhaps a fourth.** This time, you're releasing responsibility to students even more, as you ask them to both identify the signpost and discuss the anchor question. If they need help, divide this into two steps. First, let students discuss the signpost, in pairs or as a large group, and then have them talk about the anchor question with their partner. Again, the talk is for only two to three minutes. Share thoughts in the full group.
▼	**6 Read to the end of the selection.** Now, turning over a little more responsibility to students, ask them to identify the most significant example of the signpost in the entire passage, discuss the anchor question, and report to the full group.
▼ **Least Support From You**	**7 Tell students to watch for the feature in their independent reading, to mark those they find, and jot down their thoughts as they think about the anchor question.** At this point you've turned over all responsibility to students.

Think About the Generalizable Language You Will Use

Most important, plan the *generalizable language* in your explanation. Not "I notice Luke acting strangely and so I think that . . . ," but "Here I noticed a character acting in a way that *contrasts* with what I'd expect," followed by what you saw Luke doing. Then, "When I see such a contrast, I always ask myself . . ." and on to the anchor question. You want students to learn to be alert to *contrasts*, not simply to learn about Luke.

Be prepared to put the heart of the lesson on a sheet of flip-chart paper as you're teaching it. Have the paper and a bold marker at hand. That poster will include the name of the lesson, the noticeable features of the text that announce the signpost, and the anchor question to be asked. That poster should go up on the wall and remain there for a long time, reinforcing the lesson you've taught and increasing the likelihood that students will retain it.

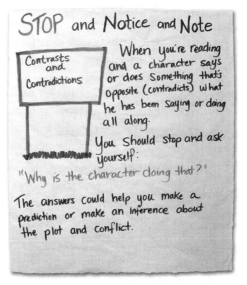

STOP and Notice and Note

Contrasts and Contradictions

When you're reading and a character says or does something that's opposite (contradicts) what he has been saying or doing all along.

You should stop and ask yourself:

"Why is the character doing that?"

The answers could help you make a prediction or make an inference about the plot and conflict.

And, of Course, Experiment

Lee Smith, a teacher in the Dallas Independent School System, told us that she taught the signpost lessons in a way we had never considered: all six at one time. She made a chart with the name of each text clue and the question to be asked. Then she briefly explained each one, and offered an example, and had students think about books they had already read and point out a scene that they thought illustrated the signpost. Finally, as a class, they began reading *A Christmas Carol*. As they read it aloud, she pointed out the signposts she saw, and soon students were doing the same. She reported that since all six signposts appeared repeatedly, students had many opportunities to practice spotting them and then discussing their implications. If you think your students are able to hold multiple lessons in mind at one time, then you might try Lee's approach.

Our experiences differ from Lee's. We returned to a classroom in Akron, Ohio, to teach Aha Moment after having taught Contrasts and Contradictions several weeks before. As we began the lesson, we reminded students that we had been there about a month ago to teach another lesson. "Who remembers that lesson?" we asked. Silence. One young man looked at us with no hint of a smile and asked, "You were here before?"

We were working with a group of seventh graders in a small, suburban middle school. Some of the students loved to read, more were what we call book-at-a-time readers. (Give them the right book and they'll read it, but they don't actively seek out books on their own.) More than several didn't like to read at all.

We had taught them Contrasts and Contradictions on one visit, Aha Moment on another visit, and Memory Moment on a third. On a fourth visit, our plan was to read aloud the first two chapters of *Among the Hidden* to see if students noticed any of those three signposts, which occur several times in the first two chapters. We didn't get the first two chapters read. Students were too busy interrupting us with their comments and their conversations with one another. We did make it through the opening scene.

> Before you read this transcript of students discussing the signposts they saw in the first couple of chapters of *Among the Hidden*, why don't you turn to page 208 of the Appendix and try this on your own.

KYLENE: It's great to be back with you guys, and we're looking forward to seeing what you notice as we read the first couple of chapters of the novel your teacher said you'd be reading soon, *Among the Hidden*. You've all got your novels, so let's just jump in and begin reading. Dr. Probst will read aloud, and we want you to follow along. Use your pencils to put light checkmarks by any lines that you notice that make you think about Contrasts and Contradictions, Aha Moments, or Memory Moments. Then, when it makes sense to pause, we'll talk about what you've found and think about the anchor questions.

BOB: OK, follow along as I read: "He saw the first tree shudder and fall, far off in the distance. Then he heard his mother call out the kitchen window: 'Luke, Inside. Now.' He had never disobeyed the order to hide. Even as a toddler, barely able to walk in the backyard's tall grass, he had somehow understood" [One student interrupted at this point.]

STUDENT 1: Hey, Dr. Probst, that's a Memory Moment because . . . [It was hard to understand because another student began speaking.]

STUDENT 2: Yeah, I thought so too because it was like . . . [Many students began speaking.]

> Four minutes into class and we had lost control, as now all students had turned to other students asking where the Memory Moment was. We let them talk for about another thirty seconds.

KYLENE: Let's come back together. [Well, that didn't work.] Hey guys, look back up this way. [Slowly students looked at us.] We're hearing a lot of you say this is a Memory Moment, while I think some of you say it's not. Who thinks this is a Memory Moment? [Hands went up. I called on student 7, and when he finished, other students offered their thoughts without us having to call on them.]

STUDENT 7: He had to be remembering that he always obeyed to know that he had never disobeyed.

STUDENT 8: But it doesn't say it's his memory. He's not saying, "I always obeyed." This is just like background knowledge.

STUDENT 6: And that's what makes it a memory.

STUDENT 10: But even if it's not a memory of his, it matters that we, you know, the readers, that we know this because look at the anchor question for Memory Moment: Why is this memory significant? That's what's important because . . . [Student 15 started talking over the remainder of this comment.]

STUDENT 15: Yeah, that's it because it says he has never disobeyed the order to hide and . . . [Student 20 started talking over remainder of this comment.]

STUDENT 20: And like you suddenly know that he's always been ordered to hide.

STUDENT 13: This was a really cool way of showing you that he's always had to hide.

STUDENT 15: So, like why is he always hiding? Maybe he was kidnapped?

Most students began talking at this point, and we decided it was time to move on.

BOB: These are all great speculations. You've noticed something very interesting early on, and some of you see that as a Memory Moment. Others don't. But all of you recognize that it's important to us, as readers, to learn that he's had to hide from something or someone his entire life. Let's keep reading to see what else we discover.

> Even as a toddler, barely able to walk in the backyard's tall grass, he had somehow understood the fear in his mother's voice. But on this day, the day they began taking the woods away, he hesitated. He took one extra breath of fresh air, scented with clover and honeysuckle and—come from far away—pine smoke. He laid his hoe down gently, and savored one last moment of feeling warm soil beneath his bare feet. He reminded himself, 'I will never be allowed outside again. Maybe never again as long as I live.' He turned and walked into the house, as silently as a shadow.

BOB: When you're ready, turn and talk with your reading partner about any of the Notice and Note Signposts you saw and your answers to the anchor questions.

Almost immediately all the students turned to their reading partners. We'd been there with them enough that they knew we wanted students working with only one other person. All around the room students were talking, pointing at sentences, listening to one another. Occasionally, we'd hear, "Oh, I get it" or "Yeah, I see what you mean" or "I just don't think that's it." What follows is the conversation of one pair.

STUDENT 11: This line here, "I will never be allowed outside again. Maybe never again as long as I live." That's a Contrast and Contradiction because I don't know anyone who ever had to like go inside and then never come out again. That's like a real contradiction to, you know, normal life. Then when you ask the anchor question, "Why would the character act that way?" then you have to like, stop and think about what's going on. I'm thinking it was like Cory said earlier that maybe he was kidnapped. See this part where it says "they are taking the wood away"? Well that means that before he could be outside, because there was like no way people could see him but now there's like no safety because the woods are being chopped down, so he has to stay hidden.

> She cites the text to support her reasoning. As you listen to students, if you keep the CCSS for reading in mind, you'll hear students attending to the standards, especially 1–3 for reading as well as standards for speaking and listening.

STUDENT 12: I didn't see it that way. I marked that same place, but I think it's an Aha Moment. He's realizing that he'll never go outside again. That's why it says, "He reminded himself." He's like really reminding himself that this is important. That's what makes it an Aha, because it is so important. And then when you think about the question "How does this change things?" and compare it with how much it meant to him to be outside—see that part about, here, this part about "fresh air, scented with clover and honeysuckle" and how he "savored one last moment of feeling warm soil," well you wouldn't know those things like clover and you wouldn't think about how warm soil feels unless you really like nature stuff and so going in, well, going inside forever, that's going to be huge for him.

> Again we see students turning naturally to the text for evidence to support their thinking.

> Here, we see this student using evidence from the text to make an inference.

STUDENT 11: Yeah, like, maybe that's the problem. He wants to be outside, but he's going to have to be inside. [pause] Did you know what that word *savored* is?

STUDENT 12: Not really, but it looks like *favored*, you know like it's your favorite, so I thought it meant he was like favoring something, you know how you *like* something on Facebook.

STUDENT 11: Yeah, that makes sense. So if you savor it, that's like you really favor it. Super favor makes savor.

> These two use evidence from the text and from their world to build their understanding of *savor*.

STUDENT 12: So, is it wrong that you say it's Contrasts and I say Aha?

STUDENT 11: I don't think so. I think it really is both. He's having an Aha Moment because his life is about to change so much from what it had been and from what ours is. And when you answer the questions, that's when you find out a lot more. Like if it's because he's been kidnapped, then it's like reading to find out if that's it, but if you think about it from Aha, then you're like thinking about how he feels about it. I think they're both right.

These two students had a rich and detailed conversation. Nearby were two other students. Their conversation is shorter, so at first glimpse, you might think it wasn't valuable. But the more we thought about what they said, the more we realized that these two boys—obviously men of few words—were saying a lot with a little.

STUDENT 17: It was a contrast.

STUDENT 18: What?

STUDENT 17: Here. "I will never be allowed outside again." That's like a real contrast to me because if I wanted out, no one would tell me I couldn't go out, but he's going to stay in. He must be a real scared kid.

STUDENT 18: OK. Or maybe it's not that he's that scared but that someone has convinced him that he'll die or something if he stays out. Like bird flu. It's coming. He's got to stay in.

STUDENT 17: Maybe. But that wouldn't be forever. Something else. But it's got to be bad because nothing would keep me in.

> Student 17, a quiet boy, jumped in with his thinking and it was evident that he was stunned that Luke was never going to be outside again. As they talked, they identified the internal conflict: Is Luke brave enough to disobey and venture forth into the world?

What we've noticed is that some students just talk more. It's easy to think that the students who talk more are doing more and better thinking than the students who talk less. That's not necessarily true. More talk means more opportunity for students to work through their thinking, but don't dismiss the few sentences from the quieter students. They often reveal insights you can use to encourage more talk.

And we've also noticed that students read texts more attentively when they read with these Notice and Note Signposts in mind. It's slower reading because it's deeper. And that's the point. Close reading isn't about skimming or surfing. It disrupts reading fluency because we're pausing to think, to consider, to speculate, to talk, to revise our initial understandings. Close reading happens when we notice and note something that makes us stop and think.

7

Assessment and the Signposts

We think the most critical question is "Do these signposts help students read more closely?" In this section, we'll explore three topics that will help us determine that. First, in the section titled "Assessing by Listening to Talk," we'll look at comments students make. Then, in the next section, titled "Assessing by Reading Their Logs" we'll look at what students write. Finally, in the section titled "Assessing with the Common Core State Standards," we'll examine how the signposts help students achieve necessary skills required by the CCSS.

We didn't develop these Notice and Note Lessons to support the Common Core State Standards. We were trying to give students a scaffold so that they could read more closely, so that they could develop the habits, dispositions, and skills we want them to have as lifelong learners.

Before we begin, though, we think it's important that you know that we didn't develop these Notice and Note Lessons to support the Common Core State Standards. We were trying to give students a scaffold so that they could read more closely, so that they could develop the habits, dispositions, and skills we want them to have as lifelong learners. But it is important to try to assess how well that's working. So let's begin by listening to their talk.

Assessing by Listening to Their Talk

The best way to consider how well these signposts help students read more closely is to look at some transcripts of student talk. These transcripts show how students' thinking about literary texts has changed as a result of learning just one signpost each. First, Erin.

Listening to Erin

Erin was in sixth grade when we met her. In September, with her class, she was reading *Tuck Everlasting*. As the class ended one day, we asked her what she thought might happen next. She replied:

Um, I think that, I think that next, well next. I think that, well, I think more is going to happen with her being with them. And then she will probably go home. Because they don't seem like forever kidnappers.

Erin's first comment lacks specificity.

While Erin has offered some tentative reasons for her assumption that Winnie will return home, we want more specificity from a sixth grader. So, we taught her class Contrasts and Contradictions. In January, when we revisited her classroom, her class was now reading *Among the Hidden*. Now, in a small-group discussion, with no prompting, this is what Erin had to say during a part of that group's conversation. You'll quickly see her use of language about Contrasts and Contradictions and her improvement in specificity about what's happening in the novel:

Here, right when Luke, he decides to go to the house, so he had just been thinking about it, but here, he decided to go, well, I noticed that because he was doing something different, like a contradiction on how he had been acting, and so I noticed that. And that made me think that Luke, he's like maybe getting braver some. But that's going to be a problem because he needs to stay hidden. So, I think maybe that what's going to happen is about him not wanting to stay hidden. Maybe like for the conflict.

Now we see that as Erin has learned to identify changes in a character, she is more focused in her comments, has identified the conflict, and has noticed how Luke is developing as a character.

When we asked Erin how learning the Contrasts and Contradictions signpost had helped her, she replied, "Now, when I'm reading, it's like I am reading the story, but I'm also watching out for what's happening. I'm like thinking about what's causing things, because all you have to do is watch for the signpost. It's there, and all you have to do is see it and then you can, you know, just think about the question and then you get all these thoughts in your head."

Listening to Megan

Now, let's hear from Megan. Megan is a seventh grader, and she's talking with Kylene about reading *Number the Stars*. She's already learned Again and Again and is delighted when she spots a recurring event:

MEGAN: Miss—look! It's that Again and Again. The story of the Denmark king. See, she's remembering it again. Where was it first? Where was it? Can you find it? I don't know where it was but this is like the, I don't know, like it was a lot, that she keeps remembering this story, remembering that her dad told her about the Denmark king and how anyone would fight for him.

FROM KYLENE: Some students will identify this story of the Denmark king as a Memory Moment. Others might say that when the character, Annemarie, remembers it she's having an Aha Moment. Don't worry about the label. Push the student to answer the question, which is what I had to do with Megan.

We're pretty sure Mrs. Lowry, an award-winning author, knew exactly what she was doing, but we're happy that Megan realized that repetition of something—especially a story about a positive trait (courage)—is worth noting.

KYLENE: Why do you think this keeps coming up again and again?

MEGAN: Because. I think it is because, oh, I know, see how she keeps remembering that anyone would do anything to save him. Oh—this is that foreshadowing. Here it is! This is foreshadowing. Oh my God. It's right here! Do you think Mrs. Lowry knows she did this?

Megan had recently finished a quiz over literary elements. On that quiz, when asked, "What is foreshadowing?" she responded with an abbreviation you might have seen: DNK (do not know). Her excitement at labeling this Again and Again as foreshadowing was probably the result of figuring out something she had missed on the quiz. Megan, excited to have spotted the foreshadowing, paused for a moment while we waited, as if exploring the discovery, and then continued, figuring out just what it was that was being foreshadowed as she talked.

MEGAN: It's like, you know, since she keeps remembering this story about courage, then, you know [pause] well, whatever is going to happen, she's going to need courage, like the people in the story about the king. That's why she keeps remembering it, because she's going to need courage. [pause] Oh, that's what the foreshadowing is, that something is going to happen, and she'll need to be courageous.

Now Megan is approaching the specificity we want. It just took a while for her to put all the pieces together.

Listening to Matt and Brittany

Matt and Brittany, seventh graders, were buddy-reading *The Watsons Go to Birmingham—1963*. Everyone in the class was reading this book, but each student was paired with one "buddy." As students read, they occasionally talked with their reading buddy about what they had been reading, and the teacher also planned to occasionally combine the pairs into groups of four. In addition, the students also participated in brief whole-class discussions about general impressions of the book.

The teacher had taught the entire class Contrasts and Contradictions, and most students were doing well finding points in the novel where characters were acting in a way that contrasted with what they had come to expect. For instance, they all quickly spotted, in the first chapter, that although Kenny is teased terribly by Byron, as soon as Byron is in pain (tongue stuck on frozen mirror), Kenny is sympathetic and concerned, and seems to forget Byron's bullying. They knew the question to ask themselves (*Why would the character act this way?*), and one girl responded that "the author is showing us that even though Byron is mean to Kenny, they are still brothers so they love each other a lot."

The teacher was waiting for the right moment to teach another signpost, the Aha Moment. She chose to do this before students began Chapter 3. She knew that there was a significant and obvious Aha Moment on page 45. On this page, the main character, Kenny, thinks to himself, "All of a sudden I started remembering how much I hated riding the bus, all of a sudden I started remembering how lunchtime under the swing set alone wasn't very much fun. . . ."

So the next day the teacher took about thirty minutes of class time to teach the Aha Moment. Then she sent the students off to read and reminded them that today she wanted to see sticky notes in their books that pointed out either Aha Moments or Contrasts and Contradictions with brief answers to the anchor question.

Not too long after students began reading, Brittany and Matt went to an area of the room labeled "Our Talk." Here, students can sit with their reading buddy to video- or audio-record a conversation about a book. They know that their conversations will be listened to by others and perhaps used by the teacher as an example.

> BRITTANY: Is it on? [pointing to the tape recorder] OK. This is Brittany and Matt, and we've found an Aha Moment. On page 45 it says, "All of a sudden" and it says it over and over. And so it's an Aha Moment. And so I noticed that. And so, and so, and so now, what's the question we're supposed to ask?
>
> MATT: You know. How might this change things? Like since he now realizes how having Rufus as a friend made things better, then how will that change what he does next?
>
> BRITTANY: Well, if you look at the whole paragraph, this part where he said that "all of a sudden I started remembering that before Rufus came to Flint my only friend was the world's biggest dinosaur thief" then well, you see, the Aha Moment isn't just about him suddenly remembering these things, but it's about starting to feel bad for not being nice to Rufus. And so, it might change things by, Kenny, he will probably try to be friends with him again. He'll have his friend back and Rufus will be happy again. Or maybe Rufus won't be his friend so easy.

The Aha Moment lesson that the teacher taught students is on page 128.

This one simple idea—give kids a place where they can record themselves—keeps the students a little more focused. The teacher used their recordings in various ways: "Look what we learned" audio or video files on the school's home page; artifacts to take to PLC meetings; and—lucky us—transcripts.

First, notice how Brittany is using evidence from the text to support her answer; second, we're pleased that even though Matt had to remind her of the question to consider, she had several things to say in response to the question. In particular, she offers a couple of predictions.

MATT: I think his Aha was that he was lonely before Rufus and that none of the kids who were making fun of Rufus had ever been his friend anyway so why did he care now if they made fun of him.

BRITTANY: So, now you have to answer, *How might this change things?*

MATT: I think this is showing us that Kenny is not going to be as connected to what other kids say and is going to do his own thing. He's like getting mature.

And now Matt offers his ideas. His comment about Kenny's maturity shows he recognizes how this character is developing.

Listening to Benjamin

Finally, let's consider Benjamin, a tenth grader, in a "regular" language arts class. In his school, regular means a class from which all the pre-AP, honors, gifted and talented, and sheltered ELL students have been removed. He is trying to discuss the theme of *Holes*. Like many students, he struggled to put the theme into words. This is what he had to say about theme in September:

> The theme, so like the message, the theme was to, it was, well, you know it never really said what the theme was. It was a good book and all, but so the message, it was, well the theme was about how Stanley had to go to this prison like camp and dig holes but he escaped to help his friend who had escaped but then they came back but they got trapped in a hole but the lizards in there didn't eat them because they had lizard juice and then they got out and got to go home.

Benjamin, not unlike other struggling readers, has confused plot with theme.

In January, after he's learned the Aha Moment, he says this about theme after he finished reading *The Giver*:

> So, when Jonas saw his dad release one of the twins, that was an Aha Moment that was going to change Jonas for forever. I think it's an Aha Moment that is showing us that things are going to change so much that Jonas won't be able to live there anymore. And so the theme is, it is that, that Jonas can't live where people are like that.

Here Benjamin has identified a signpost, is about to answer the question ("things are going to change so much that Jonas won't be able to live there anymore"), but is still struggling to identify the theme.

In April, after completing *The Outsiders*, he said:

> So, like there's this Aha Moment; it was when Ponyboy, he was talking with Randy and Randy said he wasn't going to fight and Ponyboy he remembered what Cherry had said that things are rough all over

and he said "I knew then what she meant." See, that was his Aha Moment. Until then, he didn't know. But then, when he was talking with Randy, he understood it. He realized that Cherry was saying that it doesn't matter if you are a Soc or a greaser because anyone can have problems and that it's not right to think that only you and no one else ever has it hard. I think that's a big life lesson so I think it's the theme, that we all have problems, no matter who you are.

Benjamin didn't learn the Aha Moment on Thursday and make this quick leap to being able to talk about theme on Friday. He learned the Aha Moment in October, and for the next several months, his teacher helped him identify Aha Moments and pushed him to consider the anchor question. As he encountered the Aha Moment repeatedly, in different texts, he gradually became more and more confident in discussing what the Aha Moments were showing him. More important, to us, was that at the end of the year, Benjamin reported the following:

> Before I learned these signposts, I didn't understand how everyone else knew things like how characters were changing or what was the conflict or what was the theme. Then I learned these [signposts] and now I'm like I can see it. It's been in the books all the time but I just didn't know what to be looking for. You can't just read the story. If you really want to understand all of it, you know, all that's going on, you have to really notice what's happening.

Our point is not only that you need to listen to students, but also that you need to listen to them over time. Gradually, you'll hear students move to the anchor question without prompting from you (or the Brittany of the class), offer speculations, confirm or discard those speculations as they continue reading, and have, in effect, their own Aha Moments. As you listen to students, ask yourself if they . . .

- Identify the scene that made them think of a signpost?
- Explain why they think that scene represents that signpost?
- Move to the anchor question without prompting?
- Move to the anchor question with prompting?
- Offer more than one speculative answer to the anchor question?
- Remain open to other speculative answers suggested by classmates?

Now, not only does Benjamin offer a theme, but he quotes from the text to provide his evidence. It took some time, but by gently encouraging him to find signposts and think about what they mean, he got there.

Don't forget to ask your students how spotting the signposts and considering the anchor question is affecting their understanding.

- Use evidence from the text to support their answers?
- Connect this signpost to others (same type or different) in other parts of this novel?

Assessing by Reading Their Logs

In addition to listening in on discussions and perhaps even recording and transcribing them, you might glance at the signpost logs the students are keeping. These you can examine in the long, leisurely hours of the evening when you'd rather be reading new young adult fiction. Ask yourself the same sort of questions you'd ask about the talk, and they'll give you some insight into the same issues: Are kids observing elements in the text, are they thinking about them, and how well are they doing that?

Because the intent of these signposts is to create skilled, observant, engaged, *independent* readers, at some point in some way students need to record what they're observing as they read on their own. Some teachers use the Signposts bookmark and others use the Notice and Note Reading Log like the one in Figure 9 (see the Appendix, pages 209–210, for the template). Some teachers let students place sticky notes in books as they read. In some classrooms we worked in (well, three), students got to write in the books they were reading, so they made their notes right in the margin. In one classroom, students were reading on an e-reader and they used the highlight function to immediately mark the signpost they had noticed and then used the note feature to jot down their thinking.

No matter how you have students take notes about what they've found, you should from time to time take a look at what they've written. Some teachers do this daily as they walk around from student to student while kids are doing independent reading; some teachers check logs weekly. Some have students take what they've written in their logs to use as information needed for a more formal essay. No matter your choice, as you look at logs or sticky notes, make sure that the student has done more than simply identify the signpost.

For instance, as you look at Madeline's Notice and Note Reading Log, Figure 9, you see that on page 2 of *The Giver* she's noticed something she's calling a Contrast and Contradiction. In the final column she tells you what caused her to pause, and then she answers the anchor question, writing, "Maybe it is during the war. . . ."

In the Appendix, beginning on page 211, you'll see two additional types of Notice and Note Logs that teachers made that we liked enough to include.

Madeline has also learned the Again and Again signpost. She points out this location ("Chapter 1") and labels what she's found, but her comments in the final column don't attend to the anchor question (*Why does this keep happening again and again?*). We're not sure why—perhaps she was in a hurry; perhaps she forgot; perhaps at this point she has no idea why *release* is used repeatedly and thus saw no reason to mention it. When you see this happening—and you will—prompt the student to consider the question. Labeling isn't what's important; reflecting on the passage, considering possibilities—that's what leads the student to the close reading.

Name Madeline   Class Period 3   Date Mar 16

Notice and Note Reading Log for *The Giver*

Location	Signpost I Noticed	My Notes About it
Page 2	Contrasts and Contradictions	I noticed that everyone had to run, just because a plane was flying and that isn't something I would do. It seemed like a Contrasts and Contradictions lesson where something happens that seems odd. Maybe it was during a war and they were afraid this was a bomber.
Chapter 1	Again and Again	Release is used a lot and not as a good word. Jonas points out that he got punished for saying that Asher should be released.

Figure 9: A page from Madeline's Notice and Note Reading Log

Some teachers who worked with us have shared the reading logs they created to use with their students. We now share these with you in the Appendix, beginning on page 211.

Connecting to the Common Core State Standards

Assessing the logs and the classroom conversations, by the way, will provide you with some information about how well students are meeting the requirements of the Common Core State Standards. Without going into detail about them, we'd at least mention that the first three of those standards deal with "key ideas and details," and they ask students to "read closely," to "cite specific textual evidence," to "determine central ideas . . . and summarize the key supporting details," and to analyze development "over the course of a text." In other words, they ask kids to notice and note; to read observantly, to think about their responses and the textual elements that provoked them, and to articulate and explain. The next three standards, focusing on the author's design and craft, ask students to "interpret words and phrases as they are used in a text," "analyze the structure of texts" (how specific parts relate to each other and the whole), and "assess point of view and purpose." In other words, once again, they ask readers to attend to specifics in the text and think about them—to notice something and make note of it.

> **Teachers are thus free to provide students with whatever tools and knowledge their professional judgment and experience identify as most helpful for meeting the goals set out in the Standards.**

Furthermore, as the CCSS document states, "The Standards do not mandate such things as a particular writing process or the full range of metacognitive strategies that students may need to monitor and direct their thinking and learning. Teachers are thus free to provide students with whatever tools and knowledge their professional judgment and experience identify as most helpful for meeting the goals set out in the Standards" (NGA, CCSSO 2010, p. 4). That statement seems to us to grant you the autonomy to figure out not only what you need to teach your students but also what you should do to assess how well they're learning.

As you listen to student conversations and read through their logs, it might be helpful to keep in mind a page from the CCSS that attempts to offer, not standards, but rather a "portrait" of students who meet those standards. Among the seven aspects of those successful students are these four:

- They demonstrate independence.
- They build strong content knowledge.
- They comprehend as well as critique.
- They value evidence.

You'll be able to learn at least some of what you need to know about these aspects of your students' learning through your observations of their classroom conversations and your review of their logs. This assessment, undertaken by a knowledgeable teacher, ongoing and focused, is likely to be of much more help in shaping and reshaping instruction than any battery of formal, summative tests. Assessment—not grading— is the heart of instruction. As you assess students' comments, you get a glimpse into their thinking and that in turn drives your teaching. We think listening to students, thinking carefully about their comments, and then evaluating what those comments tell us about what a student does and doesn't understand is one of the hardest—and simultaneously—most exciting parts of teaching.

> **Assessment—not grading—is the heart of instruction.**

CLASSROOM CLOSE-UP

Generalizable language, anchor questions, signposts to be watching for—at first glance, this might seem too much. It did to us! That's why getting into classrooms, working with kids, and more importantly, sending teachers into classrooms to work with their own students, became critical. Once we started teaching the lessons ourselves and having other teachers teach them, we all saw that basically we're teaching kids three things: first, the particular signpost; second, what the text clue is that points them to the signpost; third, what question to ask when they spot a signpost.

Below, you'll see a classroom close-up of a fourth-grade class as the teacher, Ms. Mitchell, introduces the idea of the signposts and anchor questions to her class of twenty-three students. This is an inner-city school in a very large school district. Most students were African American, with a few Latino students, and all were on the free or reduced lunch program. In the sidebar, you'll see our comments about her brief (about ten-minute) lesson. She does a great job of introducing three concepts the students will be learning.

MS. MITCHELL: It's group time, so let's all gather on the rug. . . . Okay, every-one, eyes on me. Today, we'll spend a few minutes talking about a series of lessons we're going to begin learning tomorrow. These lessons are called the Notice and Note Signpost lessons, and we're going to learn them to help you be a smarter reader.

> She begins by asking students to think about what a signpost might be.

Let's think about what a signpost is. Who has some ideas? Turn to your neighbor and explain what you think a signpost is. [Students turn and talk for about thirty seconds.] Okay. Back up here. What was something you heard that seems right?

NAT: Marcus said that it's like a traffic sign. Like "Stop."

ETHAN: I said it was like a sign that's on a post, you know, up high, so everyone could see it.

KEVIN: It's like on the freeway, those big signs that go across the road, you know, so you have to get in the right lane.

MS. MITCHELL: I think those are all great examples. From your examples, I'd say that a signpost is something that helps you know where you're going or tells you something about the route, something you ought to be doing while on the road. If you'll all think about it, you see one signpost right outside the school, right as you turn into the carpool drop-off lane. Which sign is it?

> It's not unusual for students to offer a definition with an example. Notice how the teacher recognizes that they've offered examples and then she provides the definition.

JANIS: There's that one with the cell phone and the line through it.

MIKEY: And that one with the, it's the yellow one, it says *slow*.

MS. MITCHELL: Those are both great signs. I hadn't remembered the cell phone sign, but it sure is there. Why do you think we have those signs? [Several students speak and she allows all to be heard.] You've each made good points. The one that says *slow* is a reminder to drivers that there are kids around who might forget to look both ways before crossing the street so drivers need to be extra cautious, and the no-cell-phone sign reminds drivers not to talk on their cell phones when in the school zone so they can be focused on all the children around the cars. Signposts on roads help us know what's happening—or might be happening—so we can be better drivers.

> Now she's connecting something students already know— signs we see on the road—to what she wants them to learn—signposts authors provide.

Now, authors do that too; they put some signposts in their stories that help us know what to watch for. These signposts tell us about the characters, about the conflicts or problems in the story, and sometimes about the big life lessons in the story. But you have to know what signposts to look for or you might just read right on past them. For example, if you see a signpost like this [points to the curvy-road-ahead road sign on the chart paper], you have to know what it means. Who can tell us? . . . Right—the road is very curvy, so slow down and be careful. In a story, most signposts tell us to slow down and think about what's happening.

If we don't know to look for the signposts authors give, and don't know what they mean, we might just breeze past them and find ourselves off the road and in the ditch.

BENJAMIN: Miss Mitchell, my mother did that with the speed sign that said thirty-five but she was going faster because she didn't see it and she got a ticket and the policeman he said that he didn't care that she didn't see it, that it was her responsibility to see it.

> We're pretty sure Benjamin's mom isn't pleased at being the class example, but it made the point!

MS. MITCHELL: Well, I hate that your mom got a ticket, but I understand what the policeman was telling her. It was her *responsibility* to be on the lookout for signs that tell us how fast to go. In the same way, it's your *responsibility* to look for the signposts that authors give you.

In the next few weeks, we're going to learn six important signposts. Here are their names: [Teacher points to the chart paper that lists them all and reads the names].

> Ms. Mitchell isn't teaching the lesson about Aha Moments here. She's simply helping the students get familiar with one of the lessons they'll be learning. You could do this with as many as you want. She chose to discuss just Aha Moments.

Let's think about some of these names. Let's start with Aha Moments. Does anyone have any idea what an Aha Moment in a book might be?

LINDA: Like when you go "aha" because you've figured something out?

CARL: Or, like when you know how you are like *Oh I get it!* That's an Aha.

MISSY: Or I was talking with my friend and she was like all weird and I didn't get it and then I was like, oh my God it was her birthday and I didn't remember it and so then it was a huge Aha.

MS. MITCHELL: Those are great examples. An Aha Moment is when we figure something out, when we realize something. Missy, when you figured out that you had forgotten your friend's birthday, when you had that Aha, what did you do next?

> Here, she's introducing the concept of an anchor question.

MISSY: I was like, oh my gosh, oh my gosh, what should I do now?

When You take a Journey through a book, don't forget to STOP! at any Notice & Note Signposts

MS. MITCHELL: That's right! When we figure something out, we usually ask ourselves a question about what we should do next. The same thing is true when an author shows us a character figuring out something in an Aha Moment in a book. Authors show us these Aha Moments to help us understand why characters are doing what they do. When we see one of those moments, we want to ask ourselves one question—it's a question we're going to call an *anchor question*. For the Aha Moment, what do you think the anchor question should be?

> Now she's named the signpost and given students the generalizable language, the rule that students can carry from one text to another.

> And now she turns to the anchor question.

ERIC: I know! *What should I do next?*

MS. MITCHELL: That's the perfect question if you're the one having the Aha, but in a book, it's going to be about what the character should do next. So we're going to ask, *How might this Aha Moment change things?* You don't need to try to remember this anchor question now. I just want you to begin thinking about what we're going to be learning over the next couple of weeks. Let's review. You're going to learn to notice some things that the author has put into the story. What are these called?

BRANDON: Signs.

ALI: Traffic signs.

AMALIE: Signposts.

MS. MITCHELL: That's right. Signposts. We're going to learn six of them— here they are. [She points back to the chart paper with all six signposts on them.] We talked today for a moment about the Aha Moment signpost. And with each signpost we're also going to learn one question to ask ourselves. When you see a traffic signpost, you know to ask yourself what it means and what you should do. And when you see one of the Notice and Note Signposts, you want to ask yourself one question that will help you see what it might mean.

KIM: Miss Mitchell, why did you say "Notice and Note Signposts"?

MS. MITCHELL: Because first you have to learn to notice them and then you ought to pause and take note about what they mean. OK. Back to your seats and let's all take out the books you're reading. . . .

8

Questions You Might Have

1. *After I teach a signpost lesson, will students really be able to spot whatever signpost they've just learned?*

Probably not. The lesson transfers responsibility to the student gradually; the student will accept that responsibility even more gradually. Keep the chart listing the name of the signpost, a brief definition, the feature they should look for in the text, and the question they should ask themselves posted on the wall for the entire year if necessary. Also, you might distribute the Notice and Note Signposts bookmark for students to keep with them as they read. The front of the bookmark reminds students of each signpost, and they can use the back to jot down the page numbers where they've spotted signposts if you don't want to use the Signpost Log. Templates for the bookmark and log are included in the Appendix.

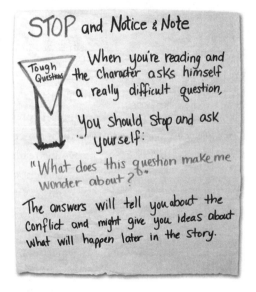

STOP and Notice & Note

When you're reading and the character asks himself a really difficult question,

You should stop and ask yourself:

"What does this question make me wonder about?"

The answers will tell you about the conflict and might give you ideas about what will happen later in the story.

2. *If students didn't seem to understand the text clue or need some review, what do I do?*

We suggest following up with a minilesson that reteaches or reviews the lesson. Now we really do mean *minilesson.* At the end of each of the lessons in Part III, we offer some other texts you can use for these much shorter lessons (seven to ten minutes).

3. *How do I know if they are finding the signposts when they are reading independently, perhaps in books I haven't read myself?*

If students are reading different books, ask them to show you what they've found. You must do this just with small groups or with individuals—doing it with the entire class would leave too many students sitting idly by, waiting, for too long.

When they become adept at finding the signposts, you can ask them to show you less frequently, though we've seen that as they are catching on, they want to show you often what they are finding. You'll also find that the very general question, *What Notice and Note Signposts have you found, and what did you think they revealed?* is a great way to begin an individual conference or a small- or large-group discussion. And you might follow it up with, *What were the scenes that didn't seem to be one of the signposts but that still seemed to be important to the story?* In addition to these six signposts, emphasized here because they are easy to spot, there is a great deal more happening in any book.

After teaching one of the signpost lessons, Bob checked on how these kids were doing. One student reported, "Once you know what to look for, signposts are everywhere."

That said, you could presume, with almost any novel or chapter book expressly written for children (*Charlotte's Web*) or in which the main character is a child even if the book was not written for young readers (*Life of Pi* or *The Kite Runner*, for example), that each signpost has a very good chance of appearing in the book. Contrasts and Contradictions, Aha Moments, and Tough Questions most certainly will appear. So, feel comfortable thinking that if in twenty pages students haven't marked at least one of those, you could say, *Has the character changed at all in this section? If so, find that scene where you think he's starting to behave or think differently.* When students find that scene, glance at it. There's probably an Aha Moment or a Contrast and Contradiction. Reread it and then ask them to speculate on the anchor question.

To help them spot a Tough Question they might have missed, ask, *Have you run across a part where the character seems really worried about something and has expressed that worry to someone else or just thought about it by himself? He might have asked someone questions that were hard to answer, or he might have said something like, "I wonder if. . . ." Let's look at those questions. Remember, when you spot tough questions, they are showing you what is really bothering the main character, and you need to pause and ask yourself what these questions make you wonder about. Chances are, you'll be wondering the same thing the character is.*

For Words of the Wiser, if you haven't read the book, just ask if the main character has learned a life lesson from someone.

For Again and Again, ask them if something—a word, an image, an event—keeps showing up again and again.

For Memory Moment, ask students if there's been a place where a character pauses to recall something. These moments are marked with phrases such as "I remember . . ." or "Mom was always telling us about when. . ." or "This memory kept popping into my mind . . ." or "I found myself remembering . . ." and so on.

4. *What do I do when a student identifies a passage that others didn't find or when students disagree about what signpost a passage represents?*

That should lead to good conversations. If students argue—politely, we hope—about whether a passage is an Aha Moment or a Tough Question, the best outcome is probably that neither of them wins but that both modify their position slightly. Consider what they will have done: They will have each noticed something significant in the text, formulated their own response to it, asked a question about it, framed a tentative answer, listened to another reader's thinking, and reshaped their own thoughts as a result of the dialogue. They will, in other words, have been engaged in the process of thinking about a text. What they label the passage is significant only in generating that intellectual activity.

5. *How many signposts might I expect to find in any novel?*

We wish we could tell you that answer, but honestly, it's a surprise in every novel. You can always count on Contrasts and Contra-dictions (as this usually indicates character development), Aha Moments (as they help move the plot along and toward the end reveal resolution of internal conflict), Words of the Wiser (though often only one or two life lessons are shared), and at least a couple of scenes with Tough Questions (though we're seeing that science fiction seems to offer many scenes with Tough Questions), and then Again and Again and Memory Moments range from many to only a few. Not too helpful, we know. We do know, though, that they appear often enough to make it valuable to your students to learn these signposts. To see an example of how often the Signposts occur in *Walk Two Moons*, by Sharon Creech, turn to page 236 in the Appendix.

6. *Are these lessons appropriate for expository texts?*

Yes, with modifications. As a history teacher pointed out to us, history is nothing but Again and Again moments, though they take a shape different from those in a novel. She put up chart paper in her classroom, one sheet for each chapter in their history textbook, and as students studied each historical period, they entered on the chart events and causes and effects. By the third chart, students realized that events (and causes and effects) kept repeating over time. She modified the Again and Again question slightly (*Why do these types of events keep showing up again and again?*), and that led students to begin discussing persistent human traits such as greed, curiosity, bravery, and honor.

Also, when teaching Contrasts and Contradictions in history, you will probably change the anchor question to *Why does the government/person/society act this way?* In science, you might say, *Why does this element/cell/cloud behave or react this way?*

Science teachers tell us that as students write their lab reports, they ask them to identify the Aha Moment the students had when conducting the experiment. "This alone has shown my students what happens when scientists repeat experiments modifying only one thing at a time." The Aha arrives when the significant variable is changed.

Don't be afraid to experiment with how these signposts work in expository texts. Change the anchor questions to better match the content—but we'd still encourage you to keep only one question per signpost.

7. *Aren't there other places in a novel, besides the six you've identified here, that are worth noticing and talking about?*

Yes, of course there are, and there are many important scenes in a novel that don't offer the easily named and observed text features that characterize the signposts. But we are working with struggling readers, and they aren't going to catch all of the subtlety and nuance in a text. Writers may tell us that they try to make every word count, but we don't linger over every word, or even every other word. Louise Rosenblatt, the literary theorist who most shaped our thinking about students' understanding of texts, pointed out that readers don't respond to an entire text; they select, sometimes intentionally and consciously but often instinctively or impulsively, what they'll focus on and think about. And if we, the more experienced readers that we are, don't closely examine every word or every page, our less experienced readers surely won't have the patience for that intensive analysis.

These six signposts are simply the textual elements that we think are easiest to keep in mind, spot, and question. We hope that learning and staying alert for the signposts will inculcate a habit of paying close attention, a readiness to slow down and reflect, and a willingness to hear and explore other responses to a text. As your students find other places in the text that strike them, applaud their diligence, encourage the discussion, and ask them what they now wonder about. Do not let students think that a novel is nothing more than a nicely arranged collection of six text elements.

> We hope that learning and staying alert for the signposts will inculcate a habit of paying close attention, a readiness to slow down and reflect, and a willingness to hear and explore other responses to a text.

8. *I worry that teachers can ruin the love of reading by constantly telling students they must be looking for something in a novel and then writing about it on a sticky note. Is that what I'm doing with these lessons?*

Only if this is reduced to mechanical hunting for text features and the signposts they announce. The purpose is not to collect signposts but to grow alert to significant moments in a text. There is a subtle but important distinction between *search for* and *be alert for*. We'd prefer to think that our students are *alert for* these text elements, not engaging in a scavenger hunt for them. We are trying to teach them to be observant and thoughtful. The lessons teach them how to be observant by showing them some patterns in the texts that they might notice; they then teach them how to become more thoughtful by suggesting a question that leads to interesting conversation. In short, we hope these lessons will teach them to notice and note.

The Lessons We Teach

In Part III, you will find the six Notice and Note lessons we use to introduce the signposts to students. We begin each of the lessons by describing the class we were teaching in, and then we move through the lesson. Toward the end of the lesson, we share some conversations that are similar to what you might hear, and then we conclude with a Q & A section.

Our hope is not only that you'll see how we teach the lessons, but also that your own ideas will begin to take shape. Should you decide that some of our language works for you, please feel free to use it. And if you like the text we chose for each lesson and think it's appropriate for your students, you'll find each reproduced in the Appendix.

Mostly, we hope that as you read you will find things in each lesson that cause you to stop and notice and note.

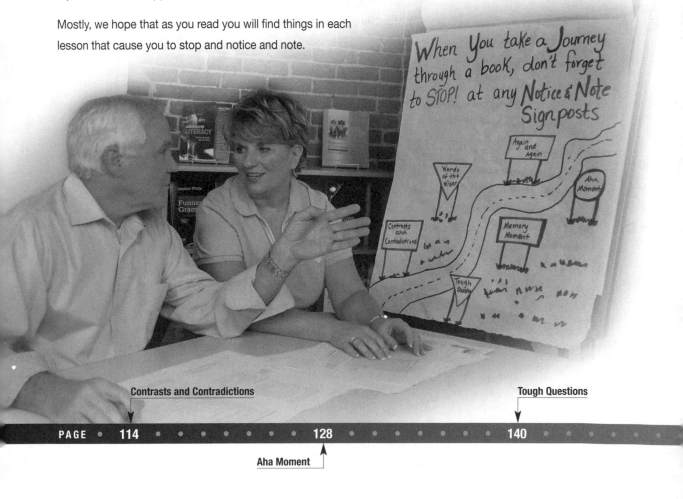

Contrasts and Contradictions

Tough Questions

PAGE • **114** • • • • • • • **128** • • • • • • **140** • • • • • • •

Aha Moment

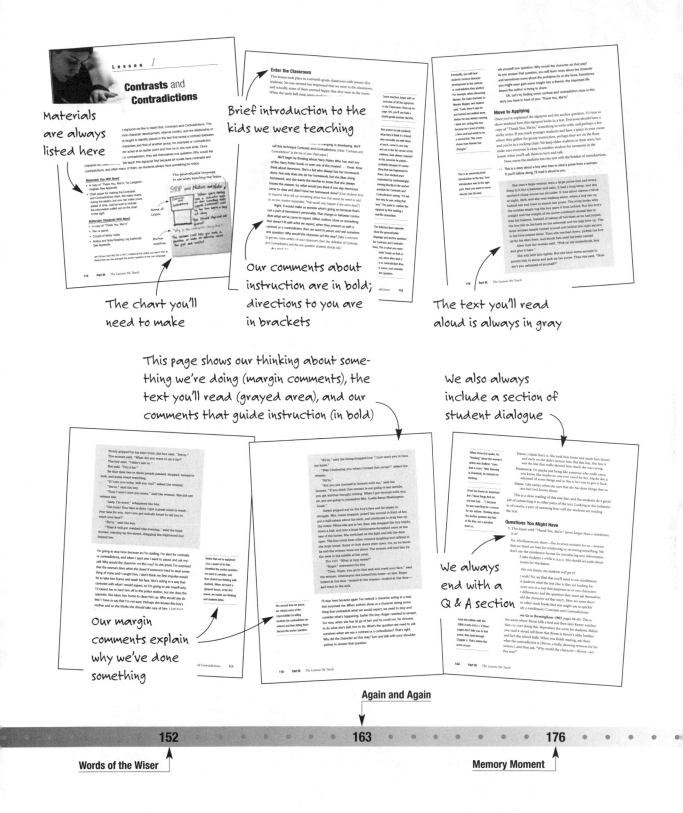

L e s s o n *1*

Contrasts and Contradictions

We begin this section with the signpost we like to teach first, Contrasts and Contradictions. This signpost helps students recognize character development, internal conflict, and the relationship of setting to the plot. Students are taught to identify places in the text that reveal a contrast (between the behavior of one group of characters and that of another group, for example) or contradiction (between how a single character acted at an earlier point and how he or she now acts). Once students identify the contrast or contradiction, they ask themselves one question: *Why would the character act (feel) this way?* We teach this signpost first because *all* novels have contrasts and contradictions, and often many of them, so students *always* have something to notice.

Materials You Will Need

- A copy of "Thank You, Ma'm," by Langston Hughes. See Appendix.
- Chart paper for making the Contrasts and Contradictions chart. We make charts during the lesson, but you can make yours ahead of time. Just be sure to include the information called out on the chart to the right.

Materials Students Will Need

- A copy of "Thank You, Ma'm"
- Pen or pencil
- Couple of sticky notes
- Notice and Note Reading Log (optional). See Appendix.

Jen Ochoa, from MS 324 in NYC, created all the charts you see in Part III. Notice that Jen has changed the anchor question to her own language.

The generalizable language to use when teaching the lesson

STOP and **Notice** and **Note**

Contrasts and Contradictions

Name of Lesson

When you're reading and a character says or does something that's opposite (contradicts) what he has been saying or doing all along.

You should stop and ask yourself:

Anchor question

"Why is the character doing that?"

The answers could help you make a prediction or make an inference about the plot and conflict.

Enter the Classroom

This lesson took place in a seventh-grade classroom with twenty-five students. No one seemed too impressed that we were in the classroom, and actually, none of them seemed happy that *they* were in the room. When the tardy bell rang, some students were talking with their buddies; a few had their heads down on their desks; one asked if we were substitute teachers, and another asked where the "real" teacher was. We quieted the students, and Bob began the lesson.

Begin by Explaining

" Let's take some time and think about one of the ways that an author shows us how a character is changing, is developing. We'll call this technique Contrasts and Contradictions. [Write "Contrasts and Contradictions" at the top of your chart paper.]

We'll begin by thinking about Harry Potter. Who has read any of the Harry Potter books or seen any of the movies? . . . Great. Now think about Hermione. She's a kid who always has her homework done. Not only does she do her homework, but she likes doing homework, and she wants the teacher to know that she always knows the answer. So, what would you think if one day Hermione came to class and didn't have her homework done? [Give students time to respond. Most will say something about how that would be weird or odd or, as one student responded, "That would only happen if she were dead."]

Right. It would make us wonder what's going on because that's not a part of Hermione's personality. That change in behavior contradicts what we've come to expect. *When authors show us something that doesn't fit with what we expect, when they present us with a contrast or a contradiction, then we want to pause and ask ourselves one question: Why would the character act this way?* [Take a moment to get two notes written on your classroom chart: the definition of Contrasts and Contradictions and the one question students should ask.]

As I read, I'm on the lookout for a place where the author shows me a character acting in a way that is a contrast or contradiction with how he or she has been acting or how I would expect the character would act. When you notice that contrast or contradiction, stop and

Some teachers begin with an overview of all the signposts. In the Classroom Close-up on page 103, you'll see how a fourth-grade teacher did this.

Bob prefers to ask students what they'd think if a friend, who normally sat with them at lunch, came in one day and sat in the far corner of the cafeteria. Kids always respond to this scenario he paints— probably because it's something that has happened to them. One student once responded by (unknowingly) moving directly to the anchor question for Contrasts and Contradictions saying, "I'd ask him why he was acting that way." The point is, explain the signpost by first making a real-life connection.

The italicized lines opposite show the generalizable language and anchor question for Contrasts and Contradictions. This is what you want in students' heads so that as they read, when they spot a contrast or contradiction they notice it, pause, and consider the anchor question.

Eventually, you will hear students connect character development to the contrast or contradiction they spotted. For example, when discussing Maniac, the main character in *Maniac Magee*, one student said, "Look, here it says he just turned and walked away. Before he was always running. I think he's acting this way because he's tired of being a hero and just wants to be a normal kid. This scene shows how Maniac has changed."

ask yourself one question: Why would the character act that way? As you answer that question, you will learn more about the character and sometimes more about the problems he or she faces. Sometimes you might even gain some insight into a theme—the important life lesson the author is trying to share.

OK. Let's try finding some contrast and contradiction clues in this story you have in front of you: "Thank You, Ma'm."

Move to Applying

Once you've explained the signpost and the anchor question, it's time to show students how this signpost looks in a text. Everyone should have a copy of "Thank You, Ma'm," something to write with, and perhaps a few sticky notes. If you teach younger students and have a space in your room where they gather for group instruction, perhaps they are on the floor and you're in a rocking chair. We keep older students in their seats, but make sure everyone is close to another student for moments in the lesson when you'll ask them to turn and talk.

Now, move the students into the text with the briefest of introductions.

This is an extremely brief introduction to the text. Your introduction was to the sign-post. Now you want to move directly into the text.

> ❝ This is a story about a boy who tries to steal a purse from a woman. If you'll follow along, I'll read it aloud to you.

> She was a large woman with a large purse that had everything in it but a hammer and nails. It had a long strap, and she carried it slung across her shoulder. It was about eleven o'clock at night, dark, and she was walking alone, when a boy ran up behind her and tried to snatch her purse. The strap broke with the sudden single tug the boy gave it from behind. But the boy's weight and the weight of the purse combined caused him to lose his balance. Instead of taking off full blast as he had hoped, the boy fell on his back on the sidewalk and his legs flew up. The large woman simply turned around and kicked him right square in his blue-jeaned sitter. Then she reached down, picked the boy up by his shirt front, and shook him until his teeth rattled.
>
> After that the woman said, "Pick up my pocketbook, boy, and give it here."
>
> She still held him tightly. But she bent down enough to permit him to stoop and pick up her purse. Then she said, "Now ain't you ashamed of yourself?"

Firmly gripped by his shirt front, the boy said, "Yes'm."

The woman said, "What did you want to do it for?"

The boy said, "I didn't aim to."

She said, "You a lie!"

By that time two or three people passed, stopped, turned to look, and some stood watching.

"If I turn you loose, will you run?" asked the woman.

"Yes'm," said the boy.

"Then I won't turn you loose," said the woman. She did not release him.

"Lady, I'm sorry," whispered the boy.

"Um-hum! Your face is dirty. I got a great mind to wash your face for you. Ain't you got nobody home to tell you to wash your face?"

"No'm," said the boy.

"Then it will get washed this evening," said the large woman, starting up the street, dragging the frightened boy behind her.

I'm going to stop here because as I'm reading, I'm alert for contrasts or contradictions, and when I spot one I want to pause and ask myself, Why would the character act this way? At this point, I'm surprised that the woman does what she does! If someone tried to steal something of mine and I caught him, I don't think my first impulse would be to take him home and wash his face. She's acting in a way that contrasts with what I would expect, so I'm going to ask myself why. I'd expect her to haul him off to the police station, but she does the opposite. She takes him home to clean him up. Why would she do this? I have to say that I'm not sure. Perhaps she knows this boy's mother and so she thinks she should take care of him. I just don't know enough about her at this point, so I'm going to keep on reading.

Notice that we've explained what caused us to stop, identified the anchor question we want to consider, and then shared our thinking with students. When we teach a signpost lesson, at the first pause, we model our thinking and students listen.

He looked as if he were fourteen or fifteen, frail and willow-wild in tennis shoes and blue jeans.

The woman said, "You ought to be my son. I would teach you right from wrong. Least I can do right now is to wash your face. Are you hungry?"

"No'm," said the being-dragged boy. "I just want you to turn me loose."

"Was I bothering you when I turned that corner?" asked the woman.

"No'm."

"But you put yourself in contact with me," said the woman. "If you think that contact is not going to last awhile, you got another thought coming. When I get through with you, sir, you are going to remember Mrs. Luella Bates Washington Jones."

Sweat popped out on the boy's face and he began to struggle. Mrs. Jones stopped, jerked him around in front of her, put a half-nelson about his neck, and continued to drag him up the street. When she got to her door, she dragged the boy inside, down a hall, and into a large kitchenette-furnished room at the rear of the house. She switched on the light and left the door open. The boy could hear other roomers laughing and talking in the large house. Some of their doors were open, too, so he knew he and the woman were not alone. The woman still had him by the neck in the middle of her room.

She said, "What is your name?"

"Roger," answered the boy.

"Then, Roger, you go to that sink and wash your face," said the woman, whereupon she turned him loose—at last. Roger looked at the door—looked at the woman—looked at the door—and went to the sink.

The second time we pause, we release some of the responsibility by telling students the contradiction we noticed and then letting them discuss the anchor question.

I'll stop here because again I've noticed a character acting in a way that surprised me. When authors show us a character doing something that contradicts what we would expect, we need to stop and consider what's happening. Earlier the boy—Roger—wanted to escape, but now, when she has let go of him and he could run, he chooses to do what she's told him to do. What's the question we need to ask ourselves when we see a contrast or a contradiction? That's right: Why did the character act this way? Turn and talk with your shoulder partner to answer that question.

As students talk in pairs, listen to what they are saying. You're focusing on two things. First, make sure they are answering the question. So if you hear, "If I had been Roger, I would have run," then say, "You've seen a sharp contrast—the contrast between what you would have done and what Roger did. Now you need to share why you think Roger might have acted this way." Second, if you have a student who is willing to let the partner's answer be her answer, then tell that student, "That's fine to share the same idea, but you need to say it, too. If you agree that Roger didn't run because he was hungry, then you need to say that." You want each student to take some ownership of an idea, even if the idea came from their partner first, and you may find that in restating the idea the second student adds something important to the thought.

Watch your time. This is only about two minutes of talk.

" Let's come back together as a big group. Tell me some of the ideas you and your partner shared. [Give students time to share their thinking—only about three or four minutes.]

OK. Those are interesting ideas. A lot of good thinking is going on. Notice how much you are able to consider just by noticing a contrast or contradiction and then asking yourself why the character would act this way. Let's keep reading, but this time, as I read, when you notice something that looks like a contrast or contradiction to you—something that surprises you—then with your pencil, put a small check mark or perhaps "C & C" in the margin. We'll come back to those points in a moment.

> "Let the water run until it gets warm," she said. "Here's a clean towel."
>
> "You gonna take me to jail?" asked the boy, bending over the sink.
>
> "Not with that face, I would not take you nowhere," said the woman. "Here I am trying to get home to cook me a bite to eat, and you snatch my pocketbook! Maybe you ain't been to your supper either, late as it be. Have you?"
>
> "There's nobody home at my house," said the boy.
>
> "Then we'll eat," said the woman. "I believe you're hungry—or been hungry—to try to snatch my pocketbook!"

When we tell students to turn and talk, we really do want them talking with only one other student, for no more than about two minutes. You'll listen in on one or two pairs, nodding, encouraging.

As students share out, encourage them to offer evidence from the text. So, if a student says, "He didn't run because he was scared of her," prompt her with "tell me more" and she'll probably point out that Mrs. Jones already had him in a "half-nelson" and was a "large" woman.

> "I want a pair of blue suede shoes," said the boy.
>
> "Well, you didn't have to snatch my pocketbook to get some suede shoes," said Mrs. Luella Bates Washington Jones. "You could of asked me."
>
> "Ma'm?"
>
> The water dripping from his face, the boy looked at her. There was a long pause. A very long pause. After he had dried his face and not knowing what else to do, dried it again, the boy turned around, wondering what next. The door was open. He would make a dash for it down the hall. He would run, run, run!
>
> The woman was sitting on the day bed. After a while, she said, "I were young once and I wanted things I could not get."
>
> There was another long pause. The boy's mouth opened. Then he frowned, not knowing he frowned.
>
> The woman said, "Um-hum! You thought I was going to say but, didn't you? You thought I was going to say, but I didn't snatch people's pocketbooks. Well, I wasn't going to say that." Pause. Silence. "I have done things, too, which I would not tell you, son—neither tell God, if He didn't already know. Everybody's got something in common. Sit you down while I fix us something to eat. You might run that comb through your hair so you will look presentable."

Now we're turning over even more responsibility to students. Each student must decide what the contrast or contradiction is and answer the question. Also, at this point, we've chosen to have students jot notes before turning to talk; we could have just as easily said turn and talk about what you found.

This is an important place to stop because I've noticed several contrasts and contradictions and I bet you did, too. Take a look at the places you put check marks, and before I let you talk with your shoulder partner, let's each take a moment to jot down our own thinking about the passages you've marked. Use one of the sticky notes you have on your desk and think about Roger or Mrs. Jones and what each has just said or done and answer this question: Why would the character act this way? OK. Let's all capture our thinking. Once you have some thoughts on paper, turn again to your partner and share your thinking.

As students write, you should walk around noticing what they are writing. With your shyer students, we find it helpful to point out that their thinking is smart and ask them quietly if, when they come back to the full group, they'll be willing to share their thinking. Since you've already affirmed that they've had a good idea, we think you'll find that they'll be much more willing to share their thinking with others. Don't let students spend more than a minute or two jotting thoughts. Your goal is to get them to turn and talk. Again, after the paired discussions, let students report to the full class. We just say, *So, what contrasts or contradictions did you find?* and that usually gets at least some talking and then others join in.

Students jot down their thoughts the third time we stop before turning to talk.

" Again, I'm so impressed with all the thinking you're doing about the characters. Remember, we're looking for places where a character does or says something that isn't what we expect. That's a contrast or a contradiction. When we find those places, we want to stop and ask ourselves, 'Why would the character act this way?' With that in mind, share with everyone some of the comments you made on your sticky notes. As many of you shared your comments, I heard excellent inferences. Remember that an inference is an idea you have that is based on what you read and what you already know. By answering this one question—Why would the character act this way?—you are able to make good inferences about how the character is thinking. As we keep reading, we'll discover which inferences might be supported and which ones turn out to be inaccurate. Let's keep reading. Again, as I read, when you find parts that you think are contrasts or contradictions, go ahead and mark them. You'll want to be able to come back to them in a moment.

Yes, you're repeating the generalizable language and the anchor question, and, yes, this will feel repetitive. It is. This is new language for students, and you need to keep reinforcing it.

We find it's important to use words such as *inference*, or if you hear students put things in a sequence, then talk about *sequencing*. In other words, let them see that by noticing Contrasts and Contradictions, they are doing thinking that involves many reading skills. Likewise, if you hear students make a *prediction* ("I bet he's still going to try to run"), then as you respond say something that uses the word *prediction*: What's happened so far that would support that prediction?

> In another corner of the room behind a screen was a gas plate and an icebox. Mrs. Jones got up and went behind the screen. The woman did not watch the boy to see if he was going to run now, nor did she watch her purse, which she left behind her on the day bed. But the boy took care to sit on the far side of the room, away from the purse, where he thought she could easily see him out of the corner of her eye if she wanted to. He did not trust the woman to trust him. And he did not trust the woman not to trust him. And he did not want to be mistrusted now.
>
> "Do you need somebody to go to the store," asked the boy, "maybe to get some milk or something?"
>
> "Don't believe I do," said the woman, "unless you just want sweet milk yourself. I was going to make cocoa out of this canned milk I got here."

She heated some lima beans and ham she had in the icebox, made the cocoa, and set the table. The woman did not ask the boy anything about where he lived, or his folks, or anything else that would embarrass him. Instead, as they ate, she told him about her job in a hotel beauty shop that stayed open late, what the work was like, and how all kinds of women came in and out, blondes, redheads, and Spanish. Then she cut him half of her ten-cent cake.

"Eat some more, son," she said.

When they finished eating, she got up and said, "Now here, take this ten dollars and buy yourself some blue suede shoes. And, next time, do not make the mistake of latching onto my pocketbook nor nobody else's—because shoes got by devilish ways will burn your feet. I got to get my rest now. But from here on in, son, I hope you will behave yourself."

She led the way down the hall to the front door and opened it. "Good night! Behave yourself, boy!" she said, looking into the street as he went down the steps.

The boy wanted to say something other than "Thank you, ma'm," to Mrs. Luella Bates Washington Jones, but although his lips moved, he couldn't even say that, as he turned at the foot of the barren stoop and looked up at the large woman in the door. Then she shut the door. And he never saw her again.

From this portion of the story, many of your students will identify the line "take this ten dollars" as a contradiction, saying people don't normally do that. Younger students often say, "People just don't give strangers money, especially as they've tried to rob them." We hear middle schoolers say, "She's trying to teach him a lesson, show him that it's better to be honest and ask than dishonest and steal." And some will reach further (as did this tenth-grader): "From the beginning, she's been a contradiction. First, she's angry that her purse was nearly stolen, then she takes him home, then she treats him nicely, then she gives him the money, and then she just shuts the door on him." By asking one question, *Why did the character act this way?* you'll encourage rich conversation that is all about differentiation because each student can enter the conversation via his or her own understanding.

Well, here we are at the end, and my head is full of thoughts. The first thing I want you to do is look back at this portion we just read and find the contrast or contradiction that you thought was most interesting. . . . OK. Now, what is the question you want to ask yourself? . . . That's right, Why did the character act this way? Now, use another one of your sticky notes to jot down your thoughts. [Only give about two minutes for this.]

Now, turn and talk with your shoulder partner and share the contrast or contradiction you thought most interesting, and then read what you wrote on your sticky note.

Again, give students only about two minutes to talk with their partners. Then bring the class back to the full group and let them share their thinking. Notice how much conversation you are getting from one question. And, if your class is anything like any of the classes we've taught, you'll see that student participation has increased. Students are now, by the end of this lesson, comfortable with this one question, and realize that they all have a chance to talk through turn and talk. When you pull students back together, let them share their thinking. Give as many students as possible the chance to share at this point. If someone offers an answer that you think isn't supported in the text, then follow up with something like, "Tell me what happened in the story that helped you make that inference." If they say, "I don't know," then push them back to the place where the contrast or contradiction occurred and tell them to do some more thinking and then move on to the next student.

By this point, all you are doing is reading the text, prompting students to recall the anchor question. They, though, must find the signpost and offer a response.

End with Reviewing

❝ Those were great comments about Roger and Mrs. Jones. And all that thinking came from the close reading you were doing. Let's review what you did that helped you make these inferences. First, we learned one text clue that authors give us. The name of this clue is . . . ? Right! Contrasts and Contradictions. [If you need to, direct students' attention to the chart you made.] When I see a character acting in a way that I wouldn't expect, then I want to stop right there and ask myself one question which is . . . Right again! "Why would the character act this way?" When I can answer that question, then I'm learning more about the story and more about the character.

   Now, as you do your reading in your own books, be sure to use your Notice and Note Reading Log or sticky note to mark any contrasts and contradictions you see. Jot down your thoughts about why the character would act that way.

While you might want to come back to "Thank You, Ma'm" for more discussion at this point, remember that you're sharing the story to teach this signpost. Summarize what they've learned about Contrasts and Contradictions and hang the chart you've created someplace in the room where it can stay for a while.

The Notice and Note Reading Log is found on pages 209–210 of the Appendix. Adaptions begin on page 211. If you want to show students an example of a student's reading log, you can find a student example on page 101.

Conversation Close-up

Let's take a close look at an exchange from two students, one typical of what you might hear.

> DREW: This line here, where she says, "You could have just asked," that was a contradiction because if you try to steal a lady's purse, then the idea that she would just give it to you, man, that is crazy.
>
> DOMINICK: Yeah, I marked that one, too. So now if you ask why she's gonna act that way, I think she is crazy! [laughter] Or maybe she just wants to show him someone cares.

When Drew first spoke, his "thinking" about the woman's action was shallow: "man, that is crazy." After listening to Dominick, he extends his thinking.

Drew has found an important line ("done things that no one but God . . .") because he was searching for a reason for her actions. Thinking about the anchor question led him to the line, not a question from us.

These page numbers are from the edition with this ISBN: 0-440-41412-1. If those pages don't take you to that scene, then look through Chapter 6. That's where this scene occurs.

DREW: I think that's it. She took him home and made him dinner and early on she didn't lecture him. But this line, this line it was the one that really showed how much she was caring.

DOMINICK: Or maybe just being like someone who really cares, you know, like maybe no one ever cared for her. Maybe she is ashamed of some things and so this is her way to give it back.

DREW: Like earlier when she says that she has done things that no one but God knows about.

This is a close reading of this one line, and the students do a good job of connecting it to other parts of the text. Looking at this behavior is, of course, a part of assessing how well the students are reading the text.

Questions You Might Have

1. *This lesson with "Thank You, Ma'm" seems longer than a minilesson. Is it?*

   Yes. Minilessons are short—five to seven minutes for us—lessons that we think are best for reinforcing or reviewing something. We don't use the minilesson format for introducing new information that will take students a while to learn. You should set aside about forty minutes for this lesson.

2. *So, after this one lesson, my students will get it?*

   Don't we wish! No, we find that you'll need to use minilessons to remind students what the text clue is they are looking for (the character acts in a way that surprises us or two characters have clear differences) and the question they must ask themselves (Why would the character act this way?). Here are some short scenes from other trade books that you might use to quickly review (truly a minilesson) Contrasts and Contradictions:

   The Watsons Go to Birmingham–1963, pages 84–85. This is the scene where Byron kills a bird and then later Kenny watches him cry over doing this. Reproduce the scene for students. Before you read it aloud, tell them that Byron is Kenny's older brother and he's the school bully. When you finish reading, ask them what the contradiction is (Byron, a bully, showing remorse for his actions), and then ask, "Why would the character—Byron—act this way?"

The Giver, page 105. The single sentence that says, "The Giver smiled, though his smile was oddly harsh." Display this sentence so all can see it. Tell students that the Giver is a wise elder of a community and his student is a boy named Jonas. The Giver is teaching Jonas how to take over his job one day, a job that will require that Jonas act as the memory keeper of the community. Ask students what the contradiction is. Someone will point out that smiles aren't harsh. Follow up with the question, "Why would the character act this way?"

This line occurs on page 105 in the edition with this ISBN: 0-553-57133-8. If you don't see this line on that page, look for it toward the end of Chapter 13.

3. *Do Contrasts and Contradictions show readers only something about a character?*

No. In historical fiction, science fiction, and fantasy, we want students to notice the contrasts between the world (time and place) of the novel and the world of the reader. When you move into those genres, remind students that in addition to seeing Contrasts and Contradictions in characters, they should look for ways in which the setting of the book contrasts with the setting of their own world. For instance, in the first chapter of *The Giver*, they'll see a community in which loudspeakers are everywhere (not just schools or airports) and see that people are instructed to go inside immediately because a plane is flying overhead. That's a characteristic of a setting that should strike them as odd. The question they ask themselves once they notice a contrast regarding setting is, *What might this mean to the character?* The "this" in that question refers to the element of the setting that the student has found to be a contrast.

4. *So, asking just* Why would the character act this way? *or* What might this mean to the character? *is all I need to teach students to ask themselves?*

Yes. We've found that we can easily overload students with text clues and questions. Students internalize this more easily if they have only one clue to keep in mind and one question to ask themselves once they find that clue. That one question will lead naturally to others. That said, we want to provide you with some additional questions you'll want to use as you talk with students. We don't suggest that you give students this list of questions; instead, keep them nearby and use one or two as needed when talking with students to help them think more deeply about the contrast or contradiction.

- Does this contradiction show us some new side of the character's personality, something we hadn't seen before? If it does, then it may be showing you that the character has been hiding something from us, or it may be revealing how the character is changing. How did it change your opinion of the character?

- Does this contrast tell us anything about the differences between individuals or groups? If so, you're probably seeing the conflict that is arising in the story.

- Is the contrast between what you would expect to see in the place portrayed and what the author actually shows you? If so, it may be revealing some unique feature of the setting.

- Is the contrast between what the character expects to find or achieve and what he or she actually does discover or accomplish? If so, we may be learning about the theme of the book.

- Is the contradiction between what the character says and what she does? Is it between her speech or actions at one point in the story and her behavior at another time? If so, we are learning something about her character and probably about her inner conflicts.

- Does the contradiction show the character making an important decision or doing something that surprises you? Try completing this statement: Once I saw [insert character's name] do _____, then I knew that he/she had learned this lesson: _____. If you can do that, then the contrast or contradiction that you noticed is probably showing you something about the theme.

5. *What do I do if a student is reading a book I've not read, and I therefore don't know if he's missed seeing a contrast or contradiction?*

This will happen often, especially if you use readers' workshop as your instructional style. So, as you talk with a student about the book he's reading, ask where he's noticed a character doing something that is a contradiction or contrast to the way he expected the character might act. Have the student take you to that point in the book. Skim that passage quickly and then make sure to have the student answer the question (all together now: *Why would the character act this way?*)

While we're both fans of readers' workshop, we think this approach to literature instruction means that students miss out on important conversations. So, use Contrasts and Contradictions as a starting point for conversations—even when students are reading various books. Have pairs of students tell each other what their book is about and point out a couple of the contrasts and contradictions they noted that day while reading. The other person has one job—to ask that all-important question!

6. *What type of comments will I hear from students as they contemplate this anchor question?*

Some students (and you know which ones) will move immediately to "I don't know." We find, though, that as we move through the lesson, even those students eventually offer ideas. Some students will offer wild ideas: "I think the lady is from outer space and she's going to do experiments on him." Just ask students to provide evidence from the text. Many students, though, will surprise you with their insight.

For example, as we read this story with a group of students in Gwinnet County, Georgia, students focused on Roger's comment that he wanted blue suede shoes. One boy said he was surprised because he thought Roger would say he was hungry. Another responded that it was honest, "Because from the beginning, even though he was trying to steal her purse, you see he was polite the way he says ma'm and the way he told her that if she turned him loose he'd run." Another joined in and said, "He wanted these blue shoes because whatever those are, they are what will make him fit in, and fitting in is what was most important. He just wanted to fit in."

We were touched by this child's understanding until he said, "Wasn't there like a singer dude from olden times who sang about blue suede shoes? My grandmother used to sing that song. Do you guys know that singer? He's like ancient."

Oh well. For a moment, it was nice.

Lesson *2*

Aha Moment

We teach the Aha Moment second. This is that moment when a character realizes or understands something that until that point he had not known. This signpost helps students better understand how the character's actions are related to the conflict, the progression of the plot, and sometimes the theme. The text clues that we teach students are the phrases that indicate either a sudden or a growing awareness, such as *I realized* and *now I understand.* Once students identify the Aha Moment, they ask themselves, *How might this change things?* It's a simple question, but it invites speculation about what the character's new understanding will lead to in subsequent chapters.

Materials You Will Need

- A copy of the excerpt from *Crash*, by Jerry Spinelli. See Appendix.
- Chart paper for making the Aha Moment chart. We make charts during the lesson, but you can make yours ahead of time. Just be sure to include the information called out on the chart to the right.

Materials Students Will Need

- A copy of the excerpt from *Crash*.
- Pen or pencil.
- Couple of sticky notes.
- Notice and Note Reading Log (optional). See Appendix.

The generalizable language to use when teaching the lesson

Name of Lesson

Anchor question

STOP and Notice & Note

Aha Moment

When you're reading and suddenly a character realizes, understands, or finally figures something out, You should stop and ask yourself:

"How might this change things?" If the character figured out a problem, you probably just learned about the conflict. If the character understood a life lesson, you probably just learned the theme.

Enter the Classroom

We were with a group of eighth graders in a suburban district. We had been in their classroom earlier in the year to teach them Contrasts and Contradictions and now returned to teach Aha Moment. It was a class of twenty-seven students, mostly African American and Latino. Some students were very skilled and were already planning to attend a dual-credit high school, while others weren't sure if they were coming to school the next day. Truly a heterogeneous classroom. The teacher tended to use the literature anthology as the primary source of materials for students to read, so everyone moved forward at the same pace. This had some reading at their frustrational level because the material was too hard, and others frustrated simply because they were bored. We were thrilled to be back with these kids and hoped they'd be happy to see us again. Most were (or were polite enough to pretend to be), though there were the two young men who were quite sure they had never seen us before. So much for making lasting impressions.

Begin by Explaining

" **Today we're going to learn another signpost you should look for as you read. This one is called Aha Moment.** [On your chart paper, in one color of marker, write at the top "Aha Moment."]

This is an easy signpost to learn because you've had many Aha Moments yourself. For instance, have you ever walked into a class, seen people looking through their class notes, and suddenly remembered what it was you were supposed to do the night before—study for that big test? That's an Aha Moment. Or have you ever been looking around your room, peering over yet another stack of dishes or clothes on the floor or papers on your bed and realized that your room really had turned into a disaster? You suddenly are aware that your room has crossed that line from messy to, well, filthy, and whether you want to or not, you just must clean it up. That's an Aha Moment. Aha Moments are those moments when we realize something, and that realization, in some way, changes our actions. Let's put that on our chart as the definition: Aha Moments are those

Although we suggest teaching this lesson after Contrasts and Contradictions, some of you will have turned to this lesson first. If that's the case, you missed our note that says if you want to begin by giving readers an overview of all the signpost lessons, take a look at the Classroom Close-up on page 103. There, you'll see how a fourth-grade teacher introduced the signposts to her students.

moments when a character realizes something, and that realization will probably change his or her actions in some way. [As you go over that definition, write it in a different color of marker on the chart paper.]

When you're reading, the author often gives you clues that the character has come to an important understanding by having the character say something like "Suddenly I realized" or "In an instant I saw" or "It came to me in a flash" or "I now knew" or "I finally understood that." There are many other possibilities, but they will all point to some understanding that the character has finally reached. Those clues are there to tell you that this moment is important, and you need to stop and give it some thought. So, once we've spotted the text clue to the Aha Moment, we have to pause and do something with it. There is a question we can ask that will help us understand what's going to happen. That simple question is: [Write this on the chart paper as you speak it] How might this change things?

Thinking about possible answers to that question will let us see why the Aha Moment is important and how it affects the story. Let's take a look at this moment in a story.

Move to Applying

You've defined the Aha Moment, so now it's time to model how you identify this when reading and how it affects your thinking.

" We'd like to share a text with you now so we can practice noticing Aha Moments. Make sure you've all got your handout and that you have a pen or pencil, and you should see two sticky notes on your desk. . . . Take a look at your handout. What you have here are several scenes we've pulled from a book titled *Crash*, by Jerry Spinelli. It's about a middle-school kid nicknamed Crash who bullies another kid. The kid he bullies is named Penn Webb, and Crash often calls him by his last name. This first scene is from the beginning of the story, page 2 in fact, when the main character, Crash, is outside and sees Penn walking down the sidewalk.

It was a sunny summer day. I was in the front yard digging a hole with my little red shovel. I heard something like whistling. I looked up. It was whistling. It was coming from a funny-looking dorky little runt walking up the sidewalk. Only he wasn't just walking regular. He was walking like he owned the place, both hands in his pockets, sort of swaying lah-dee-dah with each step. *Strollll*-ing. Strolling and gawking at the houses and whistling a happy little dorky tune like some Sneezy or Snoozy or whatever their names are.

And he wore a button, a big one. It covered about half his chest. Which wasn't that hard since his chest was so scrawny.

So here he comes strolling, whistling, gawking, buttoning, dorking up the sidewalk, onto my sidewalk, my property, and all of a sudden I knew what I had to do, like there was a big announcement coming down from the sky: Don't let him pass.

I'm going to pause here because I've spotted the phrase "all of a sudden I knew what I had to do," and I realize that the author has given me a clue that the character has suddenly discovered something. When an author shows me that a character has realized something, I want to stop and think about what that means. Spinelli then emphasizes the point even more strongly by adding, "like there was a big announcement coming down from the sky." That's another clue in the text that the character has suddenly grown aware of something. Both phrases let me know that the character has grasped something important, and that insight is going to change things.

And then Spinelli tells me what Crash has realized: He can't let that kid pass. When I see a character have an Aha Moment, I need to ask myself the question, *How might this change things?*

I think I know how, or at least I can make a good guess about what he's going to do next. I think he's going to confront this kid he has referred to as "a funny-looking dorky little runt." He's going to make him stop, and he's probably going to do something to humiliate the kid, though I'll have to keep reading to see if that's correct. When authors show us those Aha Moments, we need to pay attention. Maybe Crash has realized he wants a friend—though since he's been calling him unpleasant names, I really think he's going to bully him some. Now let's skip ahead in the book to another Aha Moment.

In this next section we find that Crash and Penn are about to compete against each other in a school race. Webb's parents and his great-grandfather, Henry Wilhide Webb III, have come to watch Penn

We want to point out that even though we don't tell students to visualize, an important comprehension process, they do visualize as they think about Aha Moments. For example, one student, in talking about this Aha Moment, said, "He knew he had to do that because that other kid was acting so stuck-up. You can just see him walking around like he's in charge." You don't need to say, "Let's visualize," but you do need to listen for language that indicates that it's happening.

At this point we're doing all the work. We've pointed out the text clues that indicate the Aha Moment, we've asked the anchor question, and we've proposed an answer. We'll give students less help the next time we pause.

run. Crash is looking at the three of them in the stands, thinking of his own grandfather, Scooter. Until now, Crash has continued to bully Penn. As I read, see if you notice the Aha that Crash has.

And this excerpt is on page 154 in the edition we're using. That's about three pages into Chapter 46 if you're using a different edition.

> The stands were empty. A school bus moved in the distance beyond the football goalpost. Under the crossbar and between the uprights, like in a framed picture, stood three people.
>
> For once, Webb's parents didn't look so old, not compared to the man standing between them. He was shorter than them, and real skinny, like the prairie winds were eroding him away. But he was standing straight and by himself—no cane, no walker, just two legs. Ninety-three years old. Maybe it was the Missouri River mud.
>
> The thought came to me: they would have liked each other, Scooter and Henry Wilhide Webb III. Two storytellers. Both from the great flat open spaces, one a prairie of grass, one of water. Both came to watch when no one else was there.

Did you hear the Aha? When I saw the phrase "the thought came to me," I knew Crash had figured something out, had an Aha Moment. Authors use these Aha Moments to show us insight, something the character now understands. Once you spot the Aha Moment, think about the question we want to ask ourselves: How might this change things? How might Crash's realization that the two grandfathers might have liked one another change Crash?

This time I'll let you think about it. On one of your sticky notes, jot down your answers to that question.

The second time we pause—actually each time—we begin by reminding students why we're pausing. We do this by always going back to the fact that authors use Aha Moments to show something that the character has figured out. With the first Aha Moment, we did all the work. This time we've directed the students to the text clues, reminded them of the anchor question, and then stepped aside to let them speculate about what the passage means. Take about two minutes.

Give students one or two minutes to jot down their thinking. As students write, stroll around the room and try to see what they are writing. You might occasionally point out an insight that you think is good and quietly encourage the student to share it later.

❝ OK. Now turn and talk with the person next to you, sharing your thinking. [Again, listen in on as many conversations as you can.]

As students talk in pairs, listen to what they are saying. You're focusing on two things. First, make sure they are answering the question, *How might this change things?* If too many say something general, such as "It means he thinks they would like each other" then they are simply restating the comment in the book. Ask them to think about a time when they've realized that two people they thought couldn't be friends indeed could have been. How might that friendship between the two change things?

“ Let's come back together as a group and hear some of the thoughts you had. . . . Good. You've pointed out that Crash is thinking about how the grandfathers liked each other. . . . Several of you have mentioned that it's hard to know what this will mean to Crash. Some of you have said it might mean that if Crash's grandfather might be a friend with Penn's, then maybe Crash could be friendly with Penn. What you've seen, regardless of what you predict might happen next, is that when an author shows us an Aha that a character has had, we need to wonder how that insight will change things and what it shows us about the character. We'll learn more as we keep reading.

I'll read on now, and you mark the place where you spot another text clue that you think might let us know that the character is having an Aha Moment. It's still before the race, and Crash is thinking about Penn's great-grandfather.

Try to encourage speculation, but speculation with support. *What's in the text to support that?* is a good follow-up for declarations students make.

Why exactly was he here? Did he know about me? Did he know his great-grandson could not win the race-off, and so would not run in the Penn Relays?

I wondered if Webb felt safe in his great-grandfather's bed.

The cinder track crunched under my feet. There were five of us in the race: me, Webb, two other seventh graders, and a sixth grader. The coach put us in lanes. Me and Webb were side by side.

Again, he hadn't said a word to me all day. We milled around behind the starting blocks, nervous, shaking out our arms and legs, everything as quiet as if the coach had already said, "Ready."

The other team members—jumpers, throwers, distance runners—had all stopped their practicing to watch. A single hawk, its wingtips spread like black fingers, kited over the school, and suddenly I saw something: a gift. A gift for a great-grandfather from North Dakota, maybe for all great-grandfathers. But the thing was, only one person could give the gift, and it wasn't the great-grandson, not on his fastest day alive. It was me.

I hated it being me. I tried not to see, but everywhere I looked, there it was.

The gift.

This excerpt begins on page 154 and ends on 155.

This one is a little tricky. Let's look at this paragraph that begins with "The other team members" once more. [Reread that paragraph.]

On your own, underline the realization Crash has had. What was it? . . . Right. It's the phrase "suddenly I saw something." It's a little hard because you might think he literally saw something. But if you think about it, you realize it means Crash saw something in his mind, saw something he's realized. Now, what question should we ask ourselves when we see an Aha Moment? . . . Once you've thought about the question and jotted down your answer on one of your sticky notes, turn and talk with a neighbor about your thoughts.

[After just a few minutes, bring them back together.] Let's talk about what you and your partner said about how this realization might change what happens next. Crash has realized that he could give Penn's great-grandfather a gift, and that he is the only one who can because he is the faster runner. And at least some of you think that he's going to let Penn Webb win the race.

Let's see what happens next. As I read through this last part of the chapter, mark any passages that show you an Aha Moment with a check mark or by underlining them.

At this point in the lesson, we've helped students identify the text clue and recall the question, but now we want them thinking about the question and then talking with a partner. We're trying to turn over more and more of the task of reading to them.

This excerpt begins on page 155 and ends on 156.

Some students will identify "it occurred to me" as an Aha Moment.

And others will mark "for the first time in my life, I didn't know if I wanted to win."

"Let's go, boys," said the coach.

A voice closer to me said, "Good luck."

It was Webb, sticking out his dorky hand, smiling that old dorky smile of his. No button. I shook his hand, and it occurred to me that because he was always eating my dust, the dumb fishcake had never won a real race and probably didn't know how. And now there wasn't time.

"Don't forget to lean," I told him. His face went blank. The coach called, "Ready."

I got down, feet in the blocks, right knee on the track, thumbs and forefingers on the chalk, eyes straight down— and right then, for the first time in my life, I didn't know if I wanted to win.

"Set."

Knee up, rear up, eyes up.

The coach says the most important thing here is to focus your mind. You are a coiled steel spring, ready to dart out at the sound of the gun. So what comes into my head? Ollie the one-armed octopus. He didn't disappear till the gun went off.

I was behind—not only Webb, but everybody. No problem. Within ten strides I picked up three of them. That left Webb. He was farther ahead of me than usual, but that was because of my rotten start.

At the halfway mark, where I usually passed him, he was still ahead, and I still didn't know if I wanted to win. I gassed it. The gap closed. I could hear him puffing, like a second set of footsteps. Cinder flecks from his feet pecked at my shins. I was still behind. The finish line was closing. I kicked in the afterburners. Ten meters from the white string we were shoulder to shoulder, breath to breath, grandson to great grandson, and it felt new, it felt good, not being behind, not being ahead, but being even, and just like that, a half breath from the white string, I knew. There was no time to turn to him. I just barked it out: "Lean!" He leaned, he threw his chest out, he broke the string. He won.

You can expect several to mark "and just like that . . . I knew."

All right. That's the end of this section. I saw you underlining passages as I was reading, phrases or words that showed you the Aha Moments Crash had. Take a moment or two and look at the passages you marked, and then on your sticky note, jot down how you think that Aha might change things. [Let them jot down their notes for several minutes, and then for several minutes have them talk in pairs, or perhaps in groups of three or four, about what they've noticed.]

Here we've left students largely on their own, with a passage that has several candidates for the Aha Moment. We're trying to move them closer and closer to independence.

All right, let's talk about what you found. Some of you said that the first one you noticed is the phrase "it occurred to me." Tell us what makes this an Aha Moment and how you answered the question. . . . We agree. Crash has realized that Penn Webb can't win the race on his own, and he doesn't have time to teach Penn how. What else did you notice? . . . Yes, "for the first time in my life, I didn't know if I wanted to win" is an Aha Moment. And how does that Aha change things? . . . OK, it does tell us that Crash has grown up enough to see that winning may not be the most important thing at this point.

Almost all of you spotted the most obvious Aha Moment of all, however, close to the end of this chapter. What is it? . . . Right. When authors use language like "I knew," that's a clear indication that the character has figured out something. How will this change things?

If you want students to use the Notice and Note Reading Log, you'll find a template of one we've created on pages 209–210 of the Appendix and you'll see some others that teachers have created beginning on page 211. Students can also use sticky notes to mark places and jot down their thinking.

These two students focused on different parts of the text—Laurie on "he knew" and Dinnie on "it occurred to me"—to reach the same conclusion: Crash had decided to let his opponent win because that was a good thing to do. Don't be surprised when students identify different parts of a text when discussing a particular signpost and then go on to reach similar conclusions. You want them noticing *something* and the signpost gives them some directions, but what each reader actually notices will vary from student to student.

End with Reviewing

❝ So, what we've been practicing here is spotting Aha Moments. Turn to your partner one last time and tell each other what you learned about this lesson. Be sure you talk about what it means, what to look for in the text, and what the anchor question is. [Give students a few minutes to do this, then perhaps let one or two share what they said.] As you read on in your own novels, watch for Aha Moments. Make a note about them, either in your reading log or on a sticky note that you place in the book itself.

Conversation Close-up

Let's take a close look at an exchange from two students, one typical of what you might hear.

LAURIE: I wrote down "He knew" because that was like he had an Aha. And I think it means that he knew his friend needed to win because it was more important to like be a good friend than just to win.

DINNIE: Yeah, that was good. I saw that one, and I wrote down "it occurred to me" because that was like having an Aha. Once he realized that he had never won a race, then I think his mind started thinking like maybe he should let him. It was like he was finally thinking about someone else.

As you listen to students, you'll hear short conversations like this one. When you hear students who say "I don't know" or "I don't see anything," point them to particular parts or even certain sentences. If one partner has something to say and the other doesn't, tell the silent one that she can borrow her partner's thinking for the moment, but that she must also say it. When kids "borrow" someone else's language, they almost always add more. That's when you offer encouragement for the independent thinking they've just done. This is, of course, a part of assessing how well the students are reading the text.

Questions You Might Have

1. *This lesson seems to offer a simple concept. Is it really important enough to teach our students?*

   We think that it is, because Aha Moments, as important as they are, rarely cause struggling readers to pause and think of the effects of such realizations. Readers, perhaps especially struggling readers, tend to focus on the action, sometimes to the neglect of the implications for character development or theme. Or, worse, they may be passing their eyes over the lines of text mindlessly, giving no thought to the significance of any of the events. Reading that way, they are sure to miss the insight. So they may see Penn crossing the finish line a split second before Crash without realizing that in that split second Crash has committed himself to giving Penn's great grandfather the gift of seeing his great grandson win the race. That split second shows us—if we pause to think about it—how much Crash has grown during the novel. Crash has been transformed from a bully into someone who can sacrifice for a friend, and that is what the entire book is about. Here the Aha Moment has led to an understanding of theme.

2. *What if my students seem to keep forgetting this lesson and I need to reteach it?*

Here are some short scenes from other trade books that you might use to quickly review (truly a minilesson) the Aha Moment.

Among the Hidden, by Margaret Haddix, page 145. Copy the passage that begins "Luke remembered how bored he'd felt before meeting Jen" and concludes, "The answer was there instantly, as if he'd known it all along and his brain was just waiting for him to come looking." Tell students that in this scene Luke, who is in great danger, has been offered false identity papers that may enable him to survive if he's willing to take them. Then ask students what they see as the text clue to the Aha Moment.

The questions in this scene led to an answer that "was there instantly." While readers won't know what that answer is (we didn't want to include that spoiler), they'll see that this answer solves a problem for Luke and therefore offers insight into an internal conflict.

Esperanza Rising, by Pam Muñoz Ryan. You might copy two scenes. Scene 1 begins on page 27 with "Esperanza avoided opening her birthday gifts" and continues for five paragraphs to page 28, ending with "She hugged the doll to her chest and walked out of the room, leaving all the other gifts behind." Tell students that in this scene, Esperanza, the daughter of a wealthy rancher in Mexico, is opening birthday presents from her father, who has recently been killed.

These page numbers are from the edition with this ISBN: 0-689-82475-0. If those pages don't take you to that scene, then look near the end of Chapter 29.

We're using the edition with this ISBN: 0-439-12042-X. This first scene is in the chapter titled "Las Papayas," and scene 2 is from the chapter titled "Los Aguacates."

Scene 2 begins on page 181 with "Esperanza was surprised at the simple things she missed about Mama," and concludes on page 182 with "Because they were the hands of a poor campesina." Tell students that in this scene, Esperanza and her mother have fled Mexico and moved to California, where they are now migrant farm workers.

Have students discuss which of these two scenes contains an Aha Moment. They should recognize that the first scene simply discusses how Esperanza felt after opening some presents. There's no new Aha.

If you're wondering why we didn't provide passages, it's our small effort at going at least slightly green. We didn't want to use the pages for examples that you might never share with your students. We expect you can find these books, if not in your classroom, in your school or local library.

But in the second scene, she realizes how much her life has changed. This moment may be difficult for some readers because it is subtly presented and easily missed. The clue to it isn't dramatic, like "it came to me in a flash," but is simply the words "she realized" in the phrase "she realized that it wouldn't matter how much avocado and glycerin she put on them, they would never look like the hands of a wealthy woman." And then what she has realized is also presented somewhat obliquely: "Because they were the hands of a poor campesina." The reader has to draw the inference that Esperanza knows now that she is no longer wealthy, but that she is a poor peasant and must accept her new status.

3. *It seems that the text clue for this lesson could be infinitely variable. How can we teach students to be alert to all the possible wordings?*

You can't. You might begin by emphasizing those moments that are signaled by the suddenness of the perception: "*in an instant* I knew," "*suddenly* it came to me," or "I was *startled* to realize." Later you might point out to them, and urge them to be alert for, those Aha Moments that are not so sudden but that are the result of a gradual realization. "I sat there for an hour, thinking about it, and gradually realized that there wasn't much question left about what I had to do." That may be harder for the student to notice and recognize as an important insight than "it hit me like a thunderbolt—I knew in a second what I had to do." Still harder to recognize will be those like the example from *Esperanza Rising* that reveal the character's insight through an action that requires us to articulate the perception. When we see Esperanza staring at her hands, thinking they are those of a poor campesina, we have to infer that she now realizes that she is no longer in the privileged class.

4. *Sometimes my students seem content to just spot the moment and paraphrase what the character has learned. How do I get them to go beyond that?*

Emphasize the question to be asked about the Aha Moment. Remind them that the point of noticing something in a book is to then be able to think about what it signifies. Encourage them to always jot down a few notes speculating about the answer to the anchor question when they have spotted an Aha Moment. And, whenever possible, give them time to discuss their answers. The more you can encourage conversation, the more you will involve students in the story, and the more they will see the significance of thinking about these moments in the novel. But remember, the ability to speculate, question, explore, elaborate upon thoughts, and qualify our judgments takes time to develop. It won't happen quickly.

> The more you can encourage conversation, the more you will involve students in the story, and the more they will see the significance of thinking about these moments in the novel.

5. *This seems simple for my more skilled readers. How do I differentiate this lesson for my more advanced students?*

There's more you can do. You could, for instance, distinguish among three kinds of Aha Moments.

- The first is that moment in which the character finally realizes what his problem is: "I suddenly realized that they were never going to accept me into their circle."

- The second is that moment in which the character sees the pathway to the resolution of the conflict or the solution of the problem: "I finally saw that I would have to find a way to be happy living my own life apart from the 'in group.'"

- And the third is that moment when the character comes to a broader understanding that might be seen as a lesson for life and possibly the theme of the book: "At last I understood that real happiness came from living up to your own principles and not simply following the crowd."

Lesson *3*

Tough Questions

At some point in virtually every children's book and young adult novel we've examined, the main character puts into words the major problem he or she is facing. The Tough Questions signpost helps students identify and recognize the importance of this moment. The clues the author provides aren't subtle. Students should simply be alert for a difficult question the character asks of himself or of a trusted other. The reader must realize that this is not a question with a simple answer, like *What's for lunch?* Instead, it troubles the main character, giving us insight into the internal conflict. When we notice tough questions, we ask, *What does this question make me wonder about?*

Materials You Will Need

- A copy of the excerpts from *A Long Walk to Water*, by Linda Sue Park. See Appendix.

- Chart paper for the Tough Questions chart. We make charts during the lesson, but you can make yours ahead of time. Just be sure to include the information called out on the chart to the right.

Materials Students Will Need

- A copy of the excerpts from *A Long Walk to Water*.

- Pen or pencil.

- Three or four sticky notes.

- Notice and Note Reading Log (optional). See Appendix.

The generalizable language to use when teaching the lesson

Name of Lesson

Anchor question

STOP and Notice & Note

Tough Questions

When you're reading and the character asks himself a really difficult question,

You should stop and ask yourself:

"What does this question make me wonder about?"

The answers will tell you about the conflict and might give you ideas about what will happen later in the story.

Enter the Classroom

This is the lesson we used while in a ninth-grade class that read mostly at about a fourth-grade level. There were twenty-three students assigned to this class, mostly boys, all from a high-poverty neighborhood. Only sixteen students were in class the day we visited. The teacher said that attendance was actually high that day. Before the tardy bell rang, most hovered in the hall, right by the classroom door, and made a dash for desks as the bell began ringing. Few students brought their textbooks. Several had pencils (if you call a two-inch stub a pencil) in the back pocket of their blue jeans. The girls were much more interested in passing around a tube of lipstick that was the "hot new color" as we were told. After a few introductory remarks in which we introduced ourselves (no one seemed impressed), we began.

Begin by Explaining

“ We all ask questions such as "What's for dinner?" or "Where are my shoes?" or "Do I really have to do my homework?" all the time. Those are questions to which we certainly want answers, but they aren't what we'd call really tough questions. Tough questions are those questions we sometimes ask ourselves, or someone else, that seem, at least for a while, not to have an answer. We might ask, "How will I ever get over this?" when we hear that a loved one has died, or we might ask, "What should I do?" when we have a difficult, almost impossible, choice to make, or we might ask, "Am I brave enough to say no?" when we're asked to do something we know we shouldn't do. If someone breaks up with you, you ask, "Why?" Tough questions are a part of life because life is, well, sometimes tough.

When you share a tough question with a friend—or just think it to yourself—you're really sharing something that bothers you. In a novel, we call that the internal conflict, and if you can spot in a novel the tough questions a character asks of himself or to a friend, then you'll have found the internal conflict.

At this point, one young man who had been watching us with his arms folded and leaning far back in his chair so that it was balanced on its back two legs, sat forward, and interrupted us: "That's it. Find the

Tough Questions and you'll get the internal conflict? Man, I miss that on every test. Why hasn't anybody told me this before?" We said that we were glad he was learning it now and that in a moment he could practice finding tough questions in a text. We thought we were doing great, that a disengaged student would now become a motivated reader. Just as we began to smile and nod at one another he brought us back to reality. "Nope. I got it. Will save it for the next test." Then he put his head down on his desk and promptly went to sleep. Perhaps you know this kid? Before he began snoring, we got back to the lesson.

" Authors often show us these Tough Questions in fairly straightforward ways: The main character either asks a trusted person or him- or herself a question that obviously doesn't have an easy answer. Often Tough Questions show up in pairs: "Why won't they talk to me anymore? Why is everyone treating me this way?" Occasionally, the character might not ask a question, but might say something like "I wonder if. . . ." Once you notice the Tough Question (or the statement that begins with "I wonder"), it's important to stop and ask yourself, *What does this question make me wonder about?*

Think about it this way. If you hear there's a party and you're not invited, you might ask yourself, "Why'd I get left out?" And from that question, you might wonder if you had done something to hurt someone's feelings or if it's really with a group you don't know well so no one figured you'd want to go. One tough question usually makes us wonder about other things.

So, let's review briefly. When authors want to show us the internal conflict—the deep problems that worry a character—they often let the character share that conflict by having him or her share some difficult questions. He might ask himself the questions or he might ask a friend. And when we see a Tough Question, we should ask ourselves, *What does this question make me wonder about?*

Move to Applying

Once you've explained the signpost and the anchor question, it's time to show students how this signpost looks in a text. Everyone should have a copy of the handout of excerpts from *A Long Walk to Water*, something to write with, and perhaps a few sticky notes. Now, move the students into the text with the briefest of introductions.

Take a moment to either share the Tough Questions chart you've already created or to put this information on the chart now. Keep it up and visible as you take students through the lesson so they can revisit the anchor question as needed.

" Let's take a look at how this works in the book *A Long Walk to Water*. This is a book about what happens to an eleven-year-old who lives in Sudan during a time in which rebels are raiding villages. In a scene early in the novel, eleven-year-old Salva has become separated from the rest of his family after rebels have attacked his small Sudanese village, and he's now alone and scared and running. You've got a handout with what I'll be reading. Follow along as I read aloud.

> Salva lowered his head and ran.
>
> He ran until he could not run anymore. Then he walked. For hours, until the sun was nearly gone from the sky.
>
> Other people were walking, too. There were so many of them that they couldn't all be from the school village; they must have come from the whole area.
>
> As Salva walked, the same thoughts kept going through his head in rhythm with his steps. Where are we going? Where is my family? When will I see them again?

Let's stop here because there are several Tough Questions: "Where are we going? Where is my family? When will I see them again?" For an eleven-year-old boy, these are obviously painful questions. When an author shows me the difficult questions that a character is considering, I want to stop and think about those questions. They show me the conflicts—the problems—that character is worried about. I want to ask myself, *What do these questions make me wonder about?* As I think about Salva's difficult questions and ask myself what they make me wonder about, I wonder if I could have survived without knowing where my family was or even if they were still alive. I have to wonder, too, how the people he is with will react. They are in desperate circumstances, too, so I wonder if they'll help or if they'll just ignore this small child. They're trying to escape, too, and might see Salva as nothing more than another burden. They might just turn their backs on him. Most of all, I wonder what he's going to have to do to survive.

Let's read on. We're skipping ahead in the story to a point where Salva, who has been on his own for a while, finds a small group of people who are trying to survive.

You might show students where Sudan is and tell them this is based on the experiences of a boy named Salva Dut. This is a difficult story because of the content, but it is an important one and appeals to reluctant readers. If you think the content is too mature, you might prefer one of the texts we mention in the Q & A section.

This first excerpt is from page 9 of the edition of *A Long Walk to Water* with this ISBN: 978-0-547-25127-1.

At this point, we do all the work. We spot the Tough Questions, call the students' attention to them, ask the anchor question, and speculate about the answers.

This excerpt is from pages 58–59.

FROM KYLENE: If I'm sharing this excerpt with younger readers, I might skip the second and third sentences of paragraph 4.

FROM BOB: But this is the reality 11-year-old Salva faced. We also know the most meaningful texts for readers—of all ages—are often the ones that present difficult moments. The horror Salva faces leads directly to the toughest question: If we are our brother's keepers, then how does this happen?

FROM BOTH OF US: We're not trying to censor works; we think there's a difference between censorship and selection. You know your students; use what's appropriate for them.

Now we point out the Tough Question and ask students to turn to each other to discuss the anchor question. We're releasing some of the responsibility to them.

Sure enough, there were now three women giving water to the men on the ground.

Like a miracle, the small amounts of water revived them. They were able to stagger to their feet and join the group as the walking continued.

But their five dead companions were left behind. There were no tools with which to dig, and besides, burying the dead men would have taken too much time.

Salva tried not to look as he walked past the bodies, but his eyes were drawn in their direction. He knew what would happen. Vultures would find the bodies and strip them of their rotting flesh until only the bones remained. He felt sick at the thought of those men—first dying in such a horrible way, and then having even their corpses ravaged.

If he were older and stronger, would he have given water to those men? Or would he, like most of the group, have kept his water for himself?

It was the group's third day in the desert. By sunset, they would be out of the desert, and after that, it would not be far to the Itang refugee camp in Ethiopia.

Obviously, the Tough Question is "Would he have given water to those men? Or would he, like most of the group, have kept his water for himself?" When you spot such a question in any text, ask yourself, "What does this make me wonder about?" With your neighbor, talk about what this makes you wonder about, and then we'll hear some of your thoughts.

Observe as many of the pairs of students as you can, looking for a variety of answers to that question. After a few minutes, ask at least several of the pairs of students to share what it is they wondered about.

“ OK, come back together as a big group. Let's hear your thoughts.

You'll probably hear students talk about being thirsty. As one student told us, "I have no idea what it would feel like to be that thirsty." Some might discuss what it would be like to have to watch people die and then just walk away, leaving them behind, unable even to call some authority to come and look after the dead. Some older students we've shared this with talked about images they remembered seeing in New Orleans from Katrina or from earthquakes in Haiti or Japan. With each comment, we just kept pushing students back to the anchor question, which encouraged them to speculate on what Salva must do next, and as they talked, they raised more questions: *What kind of country is this place? Aren't there police trying to help? What do you do when the government is out to get you?* These were authentic, dialogic questions that the students were raising, and little by little the apathy in that classroom was being replaced with curiosity. They wanted to keep reading. One student rushed us saying, "So, let's get back to what happens." We did.

" All of these are great questions. Thinking about some of them helps us to imagine ourselves in this situation, and so we'll understand what's happening better. Taking the time to think about the Tough Question helps us put ourselves in the story, visualize what's happening, and imagine how the characters are feeling. If we do that, we'll better understand what Salva is going through.

Let's read one more passage. In this scene, Salva is alone. You'll easily spot the Tough Questions.

We did want to get back to the text, but we didn't want students to forget the point of this lesson, to learn about tough questions. We find it helpful before returning to the text to just remind students what we're doing one more time.

> I am alone now.
>
> I am all that is left of my family.
>
> His father, who had sent Salva to school . . . brought him treats, like mangoes . . . trusted him to take care of the herd. . . . His mother, always ready with food and milk and a soft hand to stroke Salva's head. His brothers and sisters, whom he had laughed with and played with and looked after. . . . He would never see them again.
>
> How can I go on without them?
>
> But how can I not go on? They would want me to survive . . . to grow up and make something of my life . . . to honor their memories.

This excerpt is found on page 72.

Take a few minutes now to think about the Tough Questions you noticed and your thoughts about the anchor question. If you've forgotten the question, it's up here on the poster. Take a look at it, jot down your answer to the anchor question on one of your sticky notes, and then turn and talk with your partner about your thoughts.

As students write and talk, wander around the room and observe. This is the time to encourage less talkative students to speak up when you call all back together.

[After several minutes, ask some of the pairs to share their thoughts.] **This is a powerful scene. I want to hear what you thought about Salva's tough questions.** [Several students shared for more minutes than we had anticipated them wanting to share.] **Again, many of you wondered how we—each of us—would do in the same circumstances. We heard one of you say that you just didn't know how you'd be able to go on and that it made you wonder how you would keep on living. We heard another pair talking about how it's hard to survive here, in some of the areas around your school, but that is nothing compared to what Salva is facing and you wondered what this meant about how much faster kids there have to grow up than here. We saw that some of you had written on your sticky notes questions such as "What in his background made him this brave?" and "What if he had been a girl?"**

And several of you seemed to think that his second tough question—"How can I not go on?"—was at least part of an answer to his first question. Who can tell us more about that? [Several students explained that this question was "like a pep talk" or "a question that he knows the answer to."]

Students then took over the conversation for about five minutes, listening to one another, and not needing anything from us. They kept going back to their handout until one student said, "This isn't enough. We need the entire book." We promised we'd get them copies and then finished up the lesson.

End with Reviewing

❝ Think about all the conversations and discussions we've just had. They came from considering what the Tough Questions meant. Remember that authors show us Tough Questions to give us insight into the struggle the main character faces. When we see those questions, we should ask ourselves, What does this make me wonder about?

It's easy to read right past these tough questions because the author so seldom gives you an answer at that point. But now you know that what the author wants you to do is recognize that these questions show you what concerns the character. You should pause and ask yourself what the Tough Questions make you wonder about.

When you understand the character's situation, you are better able to contemplate how you might react in similar circumstances. When you're able to do that, you will have a much deeper understanding of the conflicts presented. So, as you read tonight's assignment, be on the lookout for Tough Questions and we'll discuss them and their implications tomorrow.

Conversation Close-up

Let's take a close look at an exchange from two students, one typical of what you might hear. We've asked them to identify the most important Tough Question.

> **AMY:** I thought "But how can I not go on?" was the most important.
>
> **SHARON:** Me, too. This was like him feeling he was in a place where he had to decide what to do.
>
> **AMY:** What was the question that we're supposed to ask?
>
> **SHARON:** So what does this make me wonder about?
>
> [pause]
>
> **SHARON:** I think, you know, I think that this makes me wonder how alone he is feeling. You know, what do I do next if I stay here? This makes me wonder if he's never going to see his family again. And it really makes me wonder if he is like really stronger. I'd just be bawling now and too afraid to do anything. But he's already thinking about what it would mean if he didn't move. He's braver than I would be.
>
> **AMY:** Miss (calling to Kylene), this is really important here. It's where you see that he has got to be like real courageous inside no matter what happens. I think he's going to make it.

We appreciated this exchange between these two girls who began the class slumped in their chairs, barely looking at us, much more interested in a note they kept passing back and forth. Amy said to us later, "It was cool how it was always the same question so we could keep just like focusing on that, so you really started thinking about what was being said and what it would mean." High praise from a girl who at the beginning of class when we asked her to take out a pencil said, "Whatever." Watching for this increasing engagement with the text is, of course, a part of assessing how well the students are reading.

The power of collaboration is apparent in this exchange. Amy has identified an important tough question but doesn't offer a reason why it's important and has forgotten the anchor question (which was on chart paper at the front of the room!). Sharon reminds her of the anchor question and then when Amy remains silent, Sharon offers her thinking. Then Amy is excited and adds her own words to Sharon's thinking. We're not sure where Amy would have gone if she had been alone. Giving students time to talk with one another sharpens their comprehension.

Questions You Might Have

1. *The Tough Question seems such an obvious place to stop that I have to wonder why readers don't pause at that point naturally. Even I seem to keep right on rolling, and I'm a good reader. Why is it so easily ignored?*

We suppose it takes some discipline to pause and think. If the Tough Question occurs during a quiet moment, when the character has gone off alone to reflect, we may be eager to get back to the faster pace of the action. If it comes at a moment when the character is under great stress, as it does several times in *A Long Walk to Water*, we may not want to slow the pace to ask ourselves what the Tough Question reveals. We may be driven more strongly by the desire to see what happens next than by the impulse to understand the character fully.

Or, if we're reading solely to experience the plot (something most readers do early in becoming lifelong readers and which is often made evident by the summary that sounds like *And then this happened and then this happened and then. . .*), we may keep on reading simply to find out how the character eventually answers his or her own question. Learning to pause and wonder, to read closely for a moment, will repay the discipline it demands. Perhaps more than anything else, it may help us to identify with the character, because in difficult moments we are very likely to wonder how we would have coped ourselves.

2. *I can get students to spot the Tough Question, and I can even get them to ask themselves the anchor question, but most of them want to say, simply, "I wonder what the answer is." Too many of them think that's enough. How do I get them to wonder more deeply?*

Yes, that simple, obvious reply comes so easily. And of course they *do* wonder what the answer is. And it's difficult to suggest to them what sort of wondering might come to them without telling them what to wonder about, doing their thinking for them. We've tried giving them examples of what we wonder about when we hit a Tough Question and hope that it suggests possibilities to them for the next Tough Question we come to in the book.

When we do give examples, we try to suggest different categories of wondering:

- How would I, the reader, feel or think in these circumstances? To refocus the student on the text, follow this with, Does the character seem to feel the same or different?

- What alternatives does the character seem to have in answering the question?

- What values will help the character make his or her choice (concern for other people, desire for great wealth, determination to appear courageous, something else)?

- What would happen if the character made *this* choice, instead of *that* one?

As we go through the year, we try to give fewer and fewer of our own speculations and instead keep asking them, "What else might we wonder about at this point?"

3. *Does the Tough Question signpost always show up as a question?*

No. It might easily show up as a statement, but it will be one implying confusion or uncertainty. For instance, a character might say, "I wonder what will happen when we have to move" or "I can't see how we'll survive without Pa." Observant readers might recognize that comments such as "I knew that I was going to have to figure out if my conscience would let me go along with my friend's plan" offer insight into an internal conflict and therefore serve as Tough Questions. We teach students to look for the questions and the statements of confusion and doubt and are thrilled when they see the more declarative rumination as a type of Tough Question.

4. *How can I help the student who sees any question as a Tough Question?*

You might explain that if the question is asking for data or information, it's probably not that tough. "Where's the office?" isn't a question that's going to deeply trouble the character or plague him or her for a long time. Somebody will come along and point down the hallway in the right direction. On the other hand, "Do I tell the principal what my friends have done and get them in trouble, or do I lie and protect them?" probably is a Tough Question. If the question requires a difficult decision or a serious commitment, if the character's values and beliefs will be tested by it, then it's a Tough Question.

5. *If I need to reteach this (or think* A Long Walk to Water *is too mature for my students), what other texts do you suggest?*

The first chapter of **Half and Half** by Lensey Namioka offers several examples of Tough Questions. Eleven-year-old Fiona is part Chinese and part Scottish. While completing an enrollment form for a dance class, she doesn't know which box to check when asked to describe her race as White, Asian, Black, Hispanic, Native American, or Other. She wonders, "Why didn't they have a box for people like me, who were half and half?" She asks her mom, "What am I?" Later she wonders, "Why do grown-ups always have to sort people into boxes anyway?" She talks with her brother, wondering if it doesn't bother him that people who don't fit into one category are "just lumped into 'Other'?" Interspersed are questions that help students see the differences between types of tough questions—those that reveal a conflict—and those asked simply to gain information.

Among the Hidden. In this book by Margaret Haddix, Luke, who is a forbidden third child, remembers that on his sixth birthday he hounded his mom, asking if his older brothers ever had to hide and, when hearing that they did not, wants to know, "Then why do I?" (page 9). Later, when he is older, and more aware of his limited life, he begins to wonder to himself, "What if something happened to them and they never came back? Would someone find him years from now, abandoned and dead?" (page 15). These are passages that will clearly illustrate the Tough Question and reveal its importance in the story.

Another good example occurs later in the same book. Jen— another hidden third child Luke has discovered living across the field from him—says to him, "Do you want to hide all your life, or do you want to change history?" (page 110). Jen has challenged Luke with a Tough Question, one that will haunt him throughout the remainder of the novel. When we notice this and other difficult questions, we begin to predict that something will probably happen to make Luke choose. He'll have to decide if he's willing to spend the rest of his life in hiding or if he has the courage to fight. We don't know what that event will be, and we don't know what he will choose, but noticing the Tough Questions and seeing his conflict helps us predict that the direction of the novel will, at least in part, be based on the choice Luke finally makes.

Any version—hard copy or paperback—will work because you're reading all of Chapter 1, which is only eight pages. Although this eleven-year-old confronts difficult issues, the book is told with humor, and most students in third and fourth grade will enjoy it.

These page numbers are from the edition with this ISBN: 0-689-82475-0. If the page numbers we list here for the quotes we've pulled don't match your book, this might help: the first quote from page 9 is in Chapter 2; the second one on page 15 is near the middle of Chapter 3; the one from page 110 is in Chapter 22; and the final one on page 145 is from Chapter 29.

So, at the end of the novel, remembering that question Jen had asked him and all of his own questions about the life in front of him, he now asks himself, "Did he want to spend the rest of his life feeling that desperate? Did he want to just . . . waste it?" (page 145).

6. *Do some genres rely more heavily on Tough Questions?*

We're not sure. Science fiction often raises difficult questions about social issues; survival and adventure novels often raise questions for the hero about his or her courage and strength of character; historical fiction often requires the main character to ask questions about choosing a side in a conflict. But all novels confront their characters with serious problems and thus with Tough Questions. If they didn't, no one would read them.

Many students have imposed this question on expository texts in ways we had not anticipated. Middle school social studies teachers in Orlando, Florida, told us that students who had learned Tough Questions in their ELA class, started using it in social studies: "When you're deciding if you should go to war, that's a Tough Question," and "So, if you move near the Nile you have the water right there, but it floods, so that's a Tough Question." Science teachers told us students did the same thing, "So when they were thinking about whether Pluto is a planet, they were really figuring out a Tough Question." These students recognized that the Tough Question does not have to be something stated by a character in fiction, but could be a dilemma anyone faces.

Lesson *4*

Words of the **Wiser**

The Words of the Wiser lesson helps students recognize the author's theme. Students are taught to identify the scene (and occasionally scenes) in which a wiser, and generally older, character offers the main character some critical advice. Once students notice the signpost, they then ask themselves, *What's the life lesson and how might it affect the character?*

Materials You Will Need

- A copy of the excerpts from *Riding Freedom*, by Pam Muñoz Ryan. See Appendix. If you're an elementary teacher and you plan to teach this novel, and you don't want to use this text to teach Words of the Wiser, look at the alternate texts in the Q & A section of this lesson.

- Chart paper for making the Words of the Wiser chart. We make charts during the lesson, but you can make yours ahead of time. Just be sure to include the information called out on the chart to the right.

Materials Students Will Need

- The excerpt from *Riding Freedom*.
- Pen or pencil.
- One or two sticky notes.
- Notice and Note Reading Log (optional). See Appendix.

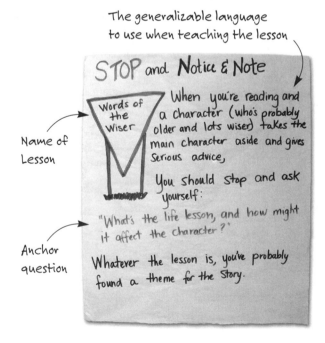

The generalizable language to use when teaching the lesson

STOP and Notice & Note

Words of the Wiser

Name of Lesson

When you're reading and a character (who's probably older and lots wiser) takes the main character aside and gives serious advice,

You should stop and ask yourself:

"What's the life lesson, and how might it affect the character?"

Anchor question

Whatever the lesson is, you've probably found a theme for the story.

Enter the Classroom

This lesson took place early in the school year in an urban tenth-grade classroom, a heterogeneous group of twenty-four boys and girls who were still excited about being back in school with their friends after summer break. The classroom had desks pushed together to form six large tables. The students obviously understood the routine: go to your table, grab your clipboard with your reading journal (a spiral labeled My Reading Journal) and a pencil, and then take a seat. Quickly (surprisingly!), the students settled down and waited for the lesson to begin.

Begin by Explaining

We usually teach this lesson fourth, after Contrasts and Contradictions, Aha Moment, and Tough Questions. If you're teaching it first, you'll recognize that our introductory remarks make sense in the context of already having taught a few lessons. If this is the first lesson you're teaching, you might take a look at the Classroom Close-up on page 103. There you'll see how a teacher introduced her class to the concept of signposts before beginning the first lesson.

“ We've been talking about the Notice and Note Signposts that you can spot in a story or novel. Remember that these signposts help us understand the plot, how characters are developing, how the conflict arises and is resolved, and perhaps even a theme the writer is exploring.

Today we're going to learn about another signpost, one called **Words of the Wiser.** [On your chart paper, in one color marker, write at the top, "Words of the Wiser."]

Let's think about what this might mean. When I was about your age, my mom was always giving me advice. She would say, "If you can't say something nice, don't say anything at all!" or "Always tell the truth" or "Haste makes waste." I remember the time she told me "Haste makes waste." I had no idea what she meant, and I kept right on hurrying through washing the dishes after dinner. I was in a huge hurry because once I finished, I could go out to play. Well, I was carrying too many dishes and I bet you can guess what happened—the top one, and then the next one, and soon the entire pile of dishes fell. And broke. And then, because I had been rushing so much, I had to spend a lot of time cleaning up a huge mess. Haste makes waste. I wasted all those dishes because they were ruined, and I wasted the time I could have been playing. My mom's words were, indeed, wise words. I just wasn't wise enough to listen to her.

Well, authors are, in some ways, like a mom or a dad or a grandparent. They include scenes in which wise words are shared. So, when I'm reading, I am always on the lookout for a place where the main character has a quiet and serious talk with a wiser character. That wiser character might be a friend, a brother or sister, a teacher, a parent, or the kindly neighbor down the street. When I find that scene, I want to read it carefully because the wiser character is probably offering the main character some good advice.

This advice is probably a life lesson, and if I pay attention to it, I'll see an important idea the author wants me to think about. Let's write our definition for Words of the Wiser. [As you say the following definition, write it in a different color marker on the chart paper.]

"The scene in which a wiser character offers the main character advice that is helpful at this moment in the story but could also be helpful throughout life." After we notice it, we want to ask ourselves one question: "What's the life lesson and how might this affect the character?" [Write this question in a third color marker on your chart.]

As you answer this question, you'll learn more about the character, the conflict he or she faces, the plot, and perhaps the message or theme the author wants you to consider. [Now, in a fourth color, write "Character Development, Conflict, Plot, and Theme."]

Move to Applying

You've defined Words of the Wiser, so now it's time to model how you identify this when reading and how it affects your thinking.

> " I'm going to read a few scenes to you that are all from a book titled *Riding Freedom*. *Riding Freedom* is about a young girl named Charlotte who lives during the mid-1800s. Her parents are dead and she lives in an orphanage. She loves horses, but the overseer of the orphanage where she lives forbids her to work with them simply because she's a girl. Life there is hard, and at some point she

realizes she cannot stay there, so she decides to run away from the orphanage. Let's look at a short scene, the one where Charlotte tells a trusted older and wiser adult at the orphanage that she must escape. The friend's name is Vern, and his job at the orphanage is to take care of the horses. One of the horses is named Justice.

> Thanks, Vern. I wish I could stay with you and work with the horses, but . . . I'd be in the kitchen and I'd be missin' Justice and frettin' 'cause I wouldn't get to see Charity's foal . . . or help you name it."
>
> "I know. I know Miss Charlotte," said Vern. "You gotta do what your heart tells you."
>
> "I won't ever forget you," said Charlotte.
>
> "I guess I'm not likely to forget you, Miss Charlotte."

I'll stop here because I've noticed that this is a scene in which an older and wiser character has offered advice to the main character. The advice I hear Vern giving Charlotte is, "You gotta do what your heart tells you." When authors create such a scene, we need to stop and ask, *How could this advice affect the character?* I think this advice will be helpful to Charlotte right now and also later on, no matter what she faces in the future. At this moment, those words may help her muster the courage to take the risk of running, and later . . . well, we'll have to see if they come back to her later and help her again. Since Charlotte says that she won't ever forget Vern, and he says he won't forget her, I'm going to bet that they won't see each other again. So, it will have to be his words, his advice, that she keeps close to her. As I keep reading, I'll discover if that's true or not.

So, Charlotte leaves the orphanage and her good friends Vern and Hayward. She eventually finds a nice older man who lets her live in his barn and begins to teach her to drive a six-horse stagecoach. Learning to drive the coach is hard work.

> Here were six strong horses waiting for her commands, her tugs on the reins, to tell them which way to go. She yelled, "Haw" and "Gee" to get them to bear left and right, like she did when she was riding one horse or driving two.

This is a longer introduction than we normally suggest, but to understand the excerpts we've chosen, students need to know what's happening. You decide how much background you think is needed.

This first excerpt is from page 38 of the edition of *Riding Freedom* with this ISBN: 978-0-439-08786-4.

This is the generalizable language that we want students to remember so they can apply it to any other text.

The first time we stop, we explain the signpost we found (the wiser character offering some advice to the main character) and then we answer the anchor question. We model our thinking while students watch and listen.

> She wished Hayward could see her. And Vern. Vern would have never let her get out of that wagon until she figured out the turns. Just like when he taught her to ride, he kept putting her back on Freedom [her horse] after each fall, saying, "Every time you fall, you learn somethin' new 'bout your horse. You learn what not to do next time."

This second excerpt is from page 64 of this edition. That's almost at the end of the first section of the book, just a few pages before the next section, titled "In the Middle," begins.

Here's another important place to stop because I've noticed another place where a wiser character has offered the main character some advice. Vern has told Charlotte that every time you fall you learn something you can use, something about what not to do the next time. Now, remember the question we need to ask ourselves once we find one of these life lessons: *How might this advice affect the character?* Take one of your sticky notes, and before you start talking with your shoulder partner, jot down some of your thinking.
[Give students about a minute to write and then have them turn and talk with a partner for about two minutes at the most.]

This time we've identified the Words of the Wiser, reminded students of the question to ask themselves, and turned over the thinking to them. We're releasing some of the responsibility to them.

As students write, walk around and see what comments they are making.

" Let's regroup. Share with me some of the thoughts you and your partner had. . . . Again, as I've walked around I've heard several possible answers to our question. You've all offered interesting thoughts. Several of you mentioned that although Vern was teaching Charlotte to ride and telling her that when she falls she needs to learn from it and get back in the saddle, this means that whenever she fails at anything, she should try to learn from it and keep on trying. In other words, it's both a lesson about riding and a lesson about life.

One student said, "Until I learned Words of the Wiser, I would've never stopped here, but when you see this as Words of the Wiser, it's like this is so much more."

Let's keep reading and see if there are any other moments like these. The story has continued, and now Charlotte is a good stagecoach driver, but on this day someone from her past wants to ride on her stagecoach and that upsets her. Ebeneezer, the man who taught her to drive a six-horse stagecoach, sees that she's upset and says:

> "What are you blabberin' about? The mail's gotta go through, same as them passengers."

This second excerpt is from page 72 of this edition. This is early in Chapter 6.

> Ebeneezer put his hand on Charlotte's shoulder. "Now listen, don't you pay them passengers no mind. You are what you are. And what you are is a fine horseman. And the best coachman I ever saw. You remember that. Under the circumstances, there ain't nothing left for you to do but your job. So get to it."
>
> Charlotte looked square at Ebeneezer.
>
> Ebeneezer looked square back at Charlotte and said, "You're the coachman. You're in charge, so load 'em up."

Well, here we are at the end of this scene, and I've seen another Words of the Wiser signpost. I want to see if you can find this one on your own. What does Ebeneezer tell Charlotte that she might remember and hold on to as good advice for the rest of her life? [Some will identify "You are what you are," and others will point to "ain't nothing left for you to do but your job," and a few might point to "You're in charge."]

Now take a moment and, on your own, jot down what you think this advice means and how it might help Charlotte. . . . Now, turn and talk with your reading partner to discuss what lesson you found and what you think it means.

Again, give students only about two minutes to talk with their partner. Regroup as a full class and let students share their thoughts. Probably, there will not be agreement on one line that represents the Words of the Wiser signpost. This is fine. You'll probably hear a lot of comments, all from raising this one question—*How did this advice help Charlotte?*

And now you'll let the students identify the Words of the Wiser and talk about what the advice means to Charlotte. You've released more of the responsibility to the students.

End with Reviewing

❝ That was smart thinking you offered about Vern's advice. Let's take a moment and review what you did. Today we learned about the Words of the Wiser. This lesson says that you should look for a scene in which a wiser and usually older character offers the main character advice that will help him or her through this moment in the story but also through much of his or her life. When you find that scene, you should ask yourself this question: *How might this advice affect the character?* When you can answer this question, then you're learning about what's very important in the story, and that might help you think about the theme.

Now that students have practiced finding Words of the Wiser in a text with you there to help and support them, you'll want to tell them what to do as they now turn to reading their own novels.

If you want students to use the Notice and Note Reading Log, you'll find a template of one we've created on pages 209–210 of the Appendix and you'll see some others that teachers have created beginning on page 211. Students can also use sticky notes to mark places and jot down their thinking.

It might be easy to think that the digression to Lady Gaga was a departure from the text; Chuck's comment, however, that "this is her [Charlotte's] Lady Gaga song" was powerful, and it was supported with evidence from the text in his next sentence.

Kahil's question is an example of a dialogic question (see pages 28–29). He's posing a question that matters to him and also is about the text.

Your homework tonight is to continue reading your novel. As you read, I want you to be on the lookout for the signpost we've called Words of the Wiser. There may be only one or two in a book, but when you find one, you know it's important. If you find one as you read the rest of your book, mark it with a sticky note and answer the question right there on your note.

If you don't find one as you're reading tonight, then listen to things your parent says to you or listen to conversations that you hear on television. Adults often give kids advice, so it's likely you'll hear Words of the Wiser from your own parent or from a parent on TV. Write it down and then answer the question: *What's the life lesson and how might it affect me or the character?* Tomorrow we'll take a look at what you found and how you answered the question.

Conversation Close-up

Let's take a close look at an exchange from two students, one typical of what you might hear.

CHUCK: I marked "You are what you are."

KAHIL: Me too. My brother is always saying, "You gotta be what you gotta be."

CHUCK: Or "Born This Way." Cool song.

KAHIL: So, they are singing Lady Gaga's song without even knowing it.

CHUCK: Yeah [laughter], and this advice, it's going to be important because her whole life is about doing what she wants to do even though no one thinks a girl could do it. This is her Lady Gaga song. It's like what Vern told her earlier about following your own heart.

KAHIL: So it's important advice, but do you think she really is being what she's gotta be? I mean shouldn't she just tell people she's a girl and to butt out because she can do the same things a man can do, even better?

CHUCK: So like my big brother; he is gay. It wasn't like anybody didn't know, but he just couldn't come out and say it. When he finally did, he said it was like the weight of the world off his shoulders. He needs to be reading this book.

KAHIL: You think she's gay?

CHUCK: No, I think she's just living in a time when no one lets women do anything other than just stay home and do stuff there and she had more ambitiousness. But this advice, you know, the wiser words, it tells her that people think she should just keep on doing what she's doing. Good advice.

Chuck's comment about his brother helps him make sense of this text. That importance of text-to-self connections cannot be overlooked or dismissed.

While this story is easy enough to be read in upper elementary school, we like sharing it with older students. This conversation, between two tenth-grade boys who rarely ever spoke in class, was one they later said they "really liked." They were making personal connections, especially Chuck, and they kept going back to the story. Is Chuck's connection important? We think it's more than important. We think the transaction he had with this one particular line was critical. Though some now say we shouldn't spend time in classrooms encouraging students to make personal connections to a text, we think that meaning is created through those personal connections.

Questions You Might Have

1. *How much time should I set aside for this lesson?*

This isn't a minilesson. Minilessons are short lessons that we believe should be used to reinforce something you've already taught. This is a lesson. You'll need thirty to forty minutes for it.

2. *Do all novels have a moment that could be considered a Words of the Wiser signpost?*

We don't know. We've looked at many children's and young adult books and so far have found this lesson in each book. We think the issue will be the age of the main character. As long as the main character is a child or young adult, then a wiser, and often older, character is likely to come along to offer sage advice. When the main character is an adult, there is probably a greater chance that we won't see this lesson. Perhaps in adult fiction it morphs into the lesson of self-awareness, with the character coming, on her own, to understand the principle that guides her.

3. *So, in a young adult or children's book, will I find several examples of the Words of the Wiser signpost?*

When we first started spotting Words of the Wiser, we thought we saw only one instance per book; however, the more we looked, the more we found. It seems that wiser characters have a strong inclination to keep offering advice to that younger main character. (Ask your own children, if you have them, if you tend to keep on offering advice even when they don't seek it!) If you think your students are identifying as Words of the Wiser comments that really are not that significant, remind them that these lessons are life lessons, guidance a wiser person shares that might shape our thinking throughout life. Words of the Wiser is, however, not a technique that the writer is going to use as frequently as others. If a writer does use it, therefore, you can be certain that it's going to be an important moment in the book, one that points the reader directly toward theme.

4. *If my students need more guided instruction from me, where can I turn?*

Take a look at page 162 of **Walk Two Moons** (most likely in your school library). Tell students that in this scene the main character, Sal, is talking with her dad. Read aloud up to the line in which her dad says, "You can't cage a person." Let students talk about what that would mean, what the life lesson he was trying to share with his daughter might be. Tell them that as you continue reading *Walk Two Moons*, you'll think about how this advice will help Sal.

Or, in **Tuck Everlasting,** read aloud the scene on pages 62–64. Tell students that this is the story of Winnie, a girl who finds the fountain of youth—a spring of water that gives eternal life. The dad, Mr. Tuck, has taken Winnie out on a pond to convince her not to drink the water or tell others about it. Read aloud that scene and then ask students what his lesson is and how it may help Winnie.

Finally, if you've used **"Thank You, Ma'm"** to teach Contrasts and Contradictions, pull out that short story. Have students reread the final several paragraphs. See if they identify the line (third paragraph from the end of the story) that says, "Shoes got by devilish means will burn your feet" as a Words of the Wiser signpost. Ask how that advice will continue to help Roger. This lesson is subtle, however, and although Mrs. Jones speaks that lesson aloud to Roger, perhaps a more important lesson is implied but left unstated. Mrs. Jones's compassionate treatment

These page numbers are from the edition with this ISBN: 978-0-06-440517-1.

These page numbers are from the edition with this ISBN: 978-0-312-36981-1.

of Roger is transforming, and perhaps the lesson, both for Roger and the reader, is that compassion and trust may sometimes be more powerful than punishment in bringing out the good in someone.

5. *What is it that students have learned when they find a scene that contains a Words of the Wiser signpost?*

They certainly have learned something about a problem the character faces, so they might have insight into character development, plot, or conflict. The most significant thing they learn, though, is something about the message the author wants to share, so they've learned something about the author's theme. If this message is important enough to create a scene in which the wiser character talks seriously with the main character, then it's a message that means much to the author.

6. *Once students find the scene in which the wiser character is sharing information, I understand that the student should ask the anchor question. But aren't there other important questions about this scene?*

Yes. We know that some students will be ready for additional questions sooner than other students. You can differentiate your instruction by keeping these additional questions close at hand, and when you find students who are ready to probe deeper as they read other books, ask them:

- The wiser has taught this lesson to the main character. How might the wiser person change this lesson for another character?

- Words of the Wiser usually gives us insight into a problem the main character is facing—even if he or she doesn't realize it. Think about this lesson. Does it give you an idea of a problem or internal conflict the main character faces?

- Words of the Wiser are often direct—"be kind to others." Sometimes, though, they are more indirect; they appear to be about just one thing when they are really about life in general. For instance, in "Thank You, Ma'm" a woman whose purse is almost stolen tells her would-be thief, "Shoes got by devilish means will burn your feet." Would it be a better lesson if she just said, "Don't steal"?

- Often the Words of the Wiser signpost appears early in the book. Did that happen in this case? If so, do you think the main character will follow the advice? How might following the advice early on change the direction of the book?

- Words of the Wiser are directed at the main character, but they often seem to be directed to us, the readers, as well. Is the lesson in this book one that you agree with and accept? How might it help shape your life?

Again and Again

We all recognize that when something is repeated we should pay attention. This lesson, Again and Again, asks students to be alert to repetitions in a text, sometimes separated by many pages but clearly intended to make a point. Once they notice the repetitions, they ask themselves, *Why does this happen again and again?* As they consider the answer, they'll learn more about the plot, about characters, and often about the theme.

Materials You Will Need

- A copy of passages from *Hatchet*, by Gary Paulsen. See Appendix.

- Chart paper for making the Again and Again chart. We make charts during the lesson, but you can make yours ahead of time. Just be sure to include the information called out on the chart to the right.

Materials Students Will Need

- A copy of the excerpts from *Hatchet*.
- Pen or pencil.
- Couple of sticky notes.
- Notice and Note Reading Log (optional). See Appendix.

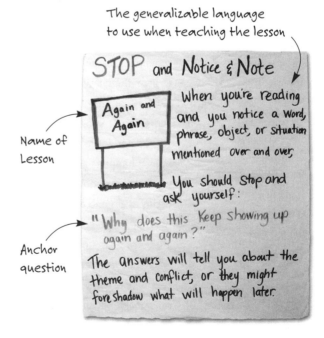

The generalizable language to use when teaching the lesson

STOP and Notice & Note

Again and Again

Name of Lesson

When you're reading and you notice a word, phrase, object, or situation mentioned over and over,

You should stop and ask yourself:

Anchor question

"Why does this keep showing up again and again?"

The answers will tell you about the theme and conflict, or they might foreshadow what will happen later.

Enter the Classroom

Think of a heterogeneously grouped sixth-grade classroom, but missing the ones put into a gifted/talented classroom. The classroom is diverse ethnically and economically, and the level of interest in reading ranges from that of the five or six kids who obviously love to read to that of the five or six who obviously (because they tell you often!) hate to read. The rest fall into that silent group in the middle, the kids who will enjoy reading only if given the right book. Reading *levels* range from students able to understand the subtle messages in sophisticated texts to those who read haltingly and generally see only the most literal meaning. Mostly, though, these kids are still young enough to be interested in what we have to say. The struggling readers want to get better, and the cool kids sometimes forget to be cool and reveal themselves to be what they really are: twelve-year-olds who want approval.

Begin by Explaining

We began with defining the lesson, and at this point, we've moved to applying it to a real-world example. If you've not taught any of the lessons, we'd encourage you to start with Contrasts and Contradictions. But, if you're about to begin a book that you know has a lot of repetition in it (for instance, the use of the word *release* in *The Giver*) and you want to begin with this lesson, that's fine. However, you might want to give students an overall idea of all the signposts. If so, take a look at the Classroom Close-up on page 103. There, you'll see how a fourth-grade teacher introduced all the signposts to her students.

" Much of what we learn about our friends—enemies, too, I suppose— we learn by noticing patterns. This lesson, Again and Again, is about some of those patterns. In this case, the pattern is repetition. When something happens over and over again, that repetition begins to tell us something if we notice it and give it some thought. For example, one day you may be sitting with a few friends when another one joins you. One of the original group grows quiet and after a few minutes gets up and leaves. You may not think anything of it at that moment, but if it happens again the next day and then again the next week, you'll probably notice it. It's the pattern, the repetition, the event that occurs again and again, that lets you know something is up—if you notice it. And if you think about it.

Obviously, noticing it isn't enough. You have to do something with what you've noticed or it's lost. You have to wonder about it, speculate about what it might mean, and perhaps compare it with other incidents, or it won't help you understand what's going on. So you make some mental (or actual) notes about that repetition and what it might mean. Ultimately, you'll figure it out. Your friends may have had a falling out, or perhaps they've discovered that they're in competition for the same prize. Or, maybe, on the other hand, they've realized that they like each other more than they thought, and they don't know what to do about that. The event may not seem significant at all the first time it occurs, but by the third time, you'll begin to wonder what's going on and start watching your friends more closely. You'll probably ask yourself something like, *Why does this happen again and again?*

And here we've introduced the anchor question.

Again and Again moments also happen in books. When authors repeat something—a word or an image or an event—it means something, and when we see those words or images or events again and again, we ought to stop and ask ourselves, *Why does this happen again and again?* The answer will generally tell us something about the character or the plot or perhaps even the theme.

Now we connect this lesson to what authors do. If you've not made your chart, then make it now, using the above paragraph to guide what should go on it: name of lesson, brief definition, and anchor question.

Move to Applying

Once you've explained the signpost and the anchor question, it's time to show students how this signpost looks in a text. Everyone should have a copy of the *Hatchet* handout, something with which to write, and perhaps a few sticky notes. Before you begin, make sure everyone is close to another student for moments in the lesson when you'll ask them to turn and talk.

❝ Now, let's look for this lesson in a book you might have read, *Hatchet*, by Gary Paulsen. Follow along as I read from the first pages of the opening chapter. Brian, the main character, is seated next to the pilot in a small plane flying over the forests in the far north.

Brian Robeson stared out the window of the small plane at the endless green northern wilderness below. It was a small plane, a Cessna 406—a bush-plane—and the engine was so loud, so roaring and consuming and loud, that it ruined any chance for conversation.

Not that he had much to say. He was thirteen and the only passenger on the plane with a pilot named—what was it? Jim or Jake or something—who was in his mid-forties and who had been silent as he worked to prepare for take-off. In fact since Brian had come to the small airport in Hampton, New York, to meet the plane—driven by his mother—the pilot had spoken only five words to him.

This first excerpt is the first two pages of the edition of *Hatchet* with this ISBN: 978-4169-3647-3.

"Get in the copilot's seat."

Which Brian had done. They had taken off and that was the last of the conversation. There had been the initial excitement, of course. He had never flown in a single-engine plane before and to be sitting in the copilot's seat with all the controls right there in front of him, all the instruments in his face as the plane clawed for altitude, jerking and sliding on the wind currents as the pilot took off, had been interesting and exciting. . . .

Now Brian sat, looking out the window with the roar thundering through his ears, and tried to catalog what had led up to his taking this flight.

The thinking started.

Always it started with a single word.

Divorce.

It was an ugly word, he thought. A tearing, ugly word that meant fights and yelling, lawyers—God, he thought, how he hated lawyers who sat with their comfortable smiles and tried to explain to him in legal terms how all that he lived in was coming apart—and the breaking and shattering of all the solid things. His home, his life—all the solid things. Divorce. A breaking word, an ugly breaking word.

At this point, we do the noticing, we ask the question, and we suggest answers (or at least speculate about possibilities). In subsequent steps, we'll gradually turn that all over to the students.

Let's pause for a moment. I notice right away that Paulsen is using the Again and Again signpost. Paulsen has Brian speak that word, *divorce*, twice. He emphasizes it, too, by letting it stand alone as a one-word sentence. And Brian has obviously thought of it many times before because he says that his thinking always started with that word. If the thinking "always" starts this way, he's thought of "divorce" many times before.

Now, at this point I don't know exactly how divorce plays a part in this story. I can guess that his parents are probably divorced, but I have no idea what that has to do with his situation at the moment, being in a small plane flying over the north woods. I'll ask myself the anchor question, *Why does this keep showing up again and again?* At this point I don't have a good answer, but I can bet that divorce will be mentioned again. Let's read on:

> Divorce.
>
> Secrets.
>
> No, not secrets so much as just the Secret. What he knew and had not told anybody, what he knew about his mother that had caused the divorce, what he knew, what he knew— the Secret.
>
> Divorce.
>
> The Secret.

This excerpt is from page 3.

That was quick. Just a few more lines and we see the author using this strategy, repetition, yet again. What have you spotted in this passage? . . . Take two minutes to discuss with one other person what you noticed. Then talk about why you think this might keep showing up again and again. See how many possible answers to that question you can come up with.

As you walk around the room, if you see students settling for the simple answer, something like, "His folks are divorced and he knows why," push them gently. Urge them to think about why that might be important, out here in a plane flying over the wilderness. This Again and Again sign-post is exceptionally easy to spot, but to realize that Brian's thoughts reveal how alone he is and how abandoned he feels takes some reflection. Later, when the plane crashes, he will be, quite literally, alone and abandoned, so this moment prepares us for what will come. These moments essentially foreshadow just how alone and isolated Brian will be later in the story when the pilot dies and the plane goes down in the north woods.

After a few minutes, call them back together.

❝ OK. You all spotted that *divorce* was repeated several more times, and most of us noticed the repeated mention of the Secret. So we're beginning to see that Brian knows something about the break-up, something that he's never shared. But why do you think this is important? Why is Paulsen driving this home, again and again? What are we learning about the character and his situation?

Now, after this short passage, you're giving them the chance to do their own thinking about the repetition.

If students don't have many (or any) thoughts about this, you may have to help. Suggest to them that Brian must feel a heavy burden, knowing such a damaging secret and keeping it entirely to himself. He must feel very alone. Perhaps that feeling is going to become important as the story progresses. If you think they can carry their thinking a bit further, you might ask them to talk about what they might be learning about Brian from this moment.

❝ Let's read on. This time, as I read, put a check mark next to or underline anything that you think is repeated, something the author probably wants us to notice as repetitious.

This excerpt is from pages 3–5.

> Brian felt his eyes beginning to burn and knew there would be tears. He had cried for a time, but that was gone now. He didn't cry now. . . .
>
> The pilot sat large, his hands lightly on the wheel, feet on the rudder pedals. He seemed more a machine than a man, an extension of the plane. . . .
>
> When he saw Brian look at him, the pilot seemed to open up a bit and he smiled. "Ever fly in the copilot's seat before?" He leaned over and lifted the headset off his right ear and put it on his temple, yelling to overcome the sound of the engine.
>
> Brian shook his head. . . .
>
> "It's not as complicated as it looks. Good plane like this almost flies itself." The pilot shrugged. "Makes my job easy." He took Brian's left arm. "Here, put your hands on the controls, your feet on the rudder pedals, and I'll show you what I mean."
>
> Brian shook his head. "I'd better not."
>
> "Sure. Try it. . . ."
>
> Brian reached out and took the wheel in a grip so tight his knuckles were white. He pushed his feet down on the pedals. The plane slewed suddenly to the right.
>
> "Not so hard. Take her light, take her light."
>
> Brian eased off, relaxed his grip. The burning in his eyes was forgotten momentarily as the vibration of the plane came through the wheel and the pedals. It seemed almost alive.
>
> "See?" The pilot let go of his wheel, raised his hands in the air and took his feet off the pedals to show Brian he was actually flying the plane alone. "Simple. Now turn the wheel a little to the right and push on the right rudder pedal a small amount."
>
> Brian turned the wheel slightly and the plane immediately banked to the right, and when he pressed on the right rudder pedal the nose slid across the horizon to the right. He left off

on the pressure and straightened the wheel and the plane righted itself.

"Now you can turn. Bring her back to the left a little."

Brian turned the wheel left, pushed on the left pedal, and the plane came back around. "It's easy." He smiled. "At least this part."

The pilot nodded. "All of flying is easy. Just takes learning. Like everything else. Like everything else." He took the controls back, then reached up and rubbed his left shoulder. "Aches and pains—must be getting old."

Brian let go of the controls and moved his feet away from the pedals as the pilot put his hands on the wheel. "Thank you. . . ."

But the pilot had put his headset back on and the gratitude was lost in the engine noise and things went back to Brian looking out the window at the ocean of trees and lakes. The burning eyes did not come back, but memories did, came flooding in. The words. Always the words.

Divorce.

The Secret.

Fights.

Split.

The big split. Brian's father did not understand as Brian did, knew only that Brian's mother wanted to break the marriage apart. The split had come and then the divorce, all so fast, and the court had left him with his mother except for the summers and what the judge called "visitation rights." So formal.

That was a long passage. What repetitions did you notice? Take a moment to jot down the repetitions that you saw—the Again and Again—and then ask yourself that anchor question: Why does this show up again and again? When you've had a few minutes to think about it, turn to your neighbor and discuss what you've observed and thought.

As you walk around the room, listen for a willingness to speculate. The students will have noticed that divorce is mentioned yet again, and most will also probably see the Secret as another Again and Again moment. Encourage them to ask the anchor question, *Why might the*

And now, you've turned most of the work over to the students. They've identified what they think represents an Again and Again moment and are sharing their thoughts about it with a partner.

author bring this up again and again? They might wonder if Brian feels responsible for the divorce, perhaps because of a secret he knows and should have shared with someone. Or perhaps he's plagued by the Secret because he wishes he didn't know it at all.

" OK. You've noticed that another word is beginning to appear again and again—*Secret*. And you noticed that it's apparently important because it's capitalized. Brian knows the Secret that caused the divorce, and he hasn't told anyone about it. When we ask why the author might be returning to this again and again, what can we say? All that we know with certainty is how deeply troubled Brian is. But we've also thought about how alone he must feel, with his parents splitting up. And he must feel alone in that small cockpit with a pilot who barely speaks. As we read on in the novel, we'll have to see if this divorce and his feeling so alone because of it play the important role in the story that we've been led to expect.

End with Reviewing

" The Again and Again signpost reminds us to be alert to repetitions—those words or phrases or actions or situations—that the author shows us over and over. When we see them, we know that we need to pause and ask why the author is doing this. That's what we'd do if we saw a friend doing or saying much the same thing repeatedly. We'd ask ourselves what that repetition revealed.

As you do today's reading, I want you to be on the lookout for Again and Again signposts. And tonight, when you're home, think about the power of repetition and jot down what you hear in your home or on television that represents this pattern we're looking for. Be sure to ask yourself why something—a word or event or image—shows up again and again.

Conversation Close-up

Let's take a close look at an exchange from two students, one typical of what you might hear.

TAMINA: Well, Secret, it's like again and again and again.

CHARMAIN: How come he keeps saying it over and over?

TAMINA: It keeps coming up again and again because it's on his mind a lot. He's like worried about that more than

We have occasionally wrapped up this lesson by asking students to discuss why jingles and campaign slogans are effective. This always leads to some interesting Aha Moments!

If you want students to use the Notice and Note Reading Log, you'll find a template of one we've created on pages 209–210 of the Appendix and you'll see some others that teachers have created beginning on page 211. Students can also use sticky notes to mark places and jot down their thinking.

anything. Hey—this is a predicting thing. You know it—hey, Mr. Probst—come over here. [Bob joins the two girls.] Here's a predicting thing. You can look at how much it comes up, you know about the Secret, and you just know that this is so bothering him that it is going to have to be explained.

CHARMAIN: Hey, it's predicting. We did it! So, you see it again and again and then you can say it is because he's worried and then you know that you're just going to have to find the answer or why would it be there all the time. It's predicting!

These students were so excited that they spoke up first when we brought the class back together. As they reported to the class, another boy spoke up: "Yeah, my mom keeps saying that if I don't clean my room I'm going to be grounded. And yesterday she was so angry about it that I'm predicting I better get it done!"

Questions You Might Have

1. *This seems to be such a simple idea. Do we really need to teach it? What do students learn by noticing repetitions?*

It is a simple idea. And it's a simple text clue, easy for the author to use as a subtle way of planting an idea, and easy for the reader to use as a tool to unlock aspects of a text. But it's also easy for students to miss. The repetitions don't seem important at the time and may even seem to impede the forward motion of the plot, since the repeated element may be mentioned briefly, may seem a trivial detail, and will certainly be left unexplained—at least at first. Struggling readers may simply dismiss it and move on. If we can teach students to pause and wonder about the signpost's significance, they will have a powerful tool for thinking critically about the novel.

Furthermore, we like the Again and Again signpost because authors use repetition for so many reasons. Sometimes they use it to reveal an aspect of the setting; other times it might be to give insight into theme or conflict; sometimes it helps establish the mood or the tone. This, of course, means that once students recognize the repetition, they then must consider what the repetition tells them. Don't be surprised if discussion reveals a difference of opinion.

A powerful outcome of the Notice and Note Signposts is that as students notice a signpost, they naturally begin to predict or visualize or make connections—all the things we want readers doing. It's not natural, though, to tell students to read and pause to make a prediction or pause and visualize. What skilled readers do is see something that captures their attention, and then as they reflect on that, they might realize they are predicting—as in this situation.

For instance, in the novel *Maniac Magee*, by Jerry Spinelli, the main character, Maniac, runs constantly. One student reported that this repetition "shows me something about Maniac, that he doesn't want to be hurt anymore, so he keeps on running." Another student in class spoke up and said, "I saw that same thing [Maniac's running] as an Again and Again signpost, but I think it tells me about the theme because eventually Maniac stops running and so you learn that running away doesn't solve your problems. You have to just face them." A third student, who had not identified this as an Again and Again signpost, added his thoughts: "I hadn't noticed that, that it was an Again and Again because it was just there all the time. It was just what Maniac did. But now that I listen to what they said, I think it is Again and Again, but I think it is about the conflict. Like it was because he was hurt in places when he stopped running that he kept running. But he didn't want to run. He wanted a home. So it was a good way to show conflict."

2. *Does it matter that one student thought that the Again and Again signpost in* Maniac Magee *revealed something about the character while another thought it suggested the theme and another thought it was about conflict? Of those three ideas, isn't one of them right? Isn't one at least more correct than the others?*

What we want readers to learn to do is to pause when they notice a significant feature in the text. Then we want them to reflect on what it might mean. Regardless of what they infer, they'll be able to participate in the discussion. In fact, the discussion is likely to be more interesting and insightful if some students feel that they have learned more about character, others more about theme, and still others more about conflict. Those differences may lead to thinking about aspects of the novel that had been overlooked at first, may lead students to develop a more tentative approach to texts as they see the possibility of other readings, and may show them the power of collaboration in making sense out of texts and the world.

What you'll begin to notice as you listen to your students talk about Again and Again is that your more sophisticated readers are more likely to connect repetition to conflict and theme, while your less skilled readers are more likely to connect it to character and plot. There's a good reason for this.

On the journey to becoming lifetime readers, we all tend to progress through some similar stages. Margaret Early (1960) and G. Robert Carlsen (1980) have written about these stages, and both explain that early in a lifetime of reading we read mostly to enjoy the plot. Later (early adolescence), we begin to read through the eyes of the main character. At this stage, young adolescents are testing out the choices they would make in situations by living vicariously through the main character. Later (late adolescence), we begin to ponder life's bigger questions and find ourselves (while still enjoying the plot and the characters) considering the themes of the novel. Finally (adulthood), some people reach the stage where they read primarily to enjoy the beauty of the words on the page.

With these stages in mind, as you hear a student relate almost every Again and Again moment to characters or the conflicts they experience, you have a glimpse into his primary purpose for reading—to see the world through the character's point of view. If you hear another student almost always connect the Again and Again moment to the setting or what will happen next, then you recognize that this student is simply reading with a different purpose in the front of his (subconscious) mind. Interestingly, one way to gently nudge a student from one stage to the next is to let the student hear what others, at a different stage, have to say about a book. When you hear kids say, "I never saw it that way," you'll know that they are developing an awareness of a different way to see, or read, a book.

3. *Then should I let my students see what they see in the Again and Again signpost and not try to help them see something else?*

No. We can respect the stage of a student's development and at the same time help her see other responses. Think of it this way: We know that a baby's oral language development begins with babbling. That's the first stage. At the same time that we enjoy a baby's babbling, we don't babble back. We keep using real language. Sometimes we make the language we use very specific. Baby reaches for the cup and we hand it to her and say "Cup!" We don't offer her a long explanation of why it is a cup and not a wine glass or made of plastic and not glass. We just say "Cup!" Then we add our own extensions—"Oh, you want your cup!"—but we start with "Cup!"

In a similar way, if you notice that a student always connects Again and Again to something about the character, and you know that sometimes it's showing us more about the setting or the theme, you can accept that first response and then offer a prompt that might get him thinking at a different level. Here are some prompts that you might use:

- Does this repetition make you think about where or when this story takes place? If so, then it is probably giving you information about the setting.

- Does this repetition tell you something about a character's habits? If so, then it's probably offering insight into the character.

- What does this Again and Again signpost suggest will happen the next time our main character finds himself in a similar situation? Now you might be considering the plot.

- Does this repetition push you to think about how someone feels, or what someone wants, or what bothers someone? If so, then it is probably giving you information about conflict.

- Does the repetition make you think about a life lesson? Or is it a repetition of something said in a Words of the Wiser moment? For instance, does someone repeat that you have to be willing to stand up for what you know is right? If that's the case, then it's probably helping you think about the theme.

4. *What are the texts I could use for minilessons when I need to reteach or review?*

The short story *"The Most Dangerous Game,"* by Richard Connell, offers the chance to talk about a very particular type of Again and Again moment: the repetition of a single word that carries multiple meanings. Take a look at the story (easily found online and also anthologized in several literature textbooks); as you read through it, you'll find many places where the word *game* is used. What you want students to see is that the repetition helps establish the importance and double meaning of the word. Game is both what is hunted and something that is played.

More suitable for older students is the short story *"The Chaser,"* by John Collier (also easily found online). We would read it aloud as students follow along, asking them to listen for words that are repeated. This story provides several different examples of words or phrases that are repeated. For example, early in the story they'll see, "Here is a liquid as colorless as water, almost tasteless, quite imperceptible in coffee, milk, wine, or any other beverage. It is also quite imperceptible to any known method of autopsy." Later, we see the word, imperceptible, again: "Give one tiny measure of this to the young lady—its flavor is imperceptible in orange juice, soup, or cocktails—and however gay and giddy she is, she will change altogether."

For high school students, this is also an excellent story for pointing out Contrasts and Contradictions. For instance, in the first three paragraphs we see that the main character, Alan, has been searching for someone who seems to have been expecting him; yet the name on the door that would lead Alan (and others) to the person he is seeking is "written obscurely." Why would the man in the room, who has given out his card for people to find him, act this way—allow his name to be obscured? Finally, see if they notice the critical contradiction—the love potion costs only a dollar while the other mixture, the "life-cleanser," is extremely expensive. Why would a man act (set his prices) this way?

Finally, you could pull some scenes from *The Outsiders*. For instance, early in the novel, in quick succession, we see repeated references to the importance of loyalty to one's friends. Ponyboy, on page 26, says, "You take up for your buddies, no matter what," and only three pages later, on page 29, he reminds us that their most important rule, the first of only two, is to "stick together." As the story moves on, this principle is perhaps spoken of less, but is revealed again and again when Ponyboy and Johnny go off into hiding together, supporting one another. There are other instances of the Again and Again signpost, to do with hair as a symbol of identity and with the imagery of gold and golden as qualities that can't last.

These page numbers are from the edition with this ISBN: 0-14-240733-X.

L e s s o n *6*

Memory Moment

Memory Moments are the points in a novel where a character remembers something from the past. When students learn to be alert to these moments, they quickly see that memories often play an important role in the book, telling us much about the character and his or her background that we wouldn't otherwise know. When students identify the Memory Moment, they ask, *Why might this memory be important?* As students speculate, they are making predictions about characters and theme.

Materials You Will Need

- A copy of the passages from *Hope Was Here*, by Joan Bauer. See Appendix.
- Chart paper for making the Memory Moment chart. We make charts during the lesson, but you can make yours in advance. Just be sure to include the information shown on the chart at right.

Materials Students Will Need

- A copy of the excerpt from *Hope Was Here*.
- Pen or pencil.
- Couple of sticky notes.
- Notice and Note Reading Log (optional). See Appendix.

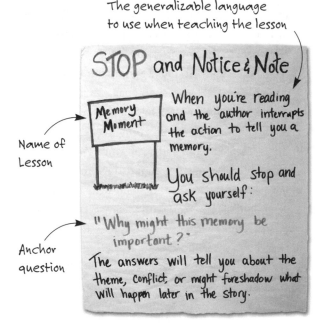

The generalizable language to use when teaching the lesson

STOP and Notice & Note

Memory Moment

Name of Lesson

When you're reading and the author interrupts the action to tell you a memory.

You should stop and ask yourself:

Anchor question

"Why might this memory be important?"

The answers will tell you about the theme, conflict, or might foreshadow what will happen later in the story.

Enter the Classroom

It's late in the school year, in an eighth-grade classroom, with students who, though generally well behaved, are on some days best described as bored and other days apathetic. They seem to be going through the motions. They are word-callers when it comes to reading and at best read primarily for the plot. In the class of thirty-one, there are more girls than boys, and most of the students speak Spanish as their home language. They are energetic, vocal, and inquisitive in the hallway. But here, in the classroom, during sixth period, as they might say, not so much.

Begin by Explaining

" Today we're going to take a look at a Notice and Note signpost that helps you understand why characters do what they do. We call this signpost Memory Moment. [On your chart paper, write at the top, "Memory Moment."] A Memory Moment is the point in the book when the writer interrupts what's happening in the story to show us the main character as he or she remembers something important. [As you give that definition, write it on your chart.]

Sometimes the clue to the Memory Moment is very obvious. The character will say something like "I remembered the first time I met him" or "In that very moment the memory came flooding back." Other times, the clue is more subtle. The character might say, "My dad liked to tell the story about . . ." or "This picture always reminded me of . . ." Often those moments are highlighted with words such as *remember* or *memory* or *reminded*. We want to be on the alert for times when a character shares a moment from the past because it's likely to tell us something important, either about the character or about the plot.

But we're going to have to figure out what it might tell us, and so, when we find this moment in the novel, we want to pause and ask ourselves one question: *Why might this memory be important?*

This is the only signpost lesson that begins by just jumping into the definition instead of making a real-life connection. We've found that if we do that, everyone jumps in with memories and before you know it, too much class time has passed. This is an easy lesson, and so we go straight to the definition. But if your students need that real-world connection, start there.

Move to Applying

Once we've explained the Memory Moment, we show students how it appears in *Hope Was Here*.

There is enough explanation in the excerpt we've pulled for students to understand what's happening with this brief introduction.

This first excerpt is from pages 4–5 of the edition of *Hope Was Here* with this ISBN: 0-399-23142-0.

❝ Let's take a look at how this works in a text. I'll read you a few passages from *Hope Was Here*, by Joan Bauer, while you follow along in your handout. This book is about a girl named Hope who, once again, must leave a place she's called home to move. We pick up in the novel as she and her aunt are getting in their car to begin their latest move.

> We walked across the street to the old Buick that was packed to the hilt with everything we owned and had a U-Haul trailer chained to the back.
>
> It was May 26. We were heading to Mulhoney, Wisconsin, to start work in a diner there that needed a professional manager and cook (Addie), was short on waitresses (me), and was giving us an apartment. The man we were going to work for had been diagnosed with leukemia and needed help fast. I don't mean to sound ungenerous, but working for a close-to-dying man didn't sound like a great career move to me. I had to leave school right before the end of my undistinguished sophomore year, too.
>
> I hate leaving places I love.
>
> We were about to get into the car just as Morty the cabdriver double-parked his Yellow taxi.
>
> Good old Morty. The first time I waited on him, he unloosened his belt a notch before he even looked at the menu. I knew I had a true believer.
>
> I raised my hand to a great tipper.
>
> "You always took care of me, kid!" He shouted this from across the street as a UPS truck started honking at him to move his cab.
>
> "I tried, Morty!"
>
> "Wherever you go, you'll do okay. You got heart!"
>
> The UPS driver screamed something heartless at Morty, who screamed back, "Watch your mouth, big man in a brown truck!"
>
> I didn't know what kind of customers I'd get in Wisconsin.

OK. Let me pause now. I've noticed that Bauer interrupts her narrative to have Hope, the main character, tell us about a memory. I know that memories are important to characters, just as memories are important to each of us. Here, Hope is walking across the street toward the car and the U-Haul trailer when she sees Morty stop in his cab. Seeing Morty reminds her of the first time she had waited on him—a memory from her earlier days working in the restaurant—and she recalls that even on that first encounter she had known that he'd be an appreciative customer.

When I see a memory interrupt the flow of the narrative, I have to ask myself, *Why might this memory be important?* Even though Hope doesn't make a big issue of this memory, it's in the story for a reason. What could that reason be?

I think it helps me see how Hope is feeling about leaving home. She's going to miss Morty and others like him. And then, when I get to the line in which she wonders what sort of customers she'll find in Wisconsin, I realize, too, that her warm memory of serving Morty has made her worry about what she'll face in Wisconsin. Will her new customers be as friendly and pleasant as Morty had been? I'm beginning to understand, through this simple memory, what leaving town means to her—that she's leaving behind a comfortable, happy situation for one filled with uncertainty and anxiety.

Let's take a look at another passage, from about the same point in the book. Hope has gotten in the car with her aunt, Addie, about to set out on the trip to a new life in Wisconsin. Addie is trying to reassure her. As we read, see if you notice the Memory Moment. Put a check mark where you think it appears.

> She grabbed my hand and gave it a squeeze.
>
> Addie never promised that life would be easy, but she did promise that if I hung with her the food would be good.
>
> Believe me when I tell you, I know about survival.
>
> I was born too early and much too small (two pounds and five ounces). For the first month of my life I kept gasping for air, like I couldn't get the hang of breathing. I couldn't eat either; couldn't suck a bottle. The doctors didn't think I would make it. Shows what they know. My mother didn't want the responsibility of a baby so she left me with Addie, her older sister, and went

This is the generalizable language—the reminder to always be alert for the Memory Moment and to always ask this question about it. Students can apply this concept to any book they're reading.

At this point we're telling the students everything—where we would stop, why this is a memory moment, and what our own answer to the anchor question would be. The next time, we'll identify the moment but ask the students to think about the question and possible answers to it.

This excerpt is from pages 5–6.

off to live her own life. I've seen her exactly three times since I was born—when she visited on my fifth, eighth, and thirteenth birthdays.

Each time she talked about being a waitress. What made a good one ("great hands and personality"). What were the pitfalls ("crazed cooks and being on your feet all day"); what was the biggest tip she ever got ($300 from a plumber who had just won the instant lottery).

Each time she told me, "Hon, leaving you with Addie was the best thing I could have done for you. You need constants in your life." She had a different hair color each time she said it.

Addie's been my number-one constant. . . .

Because of this, I don't buy into traditional roles. My favorite book when I was little had pictures of baby animals, like foxes and lambs and ducklings, who were being raised by other animals, like dogs, geese, and wolves. Addie said it was our story.

Now we identify the Memory Moment, but we ask students to remember the anchor question and to answer it. When we stop the next time, we'll ask them to both identify the Memory Moment and apply the question. We're trying to gradually back off and leave them more and more on their own.

Again, I'll stop. Hope and Aunt Addie are heading off to Wisconsin, but instead of thinking ahead to the trip, Hope thinks back and remembers her mother, especially the three times—the only three times—she had visited. Remember that when we come to such a moment we ask ourselves the question, *Why might this memory be important?* Turn to your neighbor and talk about that for two minutes. Why is the memory of her mother important at this moment, and what do we learn about Hope?

The students should be in pairs for this conversation, and as you wander the room, listening in on their talk, check first to see that they have understood why this is a Memory Moment (the action—their start of the trip—is interrupted to share the memory of her mother). Then make sure they're asking the anchor question and speculating about it. They should, of course, learn from the memory that Hope's mother essentially deserted her, and they should infer that Addie, her substitute mom, is thus extremely important to Hope.

After several moments ask students what they identified and why they think the memory is important. If you need to do so, you might summarize by saying,

" You've made several good points. When we are young, we look to our mothers for security, and at this anxious moment—about to leave for a new home—she thinks back about the failures of her mother to give her that security. This seems to remind her just how important Addie is to her. We've learned that Hope's mother isn't present very much in her life and that Addie has become a substitute mom for her. In fact, Addie is so important that I begin to worry that the story will be about losing that support. But we'll have to read on through the novel to find out if that prediction is correct.

Let's keep reading about Hope. As we read, mark any memory or memories that you see, and when we finish reading it, I'll ask you first to jot down on your sticky note why you think the memories you found are important and then to turn and talk with your neighbor about the passages you found. Remember the question that you need to ask yourselves at this point.

Here's the passage.

I stared out the window as the Buick roared west to whatever.

Harrison Beckworth-McCoy, my best male friend at school, . . . had given me a goodbye present, and I was opening it now as Addie pushed the Buick through Ohio. Inside the box was a small glass prism that caught the sun. A hand-printed note from Harrison read, "New places always help us look at life differently. I will miss you, but won't lose you."

Harrison was always saying sensitive things like that, which put him instantly on Jocelyn Lindstrom's male sensitivity chart. He was the only male either of us knew who had made the chart consistently over twelve months. Donald Raspigi, who occasionally said sensitive things like "Nice sweater," had been on twice.

Enter memories, sweet and sour.

Harrison and me baking enormous mocha chip cookies for the high school bake sale and having them stolen on the Lexington Avenue subway.

Harrison's African fighting fish, Luther, who ate Chef Boyardee Ravioli without chewing.

Harrison reading my mother's photocopied annual Christmas letter that she sent to family and friends—"Dear Friends, . . ."

This excerpt is from pages 10–11.

(She'd cross out "Friends" and write in "Addie and my little Tulip.") Harrison commenting that motherhood should be like driving a car—you should have to pass a test before you get to do it legally.

I held the prism up to the light. The sun hit it and showered colors through the windshield. "Now isn't that something?" Addie said, smiling at the sight. "Yeah." I looked out the window, trying not to cry.

This time, we don't tell the students what the memory is, as we did when we stopped the first time. We're trying to give them a tool and then get out of the way so they can use it on their own. If time is short, don't have students stop and jot first; just have them turn and talk with their partners.

If you hear too many students making comments that are too general, just interrupt, reread with them, and talk about it as a large class. Part of a gradual release model is knowing when you need to slow down the release of work to the students.

All right. Take a moment and jot down your thoughts and then turn to your neighbor and share what you've noticed as the Memory Moment. Use the anchor question to help you think and talk about the passage. Take about two minutes.

Again, circulate and listen to their conversations. Look for the students to talk about why these memories come to Hope's mind, to summarize what they're learning about her life, and to draw inferences about her character. Encourage them to examine the shades of meaning that might emerge. If one student says that Hope is merely unhappy about having to move on and another suggests that she is heartbroken to leave the love of her life behind, urge them to look back at the text and try to figure out why the various readers drew the differing inferences.

Then bring the class back together as a full group to discuss. After students have shared their thoughts, you might add,

❝ Yes, the memories are easy to spot. As you said, this passage began with one—Hope thinking back to Harrison giving her the prism. Then, as you noticed, she mentions his sensitivity, the pleasant times they had together, and his sarcastic comments about her mother. As I think about why these memories are important, I realize that this is a powerful way for the author to show me, the reader, just how attached Hope is to her friends. She probably doesn't know if she'll ever see Harrison again and wonders if she'll make new friends.

Looking at these memories should give us a good introduction to the character Hope. Take a minute now and write down a quick summary of what these Memory Moments have shown you about

Hope in just these few passages. When you've jotted down your ideas, we'll take another few minutes for you to discuss them with the students around you.

Let's hear what you came up with. . . .

End with Reviewing

" Now that students have practiced finding Memory Moments in a text with you there to help and support them, you'll want to tell them what to do as they now turn to reading their own novels. You also might want them to consider how Memory Moments often turn into Again and Again moments. Perhaps there's a "When-I-was-your-age" story a parent or grandparent shares again and again. Ask them to consider the point of the Memory Moment and why it might get repeated often.

Tell students that as they read they should look for Memory Moments and jot down notes about what these might suggest. When students later discuss what they found, be sure they don't just label the moment but discuss its significance.

If you want students to use the Notice and Note Reading Log, you'll find a template of one we've created on pages 209–210 of the Appendix and you'll see some others that teachers have created beginning on page 211. Students can also use sticky notes to mark places and jot down their thinking.

Conversation Close-up

Let's take a close look at an exchange from two students, one typical of what you might hear.

ROBERTO: I underlined the stuff here about Harrison.

MARIA: Yeah. Me, too. I mean it said it was memories. [pause] So like why were they important?

ROBERTO: Like all she has is memories because she keeps having to leave.

MARIA: I think she liked him a lot so these are sad memories. They are like important because it shows you how much she hates just having memories. See this part where she is looking at the prism and was trying not to cry. She's not happy and she hates moving.

ROBERTO: Maybe like all these memories early on, remember the other one was about her mom leaving her and now she's leaving Harrison, maybe this is all about leaving and how hard that is. Do you think so?

MARIA: Yeah. And maybe this is about her wanting not to have to ever leave someplace again, because that always makes her sad.

Both students are making inferences, not because we asked them to stop and do that, but because they were discussing the Memory Moment they had identified.

Notice the difference in Roberto's first comment and this one. With just a little bit of talk, he's now going back into the text for examples and has added his own question.

They moved from a discussion of the Memory Moment to making a prediction ("Maybe this is about her wanting not to have to ever leave someplace again") and identifying an internal conflict (moving makes her sad). All of that from noticing a Memory Moment and then noting what it might mean. The discussion was text-dependent, but they were in charge of the conversation. They were engaged because their comments and questions to one another were authentic (a dialogic moment). This is, of course, a part of assessing how well the students are reading the text.

Questions You Might Have

1. *The idea of the Memory Moment seems very simple. Is it really necessary to teach the kids to identify it?*

It definitely is a simple concept, but it's also subtle. A Memory Moment is so easy to miss. A good writer, first of all, will make a smooth, barely noticeable transition from the ongoing action into the memory. After all, the memory is probably triggered by something going on at the moment, some action in the plot, and so, even though it intrudes, it doesn't really disrupt the flow of the narrative badly. That makes it all too easy for the casual reader to slide right past it, perhaps thinking that it's nothing more than the character's mind wandering to irrelevancies during a slow moment in the story. That is compounded by struggling readers' difficulties in holding things in mind as they read. They may be working hard enough just to grasp the basics of the story, keep the various characters straight, visualize what's happening, and keep the sequence of events clear and comprehensible.

But even though Memory Moments are subtle and easy to miss, they can be extremely important. We usually come into the story somewhere in the middle, and so the only way we have of learning about the character's past and all the events that have shaped him or her is to look back. These memories are one of the writer's best tools for creating a character on paper who appears to the reader as a real person moving through the world.

Perhaps the best reason for teaching the Memory Moment signpost came from one of the students in the class we just highlighted. A reluctant reader, one who said little during the class, told us the next week, "If someone had just shown me this memory thing earlier, I could have been a lot smarter sooner."

2. *If the Memory Moment is so easily overlooked, isn't it important that I revisit it fairly often, to remind students to stay alert for it?*

Yes, it probably is. If you keep the poster you made at the beginning of the lesson from *Hope Was Here* somewhere on the classroom wall, you will be able to refer to it easily and often, reminding students both of the signpost and the question that helps them reflect on it. You might also give your students a brief minilesson based on a useful Memory Moment from another book that you are familiar with. Here are a few suggestions.

The Watsons Go to Birmingham–1963, page 64. This chapter begins with a memory. Curtis lets us know that we're looking back in time with the clue, "She told us that same sad old story about when she was a little girl." The story is about the day her family's home burned down, a terrifying day in her life. Byron, the older brother who seems unable to stay out of trouble, has dismissed it as that "same old story," and your students may tend to dismiss it, too. Later in this scene, however, Byron is caught by his mother playing with matches in the bathroom, and although this seems a fairly innocuous offense when compared with the other delinquency in which he has been involved, his mother erupts in fury, threatening, and even trying, to burn him to teach him some respect for the danger of fire.

> These page numbers are from the edition with this ISBN: 0-385-32175-9. If those pages don't take you to that scene, then look at the beginning of Chapter 5.

We wouldn't know why his mother is so outraged by her son's action if Curtis hadn't given us, at the beginning of the chapter, that short paragraph about Mrs. Watson's memory. If you share this passage, reproduce enough copies for your students, ask them to read it, and spot the Memory Moment. Have them speculate about why such a memory might be significant, and then let them read on to discover why Curtis shared it with us.

Hatchet, pages 1–3. Set the scene for the students by telling them that Brian is the lone passenger in a small plane, and at this moment he is sitting quietly staring out the window. Ask them to read the passage and identify the text clue that indicates this is a Memory Moment. They should all be able to identify the simple

> These page numbers are from the edition with this ISBN: 978-1-4169-3647-3.

phrase "The thinking started." Let them read on, and then ask them to discuss the anchor question and share their conversations with the class.

3. *You ask only one simple question:* Why might this memory be important? *Is that enough? Isn't there a way to further enrich the conversation about these moments?*

We've given just one question because we want the students to have an easily remembered tool that will help them begin thinking about these moments. We've found that if we keep asking different questions all the time, the students tend to wait for us. After all, they don't know what we're going to ask, so they see no sense in thinking about the passage until they know what it is we want them to think about. If we can give them a question and demonstrate that we are going to return to it regularly, it may become their own question, one that they use themselves without waiting around for us to push them in the direction we want them to go.

But you can refine the discussion of the Memory Moment if you wish.

You might, for example, teach your students that the importance of a memory may not be revealed immediately. In those cases, students have to learn to file away the questions raised by the memory and expect them to be answered later.

You might also ask:

- Is the character remembering something as a way to provide guidance or to help him or others solve a problem? If so, it might mean that this moment gives us insight into how he will solve a conflict—internal or external.

- Is the character remembering something that obviously troubles her? If so, it probably offers us insight into an internal conflict the character faces.

4. *What does the Memory Moment usually reveal in a story?*

Often it helps explain something about the plot or the conflict; when a character keeps remembering the same memory through-out the novel, the point of the memory or the lesson learned from it often reveals something about the theme.

5. *So, is the following a Memory Moment? A character says, "I remember that last week we had the same thing for dinner."*

Probably not. This seems to be just some bit of conversation from a character. On the other hand, if that memory is followed by (or immediately preceded by) the character's throwing his dinner plate against the wall, then the sharing of that memory helps us understand character motivation!

Teachers are heroes.

Chris Crutcher,
Boothbay Literacy
Retreat, 2012

And Now You Begin

So there you have it. Six lessons. Six signposts. Six anchor questions. One goal: to help teachers help students come to love thoughtful, reflective, engaged reading.

Not that they shouldn't also love getting lost in a book. That's a wonderful, if strange, metaphor—*lost in a book*. Normally, we don't think of being lost as a desirable state of affairs. Driving around a strange city, unable to find our way to the airport, no street names recognizable, no familiar buildings serving as landmarks, no idea whether to turn left or right can be unsettling, even frightening. When we hear of a friend who has "lost his way in life," we don't celebrate the joy he must be feeling but instead mourn for his confusion and discomfort and hope that he will one day find his way again. Getting lost isn't fun.

> So there you have it. Six lessons. Six signposts. Six anchor questions. One goal: to help teachers help students come to love thoughtful, reflective, engaged reading.

But getting lost in a book is a great joy. Most passionate readers have had—and loved—the feeling of being so immersed in the imaginary world that they're barely aware of the room they're sitting in or the beach they're sitting on, so caught up in the narrative that they feel what the character must be feeling and begin to tell her which door to open and which to stay far away from, hoping desperately that she will take their advice. At such moments the reader loves the hero and hates the villain, though both are mere ink spots on paper; fears the tiger behind the door, though both tiger and door are nothing but print on paper; wishes fervently that the good guys will triumph in the end and the bad suffer appropriate punishment, though, no matter how it works out, once the story is over and the book ends, both hero and villain will vanish between the cardboard covers of the book or float into cyberspace as the Kindle is turned off. But, for a few hours, that imaginary world was more real than the one around us. We were lost in the book, in the moment, an experience Margaret Early (1960) called "unconscious delight."

Much as we hope our students will have the experience of losing themselves in a book, at the same time we hope that they'll have the experience of finding themselves in a book. That is to say, we'd like them to close the book or turn off the e-reader thinking that they understand themselves, the people around them, and their world more fully than they did before they began the book. That sharpened understanding may take the form of newly acquired knowledge. That is often why we go to nonfiction—to gather information that we want or need. But it also may consist of refined understanding of the human condition, which is why we go to imaginative literature. We may read *To Kill a Mockingbird*, for instance, and close the covers with a deepened appreciation for the courage it takes to reject the assumptions and attitudes of our community. Or your class may read *Riding Freedom* and come to realize, somewhat more clearly, how much a society shapes our lives and dictates to us what we can or cannot do, who we can or cannot be. Literature enables us to see our world and ourselves more clearly, to understand our lives more fully.

Much as we hope our students will have the experience of losing themselves in a book, at the same time we hope that they'll have the experience of finding themselves in a book.

Coming to those sharpened understandings requires us not to extract something from the book but to *transact* with it. It requires us to attend to what's happening on the page just as we attend to what's happening around us, and to question and speculate. Then we are more than *lost* in a book; we are *found* in the book—through thoughtful, engaged, reflective reading. If we are to refine our understandings of ourselves and our conceptions of our world, we have to read our environment and our texts closely. We have to listen to the responsive chords struck in our own minds and see where they lead us. And we must seek evidence in the text to confirm or refute our speculations— speculations about what the text means to us, in our world, at this moment. Without that connection to us, the words on the page might just as well be mere ink spots. But if we read responsively and responsibly, we can, with those ink spots, shape our own lives into something richer than they would otherwise be.

So we must notice what's happening, ask ourselves what it means, and take note of the possible answers. We hope that *Notice and Note* will help you help your students to do just that and to come to appreciate the pleasures—intellectual, social, and aesthetic—of reading closely and thoughtfully.

Literature enables us to see our world and ourselves more clearly, to understand our lives more fully.

Appendix

In this section, you'll see many of the figures and templates from Parts I and II, as well as the texts needed to support the lessons found in Part III. All of the texts in this Appendix also appear in digital format at www.NoticeandNote.com.

1 **Surveys**

Along with the results of our surveys on commonly taught novels at grades 4–8 and 9–10, this section includes two additional surveys: one for analyzing information about students' reading habits (or your own) and a second for gathering information from students regarding their thoughts about classroom discussions. We suggest that you use these as written surveys, followed by a discussion of the students' responses. Having them begin with writing will allow everyone the quiet time needed to collect ideas, and will give you a record of their thoughts to look back at as the year progresses. Discussing them may then stimulate further thinking about the issues.

If the surveys seem too long for your class, give them only three or four items at a time. Also, for younger students, you'll probably want to revise, using language that's more appropriate for them. You can find an electronic version at www.NoticeandNote .com.

THE TWENTY-FIVE MOST COMMONLY TAUGHT NOVELS, GRADES 4–8

THE TWENTY-FIVE MOST COMMONLY TAUGHT NOVELS, GRADES 4–8

- *Among the Hidden*
- *Because of Winn Dixie*
- *Bridge to Terabithia*
- *Bud, Not Buddy*
- *The Cay*
- *A Christmas Carol*
- *The Diary of Anne Frank*
- *Esperanza Rising*
- *Freak, the Mighty*
- *The Giver*
- *Hatchet*
- *Holes*
- *Maniac Magee*

- *Night*
- *Number the Stars*
- *The Outsiders*
- *Riding Freedom*
- *Roll of Thunder, Hear My Cry*
- *Stargirl*
- *Tears of a Tiger*
- *To Kill a Mockingbird*
- *Touching Spirit Bear*
- *Tuck Everlasting*
- *Walk Two Moons*
- *The Watsons Go to Birmingham—1963*

As you look at this list, some of you will think, yes, we read that book in seventh grade, while others will consider the same book and say that book is read in eighth grade or sixth or fifth or fourth. In other words, while many respondents to our study mentioned *Esperanza Rising*, it was just as likely to be mentioned at fifth grade as it was at seventh. You can read more about this survey on page 4.

Books from this list I teach:

_____

_____

_____

_____

Books I teach NOT on this list:

_____

_____

_____

_____

THE TWENTY-FIVE MOST COMMONLY TAUGHT NOVELS, GRADES 9–10

THE TWENTY-FIVE MOST COMMONLY TAUGHT NOVELS, GRADES 9–10

- *1984*
- *The Adventures of Huckleberry Finn*
- *Animal Farm*
- *Brave New World*
- *The Crucible*
- *Fahrenheit 451*
- *Frankenstein*
- *Great Expectations*
- *The Great Gatsby*
- *Heart of Darkness*
- *Jane Eyre*
- *The Kite Runner*
- *Lord of the Flies*
- *Monster*
- *Night*
- *Of Mice and Men*
- *Othello*
- *Pride and Prejudice*
- *Romeo and Juliet*
- *The Scarlett Letter*
- *A Separate Peace*
- *Their Eyes Were Watching God*
- *Things Fall Apart*
- *The Things They Carried*
- *To Kill a Mockingbird*

We weren't too surprised at this top twenty-five. It should be noted, though, that many teachers mentioned *Tears of a Tiger, Hunger Games, The House on Mango Street, The Book Thief, Al Capone Does My Shirts, Miracle's Boys, The Absolutely True Diary of a Part-Time Indian*, and Bluford series books. Teachers noted that these books were read in "regular" or "non-academic" or "non pre-AP" classes or were for "struggling readers." We say more about this survey on page 48.

Books from this list I teach:

_____

_____

_____

_____

Books I teach NOT on this list:

_____

_____

_____

_____

Name _____ Date _____

READING HABITS SURVEY

Directions: Take a few minutes to answer these questions about your reading habits.

1. How often do you read each day at school? At home?

2. Do you mostly read books (novels and textbooks)? Do you mostly read on an e-reader such as a Nook, Kindle, or iPad? Mostly on a computer or a smart phone?

3. How is reading with an e-reader different from reading printed books?

4. What sort of material do you read online or on an e-reader or mobile device? Is this different from what you choose to read in print?

5. Do you read any blogs or websites on a regular basis? If your answer is yes, how large a part of your reading life are they?

6. How do you share with others what you are reading about? Through conversations? Comments on Facebook? By texting? By using a site such as Goodreads? Through a blog?

7. When do graphics (pictures, charts, video clips that might be a part of digital texts) help you understand what you are reading? And when are they a distraction?

8. Do you listen to audio books? Do you consider this reading?

9. Do you think that when you are reading something online or on an e-reader you are reading the same way as when you read something in a book?

10. Sometimes you choose what you want to read. Other times you are told what to read. How does choice or the lack of choice make a difference in how you read?

Name _____ Date _____

STUDENT SURVEY ON CLASSROOM DISCUSSIONS

Directions: Take a few minutes to answer these questions about classroom discussions.

1. What do you enjoy about classroom discussions? What do you not enjoy?

2. Do your classmates seem willing to listen to one another as each of you talk? If yes, what makes you say that? If no, why do you think that is?

3. What do most teachers do during classroom discussions? (Stand at the front of the room asking questions? Pull up a chair and act more like a participant? Offer some beginning comments and then let you and your classmates run the discussion?)

4. Do you think teachers already have a set of questions or topics to be discussed, or do they let you and your classmates come up with the questions and topics? Why do you think this?

5. How do discussions help you learn more about the other students in the classroom during a typical classroom discussion?

6. How does participating in a discussion change—or not change—your understanding of the topic?

7. Why do you think teachers encourage classroom discussions? Is it to check on what you're learning or to let you explore new ideas?

8. What would you like to see changed about your classroom discussions? (Here are some ideas: Have more of them? Fewer? Better ways for more people to contribute? Smaller groups of students in discussions instead of large groups? Larger groups instead of smaller groups? Students choosing the topics instead of the teacher? Sitting in a circle?)

9. Do you like having conversations online (through IM, blogging, or texting) more than discussions in a classroom? Why or why not?

10. What should you do to make discussions better?

Students and Dispositions

☐ Students are curious, as shown by comments such as "Tell me more . . ." and "Show me how . . ." and "What if we did this . . . ?"

☐ Students are reflective, as shown by comments such as "To me, this means. . . ." and "As I understand what you're saying. . . ." and "After thinking about this some more. . . ." and "When I reconsider. . . ."

☐ Students tolerate ambiguity, letting multiple ideas or positions exist side by side while evidence is being presented or sorted.

☐ Students are patient, giving ideas and others a chance to grow.

☐ Students are tentative, meaning they *offer* rather than *assert*, are open-minded rather than narrow-minded, are more interested in questions that are to be explored rather than questions that are to be answered.

Students and Texts

☐ Students use texts to expand, deepen, challenge, and clarify their own knowledge.

☐ Students use evidence from one or more texts to back up claims.

☐ Students make connections within a text.

☐ Students make connections across texts.

☐ Students refer to what was learned in previously read texts.

Students and Ideas

☐ Students change their minds about ideas from time to time.

☐ Students hypothesize.

☐ Students are able to consider alternative positions and are willing to ask "What if?"

☐ Students identify topics that they need to know more about before reaching conclusions.

Students and Reasoning and Evidence

☐ Students provide evidence for their statements and opinions.

☐ Students present information in some sort of logical order—cause and effect, sequential, lists of reasons or examples.

☐ Students avoid "just because" statements.

☐ Students recognize faulty assumptions and helpfully encourage each other to examine those assumptions.

☐ Students recognize persuasive techniques.

☐ Students question the author's motives when appropriate to do so.

Students and Vocabulary

☐ Students use language that reflects their understanding of the vocabulary specific to the topic under discussion.

☐ Students ask for clarification of words they see and hear but do not understand.

HUSWIFERY

by Edward Taylor

Make me, O Lord, thy Spinning Wheel complete.
    Thy Holy Word my Distaff make for me.
Make mine Affections thy Swift Flyers neat
    And make my Soul thy holy Spool to be.
    My Conversation make to be thy Reel
    And reel the yarn thereon spun of thy Wheel.

Make me thy Loom then, knit therein this Twine:
    And make thy Holy Spirit, Lord, wind quills:
Then weave the Web thyself. The Yarn is fine.
    Thine Ordinances make my Fulling Mills.
    Then dye the same in Heavenly Colors Choice,
All pinked with Varnished Flowers of Paradise.

Then clothe therewith mine Understanding, Will,
    Affections, Judgment, Conscience, Memory,
My Words, and Actions, that their shine may fill
    My ways with glory and thee glorify.
    Then mine apparel shall display before ye
    That I am Clothed in Holy robes for glory.

Worksheet for Analysis of Text Complexity of a Literary Text

Title of the Text: _____

Quantitative Measures: Lexile (Other) Score _____   Grade level suggested by quantitative measures: _____

Qualitative Dimensions:

Complexity of Levels of Meaning

| EASIER | Simple, single meaning. Literal, explicit, and direct. Purpose or stance clear. | ▶ | Much is explicit but moves to some implied meaning. Requires some inferential reasoning. | ▶ | Multiple levels, use of symbolism, irony, satire. Some ambiguity. Greater demand for inference. | ▶ | Multiple levels, subtle, implied meanings and purpose. Abstract, difficult ideas. Use of symbolism, irony, satire. | DEMANDING |

EVIDENCE:

Complexity of Structure

| EASIER | Clear, chronological, conventional. May support through subheads, definitions, glossary. | ▶ | Primarily explicit. Perhaps several points of view. May vary from simple chronological order. Largely conventional. | ▶ | More complex. Narrow or perhaps multiple perspectives. More deviation from chronological or sequential order. | ▶ | Complex, perhaps parallel, plot lines. Deviates from chronological or sequential. Narrator may be unreliable. | DEMANDING |

EVIDENCE:

Complexity of Language Conventionality and Clarity

| EASIER | Explicit, literal, contemporary, familiar language. Vocabulary simple. Mostly Tier One words. | ▶ | Mostly explicit, some figurative or allusive langue. Perhaps some dialect or other unconventional language. | ▶ | Meanings are implied but support is offered. More figurative or ironic language. More inference is demanded. | ▶ | Implied meanings. Allusive, figurative, or ironic language, perhaps archaic or formal. Complex sentence structures. | DEMANDING |

EVIDENCE:

Complexity of Knowledge on Demands

| EASIER | Requires no special knowledge. Situations and subjects familiar or easily envisioned. | ▶ | Some references to events or other texts. Begins to rely more on outside knowledge. | ▶ | More complexity in theme. Experiences may be less familiar to many. Cultural or historical references may make heavier demands. | ▶ | Explores complex ideas. Refers to texts or ideas that may be beyond students' experiences. May require specialized knowledge. | DEMANDING |

EVIDENCE:

Qualitative dimensions indicate text makes demands that are: Mostly easier _____   Mostly more demanding _____

Grade level suggested by qualitative assessment _____

Reader-Task Considerations

This is perhaps the most important element in judging the complexity of the text, and the most subtle. At issue is the suitability of a particular text for a particular reader. What follows are some questions to consider in making such a judgment. As you think about these questions with students in mind, make comments in the space provided.

Interest

- Is the student/class likely to be interested in the character, theme, topic, issue, subject matter, or genre?

Background and Ability

- Does the student/class have background knowledge or experience necessary to deal with the text and the task?

- Is the student/class intellectually capable of dealing with the issues presented in the text and the task?

- Does the student/class have vocabulary and inferential skills necessary for this text and the task?

Attitudes and Maturity

- Is the student/class sufficiently mature and sophisticated to deal with the subject matter?

- Does the book raise issues that might embarrass readers or be in some other way problematic?

Potential for Stimulating Thought, Discussion, and Further Reading

- Is there potential in the reading of this text for good conversation among readers?

- Does this text raise issues or questions likely to inspire the student/class to further reading, research, and writing?

Comments Summarizing the Assessments on the Three Dimensions

- How much support will be needed with this text at grade _____?

- Final recommendation for use and placement of text: _____
  Grade level? Early or late in the year? For independent reading, guided group instruction, full class?

Notice & Note

Name _____

Book _____

SIGNPOSTS YOU MIGHT NOTICE

Contrasts & Contradictions

When a character does something that contrasts with what you'd expect or contradicts his earlier acts or statements, **STOP** and ask, "Why is the character doing that?"

Aha Moment

When a character realizes, understands, or finally figures out something, **STOP** and ask yourself, "How might this change things?"

Tough Questions

When a character asks herself a very difficult question, **STOP** and ask yourself, "What does this question make me wonder about?"

Words of the Wiser

When a character (probably older and wiser) takes the main character aside and offers serious advice, **STOP** and ask, "What's the life lesson and how might it affect the character?"

Again & Again

When you notice a word, phrase, or situation mentioned over and over, **STOP** and ask yourself, "Why does this keep happening again and again?"

Memory Moment

When the author interrupts the action to tell you about a memory, **STOP** and ask yourself, "Why might this memory be important?"

Use the back to jot down page numbers of the signposts you spot.

Notice & Note

Name _____

Book _____

SIGNPOSTS YOU MIGHT NOTICE

Contrasts & Contradictions

When a character does something that contrasts with what you'd expect or contradicts his earlier acts or statements, **STOP** and ask, "Why is the character doing that?"

Aha Moment

When a character realizes, understands, or finally figures out something, **STOP** and ask yourself, "How might this change things?"

Tough Questions

When a character asks herself a very difficult question, **STOP** and ask yourself, "What does this question make me wonder about?"

Words of the Wiser

When a character (probably older and wiser) takes the main character aside and offers serious advice, **STOP** and ask, "What's the life lesson and how might it affect the character?"

Again & Again

When you notice a word, phrase, or situation mentioned over and over, **STOP** and ask yourself, "Why does this keep happening again and again?"

Memory Moment

When the author interrupts the action to tell you about a memory, **STOP** and ask yourself, "Why might this memory be important?"

Use the back to jot down page numbers of the signposts you spot.

Notice & Note

Name _____

Book _____

SIGNPOSTS YOU MIGHT NOTICE

Contrasts & Contradictions

When a character does something that contrasts with what you'd expect or contradicts his earlier acts or statements, **STOP** and ask, "Why is the character doing that?"

Aha Moment

When a character realizes, understands, or finally figures out something, **STOP** and ask yourself, "How might this change things?"

Tough Questions

When a character asks herself a very difficult question, **STOP** and ask yourself, "What does this question make me wonder about?"

Words of the Wiser

When a character (probably older and wiser) takes the main character aside and offers serious advice, **STOP** and ask, "What's the life lesson and how might it affect the character?"

Again & Again

When you notice a word, phrase, or situation mentioned over and over, **STOP** and ask yourself, "Why does this keep happening again and again?"

Memory Moment

When the author interrupts the action to tell you about a memory, **STOP** and ask yourself, "Why might this memory be important?"

Use the back to jot down page numbers of the signposts you spot.

Notice & Note

WHERE I FOUND THE LITERARY SIGNPOSTS

Contrasts & Contradictions

Aha Moment

Tough Questions

Words of the Wiser

Again & Again

Memory Moment

Notice & Note

WHERE I FOUND THE LITERARY SIGNPOSTS

Contrasts & Contradictions

Aha Moment

Tough Questions

Words of the Wiser

Again & Again

Memory Moment

Notice & Note

WHERE I FOUND THE LITERARY SIGNPOSTS

Contrasts & Contradictions

Aha Moment

Tough Questions

Words of the Wiser

Again & Again

Memory Moment

Take a look at the opening scene from *Among the Hidden*, by Margaret Haddix. As you read it, think about the Notice and Note lessons and mark any parts of the passage that bring any of those lessons to mind. Think about the anchor question for that lesson (list of anchor questions is found on page 79), and jot down your thinking in the space provided under the passage. Then, if you're reading this book as part of a study group, talk with others about what they noticed.

As you share, don't be surprised if the same lines meant different things to you and your colleagues. Talk about why you labeled a line one way and consider why your colleague made a different choice. Remember, the critical conversation emerges as you discuss the answer to the anchor question. As you listen to one another's answers, you'll see that a richer picture develops when people do see lines in different ways. Once you've completed this, you might turn to the Classroom Close-up found on page 90 to see what a group of seventh graders had to say about this first paragraph.

OK, get started.

> He saw the first tree shudder and fall, far off in the distance. Then he heard his mother call out the kitchen window: "Luke! Inside. Now."
>
> He had never disobeyed the order to hide. Even as a toddler, barely able to walk in the backyard's tall grass, he had somehow understood the fear in his mother's voice. But on this day, the day they began taking the woods away, he hesitated. He took one extra breath of the fresh air, scented with clover and honeysuckle and—coming from far away—pine smoke. He laid his hoe down gently, and savored one last moment of feeling warm soil beneath his bare feet. He reminded himself, "I will never be allowed outside again. Maybe never again as long as I live."
>
> He turned and walked into the house, as silently as a shadow.
>
> *Among the Hidden*, page 1

My Thoughts

_____

_____

_____

_____

_____

Name _____

Notice and Note Log for _____

Location	Signpost I Noticed	My Notes About It

Location	Signpost I Noticed	My Notes About It

8 Adaptations of Notice and Note Reading Logs

As we've shared these lessons, teachers have truly made them their own. Three teachers in particular, Amanda Youngblood, from Orange County Public Schools, in Orlando, Florida, and Terry Brennan and Joan Boyce, from Wauwatosa Public Schools, in Wauwatosa, Wisconsin, created their own Notice and Note Reading Logs. We thought they were great and happily share them with you here.

Name: _____ Date: _____ Period: _____

Book or article: _____ Chapter(s): _____

LESSON OF THE UNEXPECTED*
"WHY DID THE CHARACTER ACT (FEEL) THAT WAY?"

The character acts in a way that *contradicts how he or she has acted before* or that *contrasts with how we would act* or that *reveals a difference among characters.*

Look for ways a character acts that:

. . . are contradictory (opposite or different) to how the character has acted in the past.

. . . contrast with how you would act in that situation.

. . . reveal a difference among characters (a way that this character is different from another).

Ask: "Why did the character act (or feel) that way?"

What character action or feeling was unexpected?	Pg #	What was unexpected about the action/feeling?	Why do you think the character acted/felt that way?

*We call this signpost Contrasts and Contradictions.

What character action or feeling was unexpected?	Pg #	What was unexpected about the action/feeling?	Why do you think the character acted/felt that way?

Name: _____ Date: _____ Period: _____

Book or article: _____ Chapter(s): _____

AHA MOMENT

"WHY MIGHT THIS REALIZATION BE IMPORTANT?"

A character's insight or sudden understanding reveals something important about the character or the plot.

Look for the moment when the writer seems to interrupt the action, or perhaps puts a character off alone to think, and some realization occurs to him or her.

. . . I suddenly realized that. . . .

. . . At that moment, I finally understood. . . .

Ask: "Why might this realization be important?"

What words told you this was going to be an Aha Moment?	Pg #	What realization came to the character's mind?	How is this realization likely to be important in the story?

What words told you this was going to be an Aha Moment?	Pg #	What realization came to the character's mind?	How is this realization likely to be important in the story?

Name: _____ Date: _____ Period: _____

Book or article: _____ Chapter(s): _____

TOUGH QUESTIONS

"WHAT DOES THIS TOUGH QUESTION MAKE ME WONDER ABOUT?"

A time when the main character asks him- or herself, or someone else, a tough question, one that doesn't have an easy answer.

Look for the moment when a character is confused or uncertain and either asks himself (or someone else might ask him) a very hard question that will shape his life or tells us that he is wondering about something important.

You might see a character saying to herself something like:

. . . I couldn't imagine what I ought to do about. . . .
. . . I realized that I was finally going to have to figure out. . . .
. . . I just didn't know which choice to make.
. . . How could I possibly decide between. . . .

Or a friend might say or ask:

. . . No matter how tough it will be, you'll have to choose between. . . .
. . . Before you do anything you're going to have to ask yourself. . . .

Ask: "What does this tough question make me wonder about?"

How did you know this was going to be a Tough Question?	Pg #	What did you wonder about when you thought about the question?	How is this question important to the story and how do you think the character will answer it? (Or, How will his or her answer affect the events in the story that follow?)

How did you know this was going to be a Tough Question?	Pg #	What did you wonder about when you thought about the question?	How is this question important to the story and how do you think the character will answer it? (Or, How will his or her answer affect the events in the story that follow?)

Name: _____   Date: _____   Period: _____

Book or article: _____   Chapter(s): _____

Words of the Wiser
"How could this advice affect the character?"

A wiser, often older, character shares his or her experience, wisdom, or lesson about life with the protagonist, hoping to guide him or her through a difficult decision.

Look for a scene in which a wiser character offers the main character advice that is helpful at this moment in the story, but could also be helpful throughout life.

Ask: "How could this advice affect the character?"

What did you see that told you this was going to be a Words-of-the-Wiser moment?	Pg #	What advice or insight did the wiser character share?	How do you think this will affect the main character (or the one who received the advice)?

What did you see that told you this was going to be a Words-of-the-Wiser moment?	Pg #	What advice or insight did the wiser character share?	How do you think this will affect the main character (or the one who received the advice)?

Name: _____ Date: _____ Period: _____

Book or article: _____ Chapter(s): _____

AGAIN AND AGAIN

"WHY MIGHT THE AUTHOR BRING THIS UP AGAIN AND AGAIN?"

A word, phrase, or idea is repeated, making us wonder about its significance.

Look for anything that keeps happening again and again.

You might see:

. . . a single word that is repeated more often than you would expect, as if the writer is calling special attention to it

. . . a situation that a character finds him- or herself in over and over

. . . an idea that keeps coming up

Ask: "Why might the author bring this up again and again?"

What did you find that keeps coming up over and over again?	Pg #	Why do you think the author keeps repeating this word, phrase, image, idea, or situation?	What does this Again and Again signpost lead you to think is going to happen later in the story?

What did you find that keeps coming up over and over again?	Pg #	Why do you think the author keeps repeating this word, phrase, image, idea, or situation?	What does this Again and Again signpost lead you to think is going to happen later in the story?

Name: _____ Date: _____ Period: _____

Book or article: _____ Chapter(s): _____

MEMORY MOMENT
"WHY MIGHT THIS MEMORY BE IMPORTANT?"

A memory interrupts the flow of the story, but reveals something important about the character or the plot.

Look for times when:
. . . the character suddenly starts remembering something, even right in the middle of some important event
. . . a quiet moment when the character thinks back on something from his or her past

Ask: "Why might this memory be important?"

What was happening when the character recalled the memory?	Pg #	What memory came to the character's mind?	Why do you think this memory is important to the character or to the story?

What was happening when the character recalled the memory?	Pg #	What memory came to the character's mind?	Why do you think this memory is important to the character or to the story?

Contrasts and Contradictions

Definition: The character acts in a way that is contradictory
or unexpected given how he or she usually acts.

Text Clue: Author shows feelings or actions the reader hasn't seen before or doesn't expect.

Question: Why would the character act this way?

What did I notice?	*What did my partner and I say?*

What are my final thoughts?

I think the author uses this contrast or contradiction to show the reader . . .

Contrasts and Contradictions

Definition: The character acts in a way that is contradictory
or unexpected given how he or she normally acts.

Text Clue: Author shows feelings or actions the reader hasn't seen before or doesn't expect.

Question: Why would a character act this way?

Where in the text does the unexpected event or statement show up?	*What inferences can you make about why the character would act this way?*
Where in the text does the unexpected event or statement show up?	*What inferences can you make about why the character would act this way?*

Aha Moment

Definition: The character realizes or starts to realize something
that changes his or her actions or thinking.

Text clue: Characters say "I realized" or "I suddenly knew" or "Now I know why . . ."

Question: What might the character do now?

What did I notice?	*What did my partner and I say?*

Why do you think the author has the character realize this?

_____

_____

_____

_____

_____

_____

_____

Aha Moment

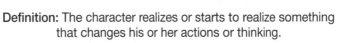

Definition: The character realizes or starts to realize something
that changes his or her actions or thinking.
Text clue: Characters say "I realized" or "I suddenly knew" or "Now I know why . . ."
Question: What might the character do now?

What is the Aha Moment?	*What inferences can you make about what the character will do now or think now?*
What is the Aha Moment?	*What inferences can you make about what the character will do now or think now?*

Tough Questions

Definition: Character asks a tough question that reveals
his or her concerns [inner conflict].

Text Clue: Character asks self or another a difficult question.

Question: What does this question make me wonder about?
What does it tell me about the character?

What is the question?	*What does this question make me wonder about? What does it tell me about this character?*
What is the question?	*What does this question make me wonder about? What does it tell me about the character?*

Tough Questions

Definition: Character asks a tough question that reveals
his or her concerns [inner conflict].

Text Clue: Character asks self or another a difficult question.

Question: What does this question make me wonder about?
What does it tell me about the character?

What did I notice?	*What did my partner and I say?*

What are my final thoughts?

This question makes me wonder if . . . _____

_____

_____

_____

_____

It tells me that . . . _____

_____

_____

Words of the Wiser

Definition: An older character (mentor, advisor, parent, etc.)
gives advice or an insight to the main character.

Text Clue: A wiser, often older, character offers a life lesson, usually in a quiet moment.

Question: What is important about that message?

What did I notice?	*What did my partner and I notice?*

What were my final thoughts?

This advice is important in the story and in life because . . .

Words of the Wiser

Definition: An older character (mentor, advisor, parent, etc.)
gives advice or an insight to the main character.

Text Clue: A wiser, often older, character offers a life lesson, usually in a quiet moment.

Question: What is important about that message?

What did I notice?	*What inferences can you make about why the message is important?*
What did I notice?	*What inferences can you make about why the message is important?*

Again and Again

Definition: The author keeps bringing up the same image, phrase, or reference.

Text clue: A repeated image, phrase, or reference

Question: Why do you think the author brings this idea up again and again?

What did I notice?	*What did my partner and I say?*

What are my final thoughts?

_____

_____

_____

_____

_____

_____

Again and Again

Definition: The author keeps bringing up the same image, phrase, or reference.

Text clue: A repeated image, phrase, or reference

Question: Why do you think the author brings this idea up again and again?

What is the idea or phrase that is repeated again and again?	*Why do you think the author keeps bringing up this idea?*
What is the idea or phrase that is repeated again and again?	*Why do you think the author keeps bringing up this idea?*

Memory Moment—Flashback

Definition: The author interrupts the flow of the story
by letting the character remember something.

Text clue: "I suddenly remembered . . ."; "I remember . . ."; or "Thinking back . . ."

Question: Why might this memory be important?

What did I notice?	*What did my partner and I say?*

What are my final thoughts?

Memory Moment—Flashback

Definition: The author interrupts the flow of the story
by letting the character remember something.

Text clue: "I suddenly remembered . . ."; "I remember . . ."; or "Thinking back . . ."

Question: Why might this memory be important?

What did the character remember?	*Why might the memory be important?*

What did the character remember?	*Why might the memory be important?*

The following chart shows you the Notice and Note Signposts we found in *Walk Two Moons*, by Sharon Creech. If you're teaching this book, you might look through these, mark the ones you think you want your students to be sure to notice, and think about what you might say to them if, after you've taught the lessons, they don't see them. If you don't teach this book, we encourage you to read it first—it's great! Whether you've read it or not, this is a good example of what the signposts look like in a book. Be warned—if you've not read the book, this chart gives away several important parts of the plot that you might want to discover through reading the novel instead of the chart. You might want to stop reading the chart at about Chapter 17 if you haven't read the book.

NOTICE AND NOTE SIGNPOSTS IN *WALK TWO MOONS*

LOCATION: *Chapter 1, Page 3* Sal's father shows her a fireplace that had been hidden behind a plaster wall.

Aha Moment	
WHAT WE NOTICED We're barely into the book and we see a critical Aha Moment, though at this point, readers won't realize just how important Sal's words are: "I realized that the story of Phoebe was like the plaster wall in our old house in Bybanks, Kentucky" (p. 3). When authors use words such as "realized" or "understood" or "figured out," we see that the character is having an Aha Moment and we want to ask ourselves how this changes things. This early in the book, we really don't know the meaning of Sal's Aha, so we'll have to keep reading. Here's what we'd say to students who have learned this lesson but weren't reading attentively enough to notice the Aha Moment signpost: "Let's reread this paragraph that begins at the bottom of page 2." [Read aloud with students or let them read on their own.] "Think about the Aha Moment we've discussed, and if you need to, review what it is by looking at the chart up here. Remember that the word 'realized' is one of those words that shows us that a character has figured something out. And once we see that, what are we supposed to ask ourselves?" [Hopefully, students will remember the anchor question, but if not then just prompt it.] "Now, let's talk about what this Aha might mean." [Again, it's early in the book, so don't worry if speculations are simply, "I'm not sure" or "Phoebe—whoever that is—is somehow like a plaster wall."] If we haven't taught the Aha Moment lesson at this point, then we wouldn't try to teach it with this as the example because the readers really won't be sure how to answer the anchor question.	YOUR NOTES

LOCATION: *Chapter 2, Page 5* Sal mentions that Gram and Gramps want to see "Momma, who was resting peacefully in Lewiston, Idaho."

Contrasts and Contradictions	
WHAT WE NOTICED This is a sophisticated use of Contrasts and Contradictions. The author has used the euphemism "resting peacefully" with no suggestion that it might mean "buried" unless the reader has noticed the word "buried" in the previous sentence. If you want, point out to students that when authors use words or terms that might mean more than one thing (the contrast between taking a peaceful nap and having died is stark), they should stop and ask themselves, "Why would the author use this term/word." In this case, why would Creech say that Sal's mom was resting peacefully? Some might speculate that she has been ill and is recuperating; some might say she's been injured; and others might wonder if this means she has died. Don't confirm, just ask for evidence in the text to support their thinking, then keep reading.	YOUR NOTES

NOTICE AND NOTE SIGNPOSTS IN *WALK TWO MOONS*

LOCATION: *Chapter 2, Pages 7–8* Sal explains how important trees are to her.

Again and Again

WHAT WE NOTICED	YOUR NOTES
Even this early in the book, Creech has already mentioned "trees" several times, first on page 1, and now, on page 7, she tells us that Sal's middle name is Tree. Noticing this repetition, and watching for it as we read on, will enable us to learn something about Sal's character and her connection to her mother and to nature. "Trees" will come up frequently throughout the book, but make note especially of pages 98–101, in which an entire chapter is devoted to "The Singing Tree." Trees will show up again on 122, 215, 257, 268, and 277, all of the references strengthening Sal's connection to both her mother and to nature. If we have taught the Again and Again lesson and students don't mention how often "tree" has appeared even by this point, we'd probably stop and simply remind students to think about the Again and Again lesson and ask them what image or word keeps reappearing. Then we'd ask why they think "trees" keep appearing again and again. We've found that most students realize, even this early, that her mother—and therefore perhaps Sal—loved nature. One student told us, "Since her mother named her after a tree, and since trees are mentioned so much, maybe this is just a way of showing how much Sal is connected to her mother." Maybe, indeed!	

LOCATION: *Chapter 3, Pages 13–14* Phoebe declares Sal brave while Sal declares herself to be afraid of many things.

Contrasts and Contradictions and Aha Moment

WHAT WE NOTICED	YOUR NOTES
When Phoebe calls Sal courageous and Sal denies it, we have a classic contradiction—one says she is and the other says she isn't. When authors show us such contradictions, we want to pause and ask ourselves, "Why would the character act this way?" In this case, we want students wondering why Phoebe would maintain that Sal is courageous while Sal would say she isn't. One student explained, "Phoebe thinks she's brave because Sal would touch a spider, but Sal knows that's not really bravery. Sal's afraid of the things she can't control. Maybe this is going to be about Sal learning that she can't be afraid of things she can't control, because most things in life that are really important, you can't control at all." Nice. We also hope students will see that in the middle of page 14, Sal has an Aha Moment that is part of this discussion of bravery. She says, "What I have since realized is that if people expect you to be brave, sometimes you pretend that you are, even when you are frightened down to your very bones." Students who notice this should then discuss "How might this Aha change things?" Another student, in answering that question said, "It's like for prediction. You can see that she's going to have to be brave about something. And she's already said that she's not brave about really hard things, like cancer. I bet her mother has cancer."	

NOTICE AND NOTE SIGNPOSTS IN *WALK TWO MOONS*

LOCATION: *Chapter 4, Page 22* Sal connects blackberries to memories of her mom.

Again and Again	
WHAT WE NOTICED	**YOUR NOTES**
Blackberries have already been mentioned again and again, and by the end of the book, will have appeared more than thirty times. While we don't expect—or want—students to interrupt their reading each time Sal or another character mentions a blackberry, we do want them to be alert to the repetition and to occasionally ask themselves why blackberries keep showing up again and again. They are often connected, in Sal's mind, to her mother and happier days, and late in the book they'll become associated with Ben, too. Here are some other points in the book in which blackberries are mentioned in some *significant* way: pages 29, 32, 35, 121, 122, 205, 214, and 215.	

LOCATION: *Chapter 5, Page 25* Sal focuses on her rush to get where they are going.

Again and Again	
WHAT WE NOTICED	**YOUR NOTES**
Once you've taught the Again and Again signpost, some students will find all the spots where frequently used words or phrases are mentioned. "Rush, rush, rush" might be one that some students key in on. If so, they'll hear the urgency that Sal is feeling. The phrase came up first on page 6, and will appear again on pages 38, 55, 57, and 72.	

LOCATION: *Chapter 6, Page 30* Sal's feelings about Mrs. Winterbottom contrast sharply with what she has observed.

Contrasts and Contradictions or Aha Moment	
WHAT WE NOTICED	**YOUR NOTES**
Your students may see this signpost as a Contrast and Contradiction, noticing the sharp contrast between what Sal has actually observed and what she nonetheless feels. Sal has been observing Mrs. Winterbottom carefully and has noticed that everything she has said indicates that she is an enthusiastic and committed homemaker. But there is something—she doesn't know what—that contradicts all of that evidence. Despite all that she has observed, Sal feels that Mrs. Winterbottom is not the happy housewife she seems to be. Noticing this, students might begin to wonder just what is happening with Phoebe's mother, and how it might shape the plot. Or they may see it as an Aha Moment. You'll want to encourage the conversation and give kids time to share their reasons. Some will see that Sal has had an important if incomplete insight into Mrs. Winterbottom. Sal continues to analyze her thoughts and feelings for several pages, never completely understanding them, but concluding for the moment that "It all seemed peculiar. They acted so thumpingly *tidy* and *respectable*." We know that something is wrong here, though we aren't sure what.	

NOTICE AND NOTE SIGNPOSTS IN *WALK TWO MOONS*

LOCATION: *Chapter 6, Pages 33–35* Sal recalls picking blackberries with her mother, and then an incident with her father and mother.

Memory Moment or Contrasts and Contradictions

WHAT WE NOTICED	YOUR NOTES
Here Sal follows one memory—of picking blackberries—to another, a memory of a strange incident involving her father and mother. When your students speculate about what they learn from this memory about Sal, her father, and her mother, they may better understand why her mother left and why Sal is struggling so desperately with her loss. Two students saw this same scene in two ways: One reported, "There's so much detail in this memory, you like just really see it, and it seems sad, the way her mom was crying, and it was like Sal was realizing that her mom just wasn't happy." The second reported, "That's how you know it's more a contrast and contradiction. See, here, it says, 'It was all sad instead of happy' (p. 35). That's a contradiction. I think that Sal's mom was trying to be happy, but she never felt like she measured up and Sal was remembering it." The first student responded: "So, the question of why is this memory important is because it was, like, the memory was the contradiction. It's like Sal knew, but didn't really understand until now that her mom wasn't happy." Note the use of evidence from the text.	

LOCATION: *Chapter 7, Page 38* Sal wonders why her mother left her.

Tough Question

WHAT WE NOTICED	YOUR NOTES
Although the question "How could she leave me?" is raised simply and without any extraordinary effort to call attention to it, it is obviously a tough and painful one for Sal. When we see a character articulate a difficult question or doubt, we can be certain that it will be a central issue in the novel. This question is the one that will trouble Sal throughout the book.	

LOCATION: *Chapter 11, Page 60* Sal and Phoebe find a second mysterious note.

Again and Again

WHAT WE NOTICED	YOUR NOTES
When this second unsigned note shows up, some students will identify this as Again and Again. In this scene, the two girls again find a mysterious note. The first note, which showed up back on page 51, was the adage, "Don't judge a man until you've walked two moons in his moccasins." This note is different— "Everyone has his own agenda." As students wonder why this keeps occurring again and again, some students will focus on the content of the notes—short messages that offer Sal and Phoebe important life lessons—and others will focus more on the act of messages being delivered.	

NOTICE AND NOTE SIGNPOSTS IN *WALK TWO MOONS*

LOCATION: *Chapter 11, Pages 63–64* Sal finds herself getting nervous around a mysterious stranger, but she can't quite figure out why.

Again and Again

WHAT WE NOTICED	YOUR NOTES
Here we noticed a mysterious character showing up again. Mysterious characters, however—those lacking a name and a clear role or relationship to the central character and who come and go with no apparent reason—should not be ignored, and we hope readers will wonder just why this one keeps appearing again and again. They know that he will play a significant role sooner or later. A quick reference to "the lunatic" first appears on page 9. Then, the character, "the Lunatic" appears on page 42. As the story continues, he appears more often as he moves from being an unknown to a known character in the story. You can find references to him on pages 69, 118–120, 127, 137–141, 154, 183–188, 204, 220, 232, 235, 239, 242, 246–250, and 277.	

LOCATION: *Chapter 14, Page 88* Sal wonders what she didn't notice about her mom.

Tough Questions

WHAT WE NOTICED	YOUR NOTES
Here, it is obvious to Sal that Phoebe's mother is worried, but Phoebe doesn't see it at all. This leads Sal to ask herself if *she*, too, had been unwilling to notice things about her own mother? As students come to understand that Sal's mother isn't coming home, they may recognize this tough question, and begin to realize this book isn't going to be so much about why Sal's mom left home, as about Sal's understanding and acceptance of it.	

LOCATION: *Chapter 16, Pages 99–100* Sal shares a memory of the singing tree.

Memory Moment

WHAT WE NOTICED	YOUR NOTES
Here, Sal remembers the singing tree that was silent the day they learned her mother wasn't coming home. We have to speculate about why that memory has come to mind at this particular moment, and what that tells us. Students may see this memory as Again and Again as the book continues.	

LOCATION: *Chapter 17, Page 106* Another mysterious message sets Sal to wondering, "What does it matter?"

Tough Questions

WHAT WE NOTICED	YOUR NOTES
In this scene, Creech gives us a tough question in the form of the mysterious message—"In the course of a lifetime, what does it matter?" Sal comes up with a tentative answer—that Prudence's cheerleading tryouts probably wouldn't matter very much, but that a mother leaving probably would matter a great deal. Figuring out how her mother's disappearance matters, and what she can do or think about it, is one of the central problems of the book.	

LOCATION: *Chapter 20, Page 126* Phoebe's mom leaves notes for her family.

Contrasts and Contradictions

WHAT WE NOTICED	YOUR NOTES
Here, Phoebe's mom, who has always been available to her family in many ways, disappears, leaving only a cryptic note. This is clearly behavior that contradicts what we've been led to expect from her. Though students won't know why until they read on, we want them to pause and wonder why she would act this way. In doing so, they begin to speculate on the internal conflict she is dealing with.	

LOCATION: *Chapter 22, Page 137* Sal's dad tells her that her excuses about her mom are "fishes in the air."

Again and Again

WHAT WE NOTICED	YOUR NOTES
Sal's dad repeats an expression we've heard before, comparing Sal's excuses to something that doesn't happen—fish don't live in the air—so he seems to be suggesting that there is something imagined or unrealistic about her thoughts, that she isn't accepting reality in some way. As we notice and then discuss this repetition, students may come to realize that much of the novel, in fact, seems to be about Sal's journey toward the discovery of the reality from which she has been hiding. The first reference to the fish was on page 6. It occurred again on page 115 (where it's also in the chapter title). And it will come up finally on page 277.	

LOCATION: *Chapter 22, Page 141* Sal's dad explains that people can't be caged like birds.

Words of the Wiser

WHAT WE NOTICED	YOUR NOTES
We noticed that at this point Sal's dad offers Sal an important lesson on how people must be treated. As students think of the key question—how might this memory be important—they may begin to speculate on how this advice might help Sal understand her mother's departure.	

NOTICE AND NOTE SIGNPOSTS IN *WALK TWO MOONS*

LOCATION: *Chapter 23, Page 150* Sal remembers her mother's story about the Napi, the creator of men and women.

Memory Moment	
WHAT WE NOTICED On this page, we noticed that Sal shared a memory about a creation myth, and the decision by Napi, the creator, that people will die rather live forever. Sal had just shared the story of the baby's death, so this memory might be important in helping her understand that the baby's death wasn't her fault—or her mother's fault—it's just what happens in this world.	YOUR NOTES

LOCATION: *Chapter 26, Page 165* Sal and Phoebe focus on the word *sacrifice*.

Again and Again	
WHAT WE NOTICED Creech repeats the word *sacrifice* four or five times on this page. This is an example of repetition not found across the book, but just on one page. If your students talk about the repetition of the word *sacrifice*, they may begin to think about who in this story made sacrifices, and what they sacrificed. They may recall that Sal's mother felt that in some way she had sacrificed herself, given up some of her identity, in order to be a good mother. They may remember the moment back on page 110, when she expressed the desire to be called by her real name, and may interpret that as a further clue that she felt she had given up—sacrificed—her real self. As they consider all the sacrifices made, they may be thinking about an important theme of the novel.	YOUR NOTES

LOCATION: *Chapter 26, Page 166* Sal realizes that her father was probably as frustrated with her behavior as she is now frustrated with Phoebe's.

Aha Moment	
WHAT WE NOTICED We noticed here that Sal suddenly recognizes that how she feels about Phoebe's behavior is probably how her father felt about her own behavior. The key question for an Aha Moment—how might this change things—pushes us to think about how Sal is maturing, coming to understand her own actions and how they affect others.	YOUR NOTES

NOTICE AND NOTE SIGNPOSTS IN *WALK TWO MOONS*

LOCATION: *Chapter 27, Page 175* Sal wonders if worry is a part of life and if death can precede birth.

Tough Questions	
WHAT WE NOTICED Here Sal asks herself several difficult questions. She asks if worry is always a part of life and reveals that she worries about something going wrong even when things seem to be going well. She also asks about the relationship between birth and death. While she's probably wondering if the baby died while still in utero, she also has posed an interesting question about having to give up something (a type of death) before moving on to something else (a type of new life).	YOUR NOTES

LOCATION: *Chapter 27, Page 176* Sal's grandparents imply that her mother's departure had nothing to do with her.

Aha Moment	
WHAT WE NOTICED This is a critical Aha Moment as Sal finally understands something her grandparents have wanted her to realize. They confirm Sal's thought that Phoebe hadn't caused her mother to leave. At that point, for "the first time," as Sal flatly tells us, it occurs to her that perhaps she hadn't been responsible for her own mother leaving. Since Aha Moments help us understand how a character is changing, be sure to encourage your students to think through the key question: How might this change things?	YOUR NOTES

LOCATION: *Chapter 30, Page 194* Sal and Phoebe discuss the letter Sal's mom had left her and why someone would leave without an explanation.

Memory Moment	
WHAT WE NOTICED Sal recalls the letter her mom had left for her. Some students might identify this as Again and Again, since the letter comes up more than once, and that's fine. The name doesn't matter. What matters is that they are noticing that Sal is referring to her mom's letter and trying to figure out what her mom has done. When characters return to something in their own past, we usually gain insight into internal conflict. The letter was first mentioned on page 110.	YOUR NOTES

NOTICE AND NOTE SIGNPOSTS IN *WALK TWO MOONS*

LOCATION: *Chapter 33, Page 221* Sal questions if Mrs. Cadaver understood what things were worth before she lost them.

Tough Questions	
WHAT WE NOTICED	YOUR NOTES
Sal has been thinking about the note that was left on the porch and wonders if Mrs. Cadaver understood the worth of what she had before it was lost. Tough Questions like this one give insight into internal conflict and theme. Although some of our notes are brief, the moments are all critical. We wanted to show a mix of longer and shorter notes.	

LOCATION: *Chapter 39, Pages 245–246* Phoebe's mother appears with short hair and lipstick.

Contrasts and Contradictions	
WHAT WE NOTICED	YOUR NOTES
Watch for dramatic contrasts. Here, Phoebe's mother's appearance has changed drastically, showing us something about character development. Obviously, something has happened.	

LOCATION: *Chapter 41, Page 257* Sal reflects on all that has happened and reaches some conclusions.

Aha Moment	
WHAT WE NOTICED	YOUR NOTES
Several times on this page, Sal tells us, "Then I started thinking . . ." or "I thought about. . . ." Although she says nothing so definite as "Suddenly I realized. . . ," it's clear that she is coming to understand something significant. When characters say repeatedly that they are thinking about something, we want readers to pay attention to those thoughts.	

LOCATION: *Chapter 44, Page 277* Sal shares what she has figured out.

Aha Moment	
WHAT WE NOTICED	YOUR NOTES
Sal has journeyed a long way. It's not unusual in young adult novels for the author to wrap up by letting the protagonist explain what she has figured out. Sometimes that is done in dialogue with another character; other times, as in this book, it is done through internal monologue. When students know that they are reading the end of a book, and they see the main character using words like "explain" and "discover," they should realize that the character is sharing all she has figured out, generally giving us one last nudge toward theme.	

On the following pages are the texts that you'll want to reproduce for students when you teach each signpost lesson. Electronic versions of most texts can also be found at www.NoticeandNote.com.

The selections appear in the following order:

THANK YOU, MA'M

by Langston Hughes

She was a large woman with a large purse that had everything in it but a hammer and nails. It had a long strap, and she carried it slung across her shoulder. It was about eleven o'clock at night, dark, and she was walking alone, when a boy ran up behind her and tried to snatch her purse. The strap broke with the sudden single tug the boy gave it from behind. But the boy's weight and the weight of the purse combined caused him to lose his balance. Instead of taking off full blast as he had hoped, the boy fell on his back on the sidewalk and his legs flew up. The large woman simply turned around and kicked him right square in his blue-jeaned sitter. Then she reached down, picked the boy up by his shirt front, and shook him until his teeth rattled.

After that the woman said, "Pick up my pocketbook, boy, and give it here."

She still held him tightly. But she bent down enough to permit him to stoop and pick up her purse. Then she said, "Now ain't you ashamed of yourself?"

Firmly gripped by his shirt front, the boy said, "Yes'm."

The woman said, "What did you want to do it for?"

The boy said, "I didn't aim to."

She said, "You a lie!"

By that time two or three people passed, stopped, turned to look, and some stood watching.

"If I turn you loose, will you run?" asked the woman.

"Yes'm," said the boy.

"Then I won't turn you loose," said the woman. She did not release him.

"Lady, I'm sorry," whispered the boy.

"Um-hum! Your face is dirty. I got a great mind to wash your face for you. Ain't you got nobody home to tell you to wash your face?"

"No'm," said the boy.

"Then it will get washed this evening," said the large woman, starting up the street, dragging the frightened boy behind her.

He looked as if he were fourteen or fifteen, frail and willow-wild in tennis shoes and blue jeans.

The woman said, "You ought to be my son. I would teach you right from wrong. Least I can do right now is to wash your face. Are you hungry?"

"No'm," said the being-dragged boy. "I just want you to turn me loose."

"Was I bothering you when I turned that corner?" asked the woman.

"No'm."

"But you put yourself in contact with me," said the woman. "If you think that contact is not going to last awhile, you got another thought coming. When I get through with you, sir, you are going to remember Mrs. Luella Bates Washington Jones."

Sweat popped out on the boy's face and he began to struggle. Mrs. Jones stopped, jerked him around in front of her, put a half-nelson about his neck, and continued to drag him up the street. When she got to her door, she dragged the boy inside, down a hall, and into a large kitchenette-furnished room at the rear of the house. She switched on the light and left the door open. The boy could hear other roomers laughing and talking in the large house. Some of their doors were open, too, so he knew he and the woman were not alone. The woman still had him by the neck in the middle of her room.

She said, "What is your name?"

"Roger," answered the boy.

"Then, Roger, you go to that sink and wash your face," said the woman, whereupon she turned him loose—at last. Roger looked at the door—looked at the woman—looked at the door—and went to the sink.

"Let the water run until it gets warm," she said. "Here's a clean towel."

"You gonna take me to jail?" asked the boy, bending over the sink.

"Not with that face, I would not take you nowhere," said the woman. "Here I am trying to get home to cook me a bite to eat, and you snatch my pocketbook! Maybe you ain't been to your supper either, late as it be. Have you?"

"There's nobody home at my house," said the boy.

"Then we'll eat," said the woman. "I believe you're hungry— or been hungry—to try to snatch my pocketbook!"

"I want a pair of blue suede shoes," said the boy.

"Well, you didn't have to snatch my pocketbook to get some suede shoes," said Mrs. Luella Bates Washington Jones. "You could of asked me."

"Ma'm?"

The water dripping from his face, the boy looked at her. There was a long pause. A very long pause. After he had dried his face and not knowing what else to do, dried it again, the boy turned around, wondering what next. The door was open. He would make a dash for it down the hall. He would run, run, run!

The woman was sitting on the day bed. After a while, she said, "I were young once and I wanted things I could not get."

There was another long pause. The boy's mouth opened. Then he frowned, not knowing he frowned.

The woman said, "Um-hum! You thought I was going to say but, didn't you? You thought I was going to say, but I didn't snatch people's pocketbooks. Well, I wasn't going to say that." Pause. Silence. "I have done things, too, which I would not tell you, son— neither tell God, if He didn't already know. Everybody's got some- thing in common. Sit you down while I fix us something to eat. You might run that comb through your hair so you will look presentable."

In another corner of the room behind a screen was a gas plate and an icebox. Mrs. Jones got up and went behind the screen. The woman did not watch the boy to see if he was going to run now, nor did she watch her purse, which she left behind her on the day-bed. But the boy took care to sit on the far side of the room, away from the purse, where he thought she could easily see him out of the corner of her eye if she wanted to. He did not trust the woman to trust him. And he did not trust the woman not to trust him. And he did not want to be mistrusted now.

"Do you need somebody to go to the store," asked the boy, "maybe to get some milk or something?"

"Don't believe I do," said the woman, "unless you just want sweet milk yourself. I was going to make cocoa out of this canned milk I got here."

She heated some lima beans and ham she had in the icebox, made the cocoa, and set the table. The woman did not ask the boy anything about where he lived, or his folks, or anything else that would embarrass him. Instead, as they ate, she told him about her job in a hotel beauty shop that stayed open late, what the work was like, and how all kinds of women came in and out, blondes, red-heads, and Spanish. Then she cut him half of her ten-cent cake.

"Eat some more, son," she said.

When they finished eating, she got up and said, "Now here, take this ten dollars and buy yourself some blue suede shoes. And, next time, do not make the mistake of latching onto my pocket-book nor nobody else's—because shoes got by devilish ways will burn your feet. I got to get my rest now. But from here on in, son, I hope you will behave yourself."

She led the way down the hall to the front door and opened it. "Good night! Behave yourself, boy!" she said, looking into the street as he went down the steps.

The boy wanted to say something other than "Thank you, Ma'm," to Mrs. Luella Bates Washington Jones, but although his lips moved, he couldn't even say that, as he turned at the foot of the barren stoop and looked up at the large woman in the door. Then she shut the door. And he never saw her again.

Excerpts from **CRASH**

by Jerry Spinelli

It was a sunny summer day. I was in the front yard digging a hole with my little red shovel. I heard something like whistling. I looked up. It was whistling. It was coming from a funny-looking dorky little runt walking up the sidewalk. Only he wasn't just walking regular. He was walking like he owned the place, both hands in his pockets, sort of swaying lah-dee-dah with each step. *Strollll*-ing. Strolling and gawking at the houses and whistling a happy little dorky tune like some Sneezy or Snoozy or whatever their names are.

And he wore a button, a big one. It covered about half his chest. Which wasn't that hard since his chest was so scrawny.

So here he comes strolling, whistling, gawking, buttoning, dorking up the sidewalk, onto my sidewalk, my property, and all of a sudden I knew what I had to do, like there was a big announcement coming down from the sky: Don't let him pass.

_____

The stands were empty. A school bus moved in the distance beyond the football goalpost. Under the crossbar and between the uprights, like in a framed picture, stood three people.

For once, Webb's parents didn't look so old, not compared to the man standing between them. He was shorter than them, and real skinny, like the prairie winds were eroding him away. But he was standing straight and by himself—no cane, no walker, just two legs. Ninety-three years old. Maybe it was the Missouri River mud.

The thought came to me: they would have liked each other, Scooter and Henry Wilhide Webb III. Two storytellers. Both from the great flat open spaces, one a prairie of grass, one of water. Both came to watch when no one else was there.

_____

Why exactly was he here? Did he know about me? Did he know his great grandson could not win the race-off, and so would not run in the Penn Relays?

I wondered if Webb felt safe in his great grandfather's bed.

The cinder track crunched under my feet. There were five of us in the race: me, Webb, two other seventh graders, and a sixth grader. The coach put us in lanes. Me and Webb were side by side.

Again, he hadn't said a word to me all day. We milled around behind the starting blocks, nervous, shaking out our arms and legs, everything as quiet as if the coach had already said, "Ready."

The other team members—jumpers, throwers, distance runners—had all stopped their practicing to watch. A single hawk, its wingtips spread like black fingers, kited over the school, and suddenly I saw something: a gift. A gift for a great grandfather from North Dakota, maybe for all great grandfathers. But the thing was, only one person could give the gift, and it wasn't the great grandson, not on his fastest day alive. It was me.

I hated it being me. I tried not to see, but everywhere I looked, there it was.

The gift.

"Let's go, boys," said the coach.

A voice closer to me said, "Good luck."

It was Webb, sticking out his dorky hand, smiling that old dorky smile of his. No button. I shook his hand, and it occurred to me that because he was always eating my dust, the dumb fishcake had never won a real race and probably didn't know how. And now there wasn't time.

"Don't forget to lean," I told him. His face went blank. The coach called, "Ready."

I got down, feet in the blocks, right knee on the track, thumbs and forefingers on the chalk, eyes straight down—and right then, for the first time in my life, I didn't know if I wanted to win.

"Set."

Knee up, rear up, eyes up.

The coach says the most important thing here is to focus your mind. You are a coiled steel spring, ready to dart out at the sound of the gun. So what comes into my head? Ollie the one-armed octopus. He didn't disappear till the gun went off.

I was behind—not only Webb, but everybody. No problem. Within ten strides I picked up three of them. That left Webb. He was farther ahead of me than usual, but that was because of my rotten start.

At the halfway mark, where I usually passed him, he was still ahead, and I still didn't know if I wanted to win. I gassed it. The gap closed. I could hear him puffing, like a second set of footsteps. Cinder flecks from his feet pecked at my shins. I was still behind. The finish line was closing. I kicked in the afterburners. Ten meters from the white string we were shoulder to shoulder, breath to breath, grandson to great grandson, and it felt new, it felt good, not being behind, not being ahead, but being even, and just like that, a half breath from the white string, I knew. There was no time to turn to him. I just barked it out: "Lean!" He leaned, he threw his chest out, he broke the string. He won.

Excerpts from *A LONG WALK TO WATER*

by Linda Sue Park

Salva lowered his head and ran.

He ran until he could not run anymore. Then he walked. For hours, until the sun was nearly gone from the sky.

Other people were walking, too. There were so many of them that they couldn't all be from the school village; they must have come from the whole area.

As Salva walked, the same thoughts kept going through his head in rhythm with his steps. *Where are we going? Where is my family? When will I see them again?*

———————————

There were now three women giving water to the men on the ground.

Like a miracle, the small amounts of water revived them. They were able to stagger to their feet and join the group as the walking continued.

But their five dead companions were left behind. There were no tools with which to dig, and besides, burying the dead men would have taken too much time.

Salva tried not to look as he walked past the bodies, but his eyes were drawn in their direction. He knew what would happen. Vultures would find the bodies and strip them of their rotting flesh until only the bones remained. He felt sick at the thought of those men—first dying in such a horrible way, and then having even their corpses ravaged.

If he were older and stronger, would he have given water to those men? Or would he, like most of the group, have kept his water for himself?

It was the group's third day in the desert. By sunset, they would be out of the desert, and after that, it would not be far to the Itang refugee camp in Ethiopia.

———————————

I am alone now.

I am all that is left of my family.

His father, who had sent Salva to school . . . brought him treats, like mangoes . . . trusted him to take care of the herd. . . . His mother, always ready with food and milk and a soft hand to stroke Salva's head. His brothers and sisters, whom he had laughed with and played with and looked after. . . . He would never see them again.

How can I go on without them?

But how can I not go on? They would want me to survive . . . to grow up and make something of my life . . . to honor their memories.

Excerpts from **RIDING FREEDOM**

by Pam Muñoz Ryan

"Thanks, Vern. I wish I could stay with you and work with the horses, but . . . I'd be in the kitchen and I'd be missin' Justice and frettin' 'cause I wouldn't get to see Charity's foal . . . or help you name it."

"I know. I know, Miss Charlotte," said Vern. "You gotta do what your heart tells you."

"I won't ever forget you," said Charlotte.

"I guess I'm not likely to forget you, Miss Charlotte."

———————————————

"Here were six strong horses waiting for her commands, her tugs on the reins, to tell them which way to go. She yelled, "Haw" and "Gee" to get them to bear left and right, like she did when she was riding one horse or driving two.

She wished Hayward could see her. And Vern. Vern would have never let her get out of that wagon until she figured out the turns. Just like when he taught her to ride, he kept putting her back on Freedom [her horse] after each fall, saying, "Every time you fall, you learn somethin' new 'bout your horse. You learn what not to do next time."

———————————————

"What are you blabberin' about? The mail's gotta go through, same as them passengers."

Ebeneezer put his hand on Charlotte's shoulder. "Now listen, don't you pay them passengers no mind. You are what you are. And what you are, is a fine horseman. And the best coachman I ever saw. You remember that. Under the circumstances, there ain't nothing left for you to do but your job. So get to it."

Charlotte looked square at Ebeneezer.

Ebeneezer looked square back at Charlotte and said, "You're the coachman. You're in charge, so load 'em up."

Excerpts from **HATCHET**

by Gary Paulsen

Brian Robeson stared out the window of the small plane at the endless green northern wilderness below. It was a small plane, a Cessna 406—a bush plane—and the engine was so loud, so roaring and consuming and loud, that it ruined any chance for conversation.

Not that he had much to say. He was thirteen and the only passenger on the plane with a pilot named—what was it? Jim or Jake or something—who was in his mid-forties and who had been silent as he worked to prepare for take-off. In fact since Brian had come to the small airport in Hampton, New York to meet the plane—driven by his mother—the pilot had spoken only five words to him.

"Get in the copilot's seat."

Which Brian had done. They had taken off and that was the last of the conversation. There had been the initial excitement, of course. He had never flown in a single-engine plane before and to be sitting in the copilot's seat with all the controls right there in front of him, all the instruments in his face as the plane clawed for altitude, jerking and sliding on the wind currents as the pilot took off, had been interesting and exciting. . . .

Now Brian sat, looking out the window with the roar thundering through his ears, and tried to catalog what had led up to his taking this flight.

The thinking started.

Always it started with a single word.

Divorce.

It was an ugly word, he thought. A tearing, ugly word that meant fights and yelling, lawyers—God, he thought, how he hated lawyers who sat with their comfortable smiles and tried to explain to him in legal terms how all that he lived in was coming apart—and the breaking and shattering of all the solid things. His home, his life—all the solid things. Divorce. A breaking word, an ugly breaking word.

———————————————————————————

Divorce.

Secrets.

No, not secrets so much as just the Secret. What he knew and had not told anybody, what he knew about his mother that had caused the divorce, what he knew, what he knew—the Secret.

Divorce.

The Secret.

———————————————————————————

Brian felt his eyes beginning to burn and knew there would be tears. He had cried for a time, but that was gone now. He didn't cry now. . . .

The pilot sat large, his hands lightly on the wheel, feet on the rudder pedals. He seemed more a machine than a man, an extension of the plane. . . .

When he saw Brian look at him, the pilot seemed to open up a bit and he smiled. "Ever fly in the copilot's seat before?" He leaned over and lifted the headset off his right ear and put it on his temple, yelling to overcome the sound of the engine.

Brian shook his head. . . .

"It's not as complicated as it looks. Good plane like this almost flies itself." The pilot shrugged. "Makes my job easy." He took Brian's left arm. "Here, put your hands on the controls, your feet on the rudder pedals, and I'll show you what I mean."

Brian shook his head. "I'd better not."

"Sure. Try it. . . ."

Brian reached out and took the wheel in a grip so tight his knuckles were white. He pushed his feet down on the pedals. The plane slewed suddenly to the right.

"Not so hard. Take her light, take her light."

Brian eased off, relaxed his grip. The burning in his eyes was forgotten momentarily as the vibration of the plane came through the wheel and the pedals. It seemed almost alive.

"See?" The pilot let go of his wheel, raised his hands in the air and took his feet off the pedals to show Brian he was actually flying the plane alone. "Simple. Now turn the wheel a little to the right and push on the right rudder pedal a small amount."

Brian turned the wheel slightly and the plane immediately banked to the right, and when he pressed on the right rudder pedal the nose slid across the horizon to the right. He left off on the pressure and straightened the wheel and the plane righted itself.

"Now you can turn. Bring her back to the left a little."

Brian turned the wheel left, pushed on the left pedal, and the plane came back around. "It's easy." He smiled. "At least this part."

The pilot nodded. "All of flying is easy. Just takes learning. Like everything else. Like everything else." He took the controls back, then reached up and rubbed his left shoulder. "Aches and pains— must be getting old."

Brian let go of the controls and moved his feet away from the pedals as the pilot put his hands on the wheel. "Thank you. . . ."

But the pilot had put his headset back on and the gratitude was lost in the engine noise and things went back to Brian looking out the window at the ocean of trees and lakes. The burning eyes did not come back, but memories did, came flooding in. The words. Always the words.

Divorce.

The Secret.

Fights.

Split.

The big split. Brian's father did not understand as Brian did, knew only that Brian's mother wanted to break the marriage apart. The split had come and then the divorce, all so fast, and the court had left him with his mother except for the summers and what the judge called "visitation rights." So formal.

Excerpts from HOPE WAS HERE

by Joan Bauer

We walked across the street to the old Buick that was packed to the hilt with everything we owned and had a U-Haul trailer chained to the back.

It was May 26. We were heading to Mulhoney, Wisconsin, to start work in a diner there that needed a professional manager and cook (Addie), was short on waitresses (me), and was giving us an apartment. The man we were going to work for had been diagnosed with leukemia and needed help fast. I don't mean to sound ungenerous, but working for a close-to-dying man didn't sound like a great career move to me. I had to leave school right before the end of my undistinguished sophomore year, too.

I hate leaving places I love.

We were about to get into the car just as Morty the cabdriver double-parked his Yellow taxi.

Good old Morty. The first time I waited on him, he unloosened his belt a notch before he even looked at the menu. I knew I had a true believer.

I raised my hand to a great tipper.

"You always took care of me, kid!" He shouted this from across the street as a UPS truck started honking at him to move his cab.

"I tried, Morty!"

"Wherever you go, you'll do okay. You got heart!"

The UPS driver screamed something heartless at Morty, who screamed back, "Watch your mouth, big man in a brown truck!"

I didn't know what kind of customers I'd get in Wisconsin.

She grabbed my hand and gave it a squeeze.

Addie never promised that life would be easy, but she did promise that if I hung with her the food would be good.

Believe me when I tell you, I know about survival.

I was born too early and much too small (two pounds and five ounces). For the first month of my life I kept gasping for air, like I couldn't get the hang of breathing. I couldn't eat either; couldn't suck a bottle. The doctors didn't think I would make it. Shows what they know. My mother didn't want the responsibility of a baby so she left me with Addie, her older sister, and went off to live her own life. I've seen her exactly three times since I was born— when she visited on my fifth, eighth, and thirteenth birthdays.

Each time she talked about being a waitress. What made a good one ("great hands and personality"). What were the pitfalls ("crazed cooks and being on your feet all day"). What was the biggest tip she ever got ($300 from a plumber who had just won the instant lottery).

Each time she told me, "Hon, leaving you with Addie was the best thing I could have done for you. You need constants in your life." She had a different hair color each time she said it.

Addie's been my number-one constant. . . .

Because of this, I don't buy into traditional roles. My favorite book when I was little had pictures of baby animals, like foxes and lambs and ducklings, who were being raised by other animals, like dogs, geese, and wolves.

Addie said it was our story.

_____

I stared out the window as the Buick roared west to whatever.

Harrison Beckworth-McCoy, my best male friend at school, . . . had given me a goodbye present, and I was opening it now as Addie pushed the Buick through Ohio. Inside the box was a small glass prism that caught the sun. A hand-printed note from Harrison read, "New places always help us look at life differently. I will miss you, but won't lose you."

Harrison was always saying sensitive things like that, which put him instantly on Jocelyn Lindstrom's male sensitivity chart. He was the only male either of us knew who had made the chart consistently over twelve months. Donald Raspigi, who occasionally said sensitive things like "Nice sweater," had been on twice.

Enter memories, sweet and sour.

Harrison and me baking enormous mocha chip cookies for the high school bake sale and having them stolen on the Lexington Avenue subway.

Harrison's African fighting fish, Luther, who ate Chef Boyardee ravioli without chewing.

Harrison reading my mother's photocopied annual Christmas letter that she sent to family and friends—"Dear Friends. . . ." (She'd cross out "Friends" and write in "Addie and my little Tulip.") Harrison commenting that motherhood should be like driving a car—you should have to pass a test before you get to do it legally.

I held the prism up to the light. The sun hit it and showered colors through the windshield. "Now isn't that something?" Addie said, smiling at the sight. "Yeah." I looked out the window, trying not to cry.

Acknowledgments and Thanks

Along the way we have said thank you to many people, but now it is nice to be able to do so in print. First, each member of our families heard far more about lessons and signposts and anchor questions, about the section that was easily written or the one paragraph that just never worked, about page proofs and drafts and revisions than any one of them ever wanted to hear. And yet they smiled through it all, nodded when nods were needed, and kept saying they believed in us and our work. Thank you to each of you for that, more than these "ink spots on paper" can impart.

When we started this project, Lisa Luedeke was our editor at Heinemann. Her wisdom, advice, observations, and smart editorial comments were always welcomed and then were sorely missed when she moved on to new professional pursuits. Other Heinemann folks also provided appreciated direction and support: Debra Doorack, Anita Gildea, Charles McQuillen, Lisa Fowler, and Stephanie Levy. The meetings with this group of people were always helpful. They know how to listen, question, explore, suggest, guide, and encourage. They know how we like our coffee, that we want vegetarian wraps for lunch, that the Oar House is our favorite end-of-day debriefing place, and that eventually they must take the manuscript from our hands because there will always be one more word we want to change, one more sentence we aren't sure reads just right.

A special thanks to Lisa Fowler, who always understood that we just needed her near, even if the meeting didn't directly involve her. We think about design as we create content, and her genius in design was, and will always be, a great inspiration to us. And though not in the Heinemann office, Carol Schanche, our longtime friend and brilliant editor, read much of this manuscript, and those parts are better because of her.

A special word about Lesa Scott, president of Heinemann. Lesa likes to talk about "author care" at Heinemann because Lesa cares deeply about the authors who publish through this company. We think that phrase, "author care," doesn't actually embody what Heinemann is all about but that the better phrase is "Heinemann cares." Heinemann cares about teachers, about students, about the direction and quality of education in this country, and about the authors who choose to link their names to the Heinemann brand. When you read a Heinemann book, you arc holding something that was published by a company that understands that profit should be measured by something more than dollars; the real profit is what a book might do in a teacher's life and in the lives of the students she teaches. This company's commitment to standing alongside teachers would not exist without a leader who stands firm in her ideals.

Literally hundreds of teachers from across the nation tried one or more of these lessons and gave us feedback. In particular, a group of about 250 teachers from South Carolina met with us repeatedly one year. They learned the lessons from us, took them to their students, and then returned to share their insights. We heard how they worked with texts from *Medea* to *Chrysanthemum*. Their feedback and suggestions were critical. Other groups in Akron, Ohio; Gwinnett County, Georgia; Orange County Public Schools, in Orlando, Florida; Dallas, Texas; and Sheridan, Arkansas, also provided needed and valuable help.

We are particularly thankful to Lee Smith, from Dallas, who showed us a new way to teach the lessons. Likewise, Jeff William, a brilliant teacher, literacy coach, and someone we're proud to call friend, in Solon, Ohio, shared his time, talent, and smart thinking with us whenever we asked. Margaret Ruppert, Deborah Leonard, and Marcy Aronson—all literacy coaches in Akron, Ohio—worked closely with us for two years, and they were always willing to help us think through concerns. Amanda Youngblood, from the Orange County Schools, in Orlando, Florida, and Terry Brennan and Joan Boyce, from the Wauwatosa School District, in Wisconsin, shared with us modifications they made to some of our templates, adapting them to their own students. Beth Vincente, a middle-school teacher in Akron, shared her students with us repeatedly so we could try lessons with them. Jennifer Ochoa, teacher extraordinaire in the New York City Public Schools, not only reviewed lessons for us, but taught them, let us into her classroom so we could teach them, shared with us the Notice and Note posters she created and that you see throughout the pages of this book, and gave us a critical idea that re-shaped much of our thinking. We turn to Jen for advice (and for dinner) whenever we can! Hal Foster—colleague, friend, and mentor—opened his home to us and, as always, opened our minds to new thoughts.

And to all the students we taught while crafting these lessons, our thanks. We owe a special thank you to students at Innes Middle School in Akron, Ohio, and Sheridan Middle School, in Sheridan, Arkansas. You are smart, funny, curious, and caring kids, and we appreciate your sharing your time with us. Our only sadness was that our time with you was too short. But our memories of you, we promise, will be long. Sha'Mia—we think of you often with smiles and hopes for all we know you will become.

But our deepest thanks go to you, our readers. You'll try what's in here; find ways to make the lessons better; change them so that they are uniquely yours. You'll keep on teaching through the foolishness that seems to be a part of education these days. When people talk of measuring the "value added" by a teacher, we tell them they don't need complicated mathematical formulas. They need only to look at you—you arrive early, stay late, celebrate your students' successes, worry over those who need more than perhaps you can give, and always you wonder what else you can do. We laugh at the thought that your value is measurable by a test score. You are a part of children's lives, a critical player in their development as lifelong learners. That is immeasurable, as is our gratitude for all that you do.

> We laugh at the thought that your value is measurable by a test score. You are a part of children's lives, a critical player in their development as lifelong learners. That is immeasurable, as is our gratitude for all that you do.

Bibliographies

Professional Works Cited

"Accountable Talk in Reading Comprehension Instruction." Accessed at http://cse.ucla.edu/products/reports/r670.pdf.

American Library Association. 2012. "The State of America's Libraries." Accessed at http://www.ala.org/tools/libfactsheets /alalibraryfactsheet06#state.

Bleich, David. 1978. *Subjective Criticism*. Baltimore, MD: Johns Hopkins University Press.

Calkins, Lucy, Mary Ehrenworth, and Christopher Lehman. 2012. *Pathways to the Common Core: Accelerating Achievement*. Portsmouth, NH: Heinemann.

Carlsen, G. Robert. 1980. *Books and the Teenage Reader: A Guide for Teachers, Librarians and Parents*. 2nd revised ed. New York: Harper & Row.

Carr, Nicholas. 2008. "Is Google Making Us Stupid?" *The Atlantic*, July/August. Accessed at http://www.theatlantic.com/magazine /toc/2008/07/.

_____. 2010. *The Shallows*. New York: W. W. Norton.

Cascio, Jamais. 2009. "Get Smarter." *The Atlantic*, July/August. Accessed at http://www.theatlantic.com/magazine/archive/2009/07 /get-smarter/7548/.

Chandler, Otis. 2012. "Goodreads: How People Discover Books Online." Paper read at Tools of Change Conference, 15 February, New York. Accessed at http://www.slideshare.net/PatrickBR/goodreads-how -people-discover-books.

Chubb, Percival. 1914. "The Blight of Literary Bookishness." *English Journal* 3 (1): 15–27.

Coleman, David, and Susan Pimentel. 2012. "Revised Publishers' Criteria for the Common Core State Standards." Accessed at http://groups .ascd.org/resource/documents/122463-PublishersCriteriaforLiteracy forGrades3-12.pdf.

Cotton, Kathleen. 1988. Classroom Questioning. North West Regional Educational Laboratory. Accessed at http://educationnorthwest.org/webfm_send/569.

Early, Margaret. 1960. "Stages of Growth in Literary Appreciation." *English Journal* 49 (3): 161–67.

Ericson, Bonnie, Mary Hubler, Thomas W. Bean, Christine C. Smith, and Joanna Vellone McKenzie. "Increasing Critical Reading in Junior High Classrooms." *Journal of Reading* 30 (5): 430–39.

Farrell, Edmund J. 2005. "A Tribute to Louise." *Voices from the Middle* 12 (3): 68–69.

Frey, Nancy, Diane Lapp, and Doug Fisher. 2012. *Text Complexity: Raising Rigor in Reading*. Newark, DE: International Reading Association.

Gewertz, Catherine. 2012. "Teachers Embedding Standards in Basal-Reader Questions." *Education Week*, April 26, 32.

Holland, Norman N. 1968. *The Dynamics of Literary Response*. New York: Oxford University Press.

Iser, Wolfgang. 1978. *The Act of Reading: A Theory of Aesthetic Response*. Baltimore, MD: Johns Hopkins University Press.

Kelly, Kevin. 2010. "Reading in a Whole New Way." *Smithsonian Magazine*. Accessed at http://www.smithsonianmag.com/specialsections/40th-anniversary/ Reading-in-a-Whole-New-Way.html.

Lesesne, Teri S. 2003. *Making the Match: The Right Book for the Right Reader at the Right Time, Grades 4–12*. Portland, ME: Stenhouse.

_____. 2010. *Reading Ladders*. Portsmouth, NH: Heinemann.

Manguel, Alberto. 1996. *A History of Reading*. New York: Viking.

Miller, Donalyn. 2009. *The Book Whisperer: Awakening the Inner Reader in Every Child*. San Francisco: Jossey-Bass.

Moyers, Bill. 1992. "Old News and the New Civil War." Editorial. *New York Times*, March 22.

National Endowment for the Arts. 2007. *To Read or Not to Read*. Accessed at http://www.nea.gov/research/ToRead_ExecSum.pdf.

National Governors Association Center for Best Practices, Council of Chief State School Officers. 2010. *Common Core State Standards for English Language Arts & Literacy in History/Social Studies, Science, and Technical Subjects*. National Governors Association Center for Best Practices, Council of Chief State School Officers, Washington,

DC. Accessed at: http://www.corestandards.org/the-standards/english-language-arts-standards/.

Nystrand, Martin, L. Lawrence, Adam Gamoran Wu, Susie Zeiser, and Daniel A. Long. 2003. "Questions in Time: Investigating the Structure and Dynamics of Unfolding Classroom Discourse." *Discourse Processes* 35 (2): 135–95.

Oatley, Keith. 2011. "In the Minds of Others." *Scientific American*, November/December 2011, 63–67.

Paul, Annie Murphy. 2012. "Your Brain on Fiction." *New York Times*, March 17.

Pew Research Center's Project for Excellence in Journalism. 2011. "The State of the News Media 2011." Accessed at http://pewresearch.org/pubs/1924/state-of-the-news-media-2011.

Pink, Daniel. 2010. "Drive: The Surprising Truth About What Motivates Us." Video created by RSA Animate. Accessed at http://www.youtube.com/watch?v=u6XAPnuFjJc.

Probst, Robert. E. 1984. *Adolescent Literature: Response and Analysis*. Columbus, OH: Charles E. Merrill.

Publisher's Weekly. 2012. "AAP Estimates: E-book Sales Rose 117% in 2011 as Print Fell." Accessed at http://www.publishersweekly.com/pw/by-topic/industry-news/financial-reporting/article/50805-aap-estimates-e-book-sales-rose-117-in-2011-as-print-fell.html.

Romano, Tom. 2000. *Blending Genre, Altering Style: Writing Multigenre Papers*. Portsmouth, NH: Heinemann Boynton/Cook.

Rosenblatt, Louise, M. 1938/1995. *Literature as Exploration*. New York: Modern Language Association.

_____. 2005. *Making Meaning with Texts: Selected Essays*. Portsmouth, NH: Heinemann.

_____. 1978/1994. *The Reader, the Text, the Poem: The Transactional Theory of the Literary Work*. Carbondale, IL: Southern Illinois University Press.

Rowntree, Derek. 1977. *How Shall We Know Them?* London: Harper & Row.

Sherman, Erik. 2012. "Facebook's IPO by the (Important) Numbers." CBSNews.com. Accessed at http://www.cbsnews.com/8301-505124_162-57435086/facebooks-ipo-by-the-important-numbers/.

U.S. Department of Education, National Center for Education Statistics. 2010. *Digest of Education Statistics 2009* (NCES 2010-013). Washington, DC: U.S. Government Printing Office.

VanDeWeghe, Rick. 2003. "Classroom Discussions of Literature." *English Journal* 93 (1): 87–91.

_____. 2007. "Research Matters: What Kinds of Classroom Discussion Promote Reading Comprehension?" *English Journal* 96 (3): 86–91.

Wilde, Sandra. 2000. *Miscue Analysis Made Easy: Building on Student Strengths*. Portsmouth, NH: Heinemann.

Trade Books/Stories/Poems Cited

Many novels are mentioned throughout *Notice and Note*. We don't include the complete list of all stories or novels in this bibliography primarily because with search engines it is easy for you to find any of those titles with a quick trip to your favorite digital (or brick-and-mortar) bookstore. We did, however, discuss some titles at such length that we felt it best to include bibliographic information for those works here.

Babbitt, Natalie. 1975. *Tuck Everlasting*. New York: Farrar, Straus & Giroux.

Bauer, Joan. 2000. *Hope Was Here*. New York: Putnam.

Collier, John. 1972. "The Chaser." *The John Collier Reader*, 508–510. New York: Knopf.

Connell, Richard. 1924. "The Most Dangerous Game." Accessed at http://manybooks.net/titles/connellrother09most_dangerous_game.html.

Coffin, Robert P. Tristram. 1949. "Forgive My Guilt." *Atlantic Monthly* 183 (May): 60.

Creech, Sharon. 1994. *Walk Two Moons*. New York: HarperTrophy.

Curtis, Christopher Paul. 1995. *The Watsons Go to Birmingham—1963*. New York: Delacorte.

Frank, Anne. 1967. *Anne Frank: The Diary of a Young Girl*. Trans. B. M. Mooyaart. New York: Bantam.

Haddix, Margaret. 2000. *Among the Hidden*. New York: Aladdin.

Hinton, S. E. 2006. *The Outsiders*. New York: Speak Penguin Group USA.

Hughes, Langston. 1997. "Thank You, Ma'm." In *Short Stories of Langston Hughes*, edited by A. S. Harper (223–226). New York: Hill & Wang.

Lowry, Lois. 1999. *The Giver*. New York: Houghton Mifflin.

Namioka, Lensey. 2003. *Half and Half*. New York: Random House.

Ryan, Pam Muñoz. 2000. *Esperanza Rising*. New York: Scholastic.

_____. 2007. *Riding Freedom*. New York: Scholastic/Apple Paperbacks.

Spinelli, Jerry. 1996. *Crash*. New York: Random House.

Taylor, Edward. 1989. "Huswifery." In *The Poems of Edward Taylor*, edited by D. E. Stanford (p. 343). Chapel Hill: University of North Carolina Press.

Park, Linda Sue. 2010. *A Long Walk to Water*. New York: Clarion.

Paulsen, Gary. 1999. *Hatchet*. New York: Simon & Schuster Books for Young Readers.

Waber, Bernard. 1973. *Ira Sleeps Over*. New York: Houghton Mifflin.

Works That Influenced Our Thinking

Though we did not reference or quote from these books, they have nonetheless affected our thinking about literacy education. We appreciate the work and dedication of these authors and encourage you to find the texts you've not read and read them, perhaps with a colleague.

Allington, Richard L. 2001. *What Really Matters for Struggling Readers: Designing Research-Based Programs*. New York: Addison-Wesley.

Appleman, Deborah. 2010. *Adolescent Literacy and the Teaching of Reading*. Urbana, IL: National Council of Teachers of English.

Baca, Jimmy Santiago, and ReLeah C. Lent. 2010. *Adolescents on the Edge*. Portsmouth, NH: Heinemann.

Beers, Kylene. 2005. "Remembering Louise Rosenblatt." *Voices from the Middle* 12 (3).

_____. 2002. *When Kids Can't Read, What Teachers Can Do: A Guide for Teachers*. Portsmouth, NH: Heinemann.

Beers, Kylene, Robert E. Probst, and Linda Rief, eds. 2007. *Adolescent Literacy: Turning Promise into Practice*. Portsmouth, NH: Heinemann.

Beers, Kylene, and Robert E. Probst. 1998. "Classroom Talk About Literature: The Social Dimensions of a Solitary Act." *Voices from the Middle* 16 (2): 16–20.

Biancarosa, Gina, and Catherine E. Snow. 2004. "Reading Next—A Vision for Action and Research in Middle and High School Literacy: A Report to Carnegie Corporation of New York." Washington, DC: Alliance for Excellent Education.

Blau, Sheridan D. 2003. *The Literature Workshop*. Portsmouth, NH: Heinemann.

Bleich, David. 1975. *Readings and Feelings: An Introduction to Subjective Criticism*. Urbana, IL: National Council of Teachers of English.

Block, Cathy Collins, and Michael Pressley, eds. 2002. *Comprehension Instruction: Research-Based Best Practices*. New York: Guilford.

Britton, James. 1969. "Talking to Learn." In *Language, the Learner, and the School*, edited by D. Barnes, J. Britton, and H. Rosen. Harmondsworth, UK: Penguin.

Brown, Rexford. 1993. *Schools of Thought: How the Politics of Literacy Shape Thinking in the Classroom*. The Jossey-Bass Education Series. San Francisco: Jossey-Bass.

Burke, Jim. 2010. *What's the Big Idea? Question-Driven Units to Motivate Thinking*. Portsmouth, NH: Heinemann.

Casner-Lotto, Jill, and Barrington, Linda. 2006. *Are They Really Ready to Work? Employers' Perspectives on the Basic Knowledge and Applied Skills of New Entrants to the 21st Century U.S. Workforce*. Washington, DC: Conference Board.

English, Cathie. 2007. "Finding a Voice in a Threaded Discussion Group: Talking About Literature Online." *English Journal* 97 (1): 56–61.

Farrell, Edmund J., and James R. Squire, eds. 1990. *Transactions with Literature: A Fifty-Year Perspective*. Urbana, IL: National Council of Teachers of English.

Foster, Harold M., and Megan C. Nosol. 2008. *America's Unseen Kids: Teaching English/Language Arts in Today's Forgotten High Schools*. Portsmouth, NH: Heinemann.

Friedman, Thomas L. 2005. *The World Is Flat: A Brief History of the Twenty-First Century*. New York: Farrar, Straus & Giroux.

Gallagher, Kelly. 2004. *Deeper Reading: Comprehending Challenging Texts, 4–12*. Portland, ME: Stenhouse.

Gee, James Paul. 2008. *Social Linguistics and Literacies: Ideology in Discourses*, 3rd ed. London/New York: Routledge.

Harvey, Stephanie. 1998. *Nonfiction Matters.* York, ME: Stenhouse Publishers.

Harvey, Stephanie, and Anne Goudvis. 2005. *Comprehension Toolkit.* Portsmouth, NH: Heinemann.

Kajder, Sara B. 2010. *Adolescents and Digital Literacies: Learning Alongside Our Students.* Urbana, IL: National Council of Teachers of English.

Keene, Ellin Oliver. 2012. *Talk About Understanding: Rethinking Classroom Talk to Enhance Comprehension.* Portsmouth, NH: Heinemann.

_____. 2008. *To Understand.* Portsmouth, NH: Heinemann.

Keene, Ellin Oliver, and Susan Zimmermann. 1997. *Mosaic of Thought: Teaching Comprehension in a Reader's Workshop.* Portsmouth, NH: Heinemann.

Kucan, Linda, and Isabel L. Beck. 1997. "Thinking Aloud and Reading Comprehension Research: Inquiry, Instruction, and Social Interaction." *Review of Educational Research* 67 (3): 271–99.

Langer, Judith, and Elizabeth Close. 2001. *Improving Literacy Understanding Through Classroom Conversation.* Center for Experiential Learning and Assessment SUNY Albany, School of Education (CELA). Accessed at http://www.albany.edu/cela/publication/env.pdf.

Lunstrum, John P. 1981. "Building Motivation Through the Use of Controversy." *Journal of Reading* 24 (8): 687–91.

Morrell, Ernest. 2008. *Critical Literacy and Urban Youth: Pedagogies of Access, Dissent, and Liberation.* New York: Routledge.

Newkirk, Tom. 2011. *The Art of Slow Reading: Six Time-Honored Practices for Engagement.* Portsmouth, NH: Heinemann.

Nystrand, Martin, and Adam Gamoran. 1991. "Instructional Discourse, Student Engagement, and Literature Achievement." *Research in the Teaching of English* 25 (3): 261–90.

_____. 1997. "The Big Picture: The Language of Learning in Dozens of English Lessons." In *Opening Dialogue: Understanding the Dynamics of Language and Learning in the English Classroom*, edited by Martin Nystrand. New York: Teachers College Press.

Peet, Anne W., and Catherine B. Snow, eds. 2003. *Rethinking Reading Comprehension.* New York: Guilford Press.

Pink, Daniel H. 2009. *Drive: The Surprising Truth About What Motivates Us.* New York: Riverhead.

Probst, Robert E. 2004. *Response and Analysis: Teaching Literature in Secondary School*. Portsmouth, NH: Heinemann.

Purves, Alan C., and Richard Beach. 1981. *Literature and the Reader*. Urbana, IL: National Council of Teachers of English.

Ravitch, Diane. 2010. *The Death and Life of the Great American School System: How Testing and Choice Are Undermining Education*. New York: Basic.

Reading Between the Lines: What the ACT Reveals About College Readiness in Reading. 2008. Iowa City, IA: ACT, Inc. Accessed at http://www.act.org/research/policymakers/pdf/reading_report.pdf.

Richardson, Will, and Rob Mancabelli. 2011. *Personal Learning Network*. Bloomington, IN: Solution Tree.

Robb, Laura. 2000. *Teaching Reading in the Middle School*. New York: Scholastic.

Seidman, Dov. 2007. *HOW: Why HOW We Do Anything Means Everything*. Hoboken, NJ: John Wiley.

Sibberson, Franki, Karen Szymusiak, and Lisa Koch. 2008. *Beyond Leveled Books*. Portland, ME: Stenhouse.

Strickland, Dorothy S., and Donna E. Alvermann, eds. 2004. *Bridging the Literacy Achievement Gap, Grades 4–12*. New York: Teachers College Press.

Tatum, Alfred W. 2009. *Reading for Their Life*. Portsmouth, NH: Heinemann.

_____. 2005. *Teaching Reading to Black Adolescent Males: Closing the Achievement Gap*. Portland, ME: Stenhouse.

Trilling, Bernie, and Charles Fadel. 2009. *Twenty-First-Century Skills: Learning for Life in Our Times*. San Francisco: Jossey-Bass.

Wilhelm, Jeff. 2001. *Improving Comprehension with Think-Aloud Strategies*. New York: Scholastic.

Photo Credits

More books by Kylene Beers and Robert E. Probst

Adolescent Literacy
Turning Promise into Practice

In *Adolescent Literacy* renowned educators Kylene Beers, Bob Probst, and Linda Rief convene a conversation with twenty-eight of the most important and widely read educational thinkers and practitioners to address crucial advances in research on adolescent learning, to assess which of our current practices meet the challenges of the twenty-first century, and to discover transformative ideas and methods that turn the promise of education into instructional practice.

Grades 5–12 / 978-0-325-01128-8 / 2007 / 432pp / $32.50

When Kids Can't Read—What Teachers Can Do
A Guide for Teachers 6–12

For Kylene Beers, the question of what to do when kids can't read surfaced abruptly in 1979 when she began teaching. That year, she discovered that some of the students in her seventh-grade language arts classes could pronounce all the words, but couldn't make any sense of the text. Others couldn't even pronounce the words. And that was the year she met a boy named George.

George couldn't read. When George's parents asked her to explain what their son's reading difficulties were and what she was going to do to help, Kylene, a secondary certified English teacher with no background in reading, realized she had little to offer the parents, even less to offer their son. That defining moment sent her on a twenty-three-year search for answers to that original question: how do we help middle and high schoolers who can't read?

In this critical and practical text, Kylene shares what she has learned and shows teachers how to help struggling readers with comprehension, vocabulary, fluency, word recognition, and motivation. Filled with student transcripts, detailed strategies, reproducible material, and extensive booklists, this much-anticipated guide to teaching reading both instructs and inspires.

Grades 6–12 / 978-0-86709-519-7 / 2002 / 400pp / $32.50

Response & Analysis, Second Edition
Teaching Literature in Secondary School

In this fully updated second edition of *Response & Analysis*, Robert Probst offers fresh methods for teaching literature that build lifelong lovers of reading by opening your classroom to the power of student-driven interpretation and analysis. *Response & Analysis* is chock-full of everything you need to plan and build a curriculum that initiates interpretative and critical conversations with and among your students while exposing them to a variety of genres.

Grades 7–12 / 978-0-325-00716-8 / 2004 / 320pp / $31.00

Kylene Beers, Ed.D., is a former middle school teacher who has turned her commitment to adolescent literacy and struggling readers into the major focus of her research, writing, speaking, and teaching. She is the author of the best-selling *When Kids Can't Read/What Teachers Can Do*, co-editor (with Bob Probst and Linda Rief) of *Adolescent Literacy: Turning Promise into Practice*, and co-author (with Bob Probst) of *Notice and Note: Strategies for Close Reading*, all published by Heinemann. She taught in the College of Education  at the University of Houston, served as Senior Reading Researcher at the Comer School Development Program at Yale University, and most recently acted as the Senior Reading Advisor to Secondary Schools for the Reading and Writing Project at Teachers College.

Kylene has published numerous articles in state and national journals, served as editor of the national literacy journal, *Voices from the Middle*, and was the 2008-2009 President of the National Council of Teachers of English. She is an invited speaker at state, national, and international conferences and works with teachers in elementary, middle, and high schools across the US. Kylene has served as a consultant to the National Governor's Association and was the 2011 recipient of the Conference on English Leadership outstanding leader award.

Robert E. Probst, author of *Response and Analysis*, (Heinemann, 2004) is a respected authority on the teaching of literature. Bob's focus on engagement and literary analysis helps teachers learn the strategies to help readers approach a text with more confidence and greater skill.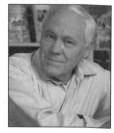

Professor Emeritus of English Education at Georgia State University, Bob's publications include numerous articles in *English Journal*, *Voices from the Middle*, and professional texts including *Adolescent Literacy: Turning Promise into Practice* (Heinemann, 2007), and the forthcoming Heinemann book *Notice and Note: Strategies for Close Reading* (with Kylene Beers). He presents at national conventions including the International Reading Association (IRA), the National Council of Teachers of English (NCTE), the Association of Supervisors and Curriculum Developers (ASCD), and the National Association of Secondary School Principals (NASSP). He has served NCTE in various leadership roles including the Conference on English Leadership Board of Directors, the Commission on Reading, column editor of the NCTE journal *Voices from the Middle*, and is the 2007 recipient of the CEL Outstanding Leadership Award.